Sound and Sense

An Introduction to Poetry

FIFTH EDITION

Sound
and
Sense

An
Introduction
to
Poetry

FIFTH EDITION

LAURENCE PERRINE
SOUTHERN METHODIST UNIVERSITY

HARCOURT BRACE JOVANOVICH, INC.

NEW YORK   CHICAGO   SAN FRANCISCO   ATLANTA

ISBN: 0-15-582604-2

Library of Congress Catalog Card Number: 76-58774

Printed in the United States of America

COPYRIGHTS AND ACKNOWLEDGMENTS

BROADSIDE PRESS for "Ballad of Birmingham" from *Poem Counterpoem.* Copyright © 1966, by Dudley Randall and Margaret Danner. Reprinted by permission of Broadside Press.

STERLING A. BROWN for "Southern Cop" from *Black Voices* edited by Abraham Chapman.

CURTIS BROWN, LTD. for "400-Meter Freestyle" from *Halfway* by Maxine Kumin. Reprinted by permission of Curtis Brown, Ltd. Copyright © 1961 by Maxine Kumin. For "The Naked and the Nude" from *5 Pens in Hand* by Robert Graves. Reprinted by permission of Curtis Brown, Ltd. Copyright © 1958 by Robert Graves.

JONATHAN CAPE LTD. for "Sea Grapes" from *Sea Grapes* by Derek Walcott. For "Sheepdog Trials in Hyde Park" from *The Gate* by C. Day Lewis. Reprinted by permission of the Executors of the Estate of C. Day Lewis and Jonathan Cape Ltd.

CHATTO AND WINDUS LTD. for "Anthem for Doomed Youth," "Dulce et Decorum Est," "The Send-Off" from *The Collected Poems of Wilfred Owen.* By permission of The Owen Estate and Chatto & Windus.

J. M. DENT & SONS LTD. for "Do not go gentle into that good night," "Poem in October," "Fern Hill" from *Collected Poems* of Dylan Thomas. By permission of the trustees for the copyrights of the late Dylan Thomas and J. M. Dent & Sons Ltd.

MS. DOROTHY DUREM for "Broadminded" from *Take No Prisoners* by Ray Durem. London, Paul Breman Ltd., 1971.

THE ECCO PRESS for "Paranoia" by Michael Dennis Browne. Copyright © 1973 *Antaeus* magazine.

NORMA MILLAY ELLIS for "Oh, oh, you will be sorry for that word!" from *Collected Poems,* Harper & Row. Copyright, 1923, 1951 by Edna St. Vincent Millay and Norma Millay Ellis.

True ease in writing comes from art, not chance,
As those move easiest who have learned to dance.
'Tis not enough no harshness gives offense,
The sound must seem an echo to the sense.

Alexander Pope from *An Essay on Criticism*

PREFACE

The fifth edition of *Sound and Sense,* like the earlier editions, is written for the college student who is beginning a serious study of poetry. It seeks to give that student a sufficient grasp of the nature and variety of poetry, some reasonable means for reading it with appreciative understanding, and a few primary ideas of how to evaluate it. The separate chapters gradually introduce the student to the elements of poetry, putting the emphasis always on *how* and *why.*

How can the reader use these elements to get at the meaning of the poem, to interpret it correctly and respond to it adequately?

Why does the poet use these elements? What values have they for the poet and the reader?

In matters of theory, some issues are undoubtedly oversimplified, but I hope none seriously. The purpose has always been to give the beginning student something to understand and use. The first assumptions of *Sound and Sense* are that poetry needs to be read carefully and thought about considerably and that, when so read, poetry gives its readers continuing rewards in experience and understanding.

The fifth edition differs from the fourth chiefly in the following respects: Over twenty-eight percent of the poems are new, and the number of poems by black poets and by women poets has been expanded. Emily Dickinson has replaced Yeats as one of the three poets (with Frost and Housman) who are represented by a sufficient number of poems to support study of them as individual artists; the number of poems by each of these poets has been increased. A Glossary of Poetic Terms has been added.

A book of this kind inevitably owes something to all who have thought or written about poetry. It would be impossible to express all indebtedness, but for personal advice, criticism, and assistance I wish especially to thank my wife, Catherine Perrine; Professor Maynard Mack, Yale University; Charles S. Holmes, Pomona College; Donald Peet, Indiana University; James W. Byrd, East Texas State University; Calvin L. Skaggs, Drew University; Willis Glover, Mercer University; and Margaret Morton Blum, Southern Methodist University.

I would also like to thank the following instructors, who have sent me helpful reactions and suggestions for this fifth edition of *Sound and Sense:* Muriel Allen, Edison Community College; Robert Anderson, Santa Ana College; James Armstrong, Fullerton College; Lloyd Bernston, Tacoma Community College; Alan K. Bickford, Macon Junior College; L. S. Bloom, Pan American University; Ann Boyce, Chabot College; Wilson C. Boynton, Holyoke Community College; Don Bozeman, Amarillo College; Diana F. Brantley, Amarillo College; Howard A. Burton, Riverside City College; M. G. Cheney, Weber State College; Marian S. Cheatham, Miami University; Ande Clark, Belmont College; Malcolm Clark, Solano College; Lawrence Clayton, Hardin-Simmons University; Lura L. Cook, Erie Community College North; Diana Cox, Amarillo College; Lynn Cox, Lincoln Land Community College; Robert Douglas, Anchorage Community College; Betty Ann Foulk, Kent State University; Carl Fowler, Amarillo College; Robert E. Foxworth, Fullerton College; Mary M. Fuller, U.S.D.A.; Rita Hammack, Judson Baptist College; Nicki Hansen, Weber State College; Edward A. Harris, Lorain County Community College; Carol T. Hayes, Holyoke Community College; Tom Hodges, Amarillo College; Merle Keiser, Norwalk Community College; Patricia C. Knight, Amarillo College; Joanne H. McCarthy, Tacoma Community College; Diane L. Miller, Springfield Technical Community College; John C. Minor, Columbia Junior College; E. J. Mooney, Amarillo College; Robert M. Nelson, University of Richmond; Kent Seltman, Pacific Union College; James W. Stone, Amarillo College; Josella Tennie, Cardinal Stritch College; Robert T. Trammel, Macon Junior College; Peter J. Ulisse, Housatonic Community College; Imogene Vaught, Odessa College; Jo Walker, Amarillo College; Joe L. Wheeler, Southwestern Union College; Robert H. Wheeler, Amarillo College; Richard White, Edison Community College; Robert Wylie, Amarillo College.

L. P.

CONTENTS

6   Figurative Language 2: Symbol, Allegory   80

7   Figurative Language 3: Paradox, Overstatement, Understatement, Irony   101

8   Allusion   122

14 Pattern   217

15 Bad Poetry and Good   237

16   Good Poetry and Great   253

II   POEMS FOR FURTHER READING

I The Elements of Poetry

1 What Is Poetry?

P oetry is as universal as language and almost as ancient. The most primitive peoples have used it, and the most civilized have cultivated it. In all ages, and in all countries, poetry has been written – and eagerly read or listened to – by all kinds and conditions of people, by soldiers, statesmen, lawyers, farmers, doctors, scientists, clergymen, philosophers, kings, and queens. In all ages it has been especially the concern of the educated, the intelligent, and the sensitive, and it has appealed, in its simpler forms, to the uneducated and to children. Why? First, because it has given pleasure. People have read it or listened to it or recited it because they liked it, because it gave them enjoyment. But this is not the whole answer. Poetry in all ages has been regarded as important, not simply as one of several alternative forms of amusement, as one man might choose bowling, another chess, and another poetry. Rather, it has been regarded as something central to each man's existence, something having unique value to the fully realized life, something that he is better off for having and spiritually impoverished without. To understand the reasons for this, we need to have at least a provisional understanding of what poetry is – provisional, because man has always been more successful at appreciating poetry than at defining it.

Initially, poetry might be defined as a kind of language that says *more* and says it *more intensely* than does ordinary language. In order to understand this fully, we need to understand what it is that poetry "says."

For language is employed on different occasions to say quite different kinds of things; in other words, language has different uses.

Perhaps the commonest use of language is to communicate *information*. We say that it is nine o'clock, that there is a good movie downtown, that George Washington was the first president of the United States, that bromine and iodine are members of the halogen group of chemical elements. This we might call the *practical* use of language; it helps us with the ordinary business of living.

But it is not primarily to communicate information that novels and short stories and plays and poems are written. These exist to bring us a sense and a perception of life, to widen and sharpen our contacts with existence. Their concern is with *experience*. We all have an inner need to live more deeply and fully and with greater awareness, to know the experience of others and to know better our own experience. The poet, from his own store of felt, observed, or imagined experiences, selects, combines, and reorganizes. He creates significant new experiences for the reader – significant because focused and formed – in which the reader can participate and that he may use to give him a greater awareness and understanding of his world. Literature, in other words, can be used as a gear for stepping up the intensity and increasing the range of our experience and as a glass for clarifying it. This is the *literary* use of language, for literature is not only an aid to living but a means of living.*

Suppose, for instance, that we are interested in eagles. If we want simply to acquire information about eagles, we may turn to an encyclopedia or a book of natural history. There we find that the family Falconidae, to which eagles belong, is characterized by imperforate nostrils, legs of medium length, a hooked bill, the hind toe inserted on a level with the three front ones, and the claws roundly curved and sharp; that land eagles are feathered to the toes and sea-fishing eagles halfway to the toes; that their length is about three feet, the extent of wing seven feet; that the nest is usually placed on some inaccessible cliff; that the eggs are spotted and do not exceed three; and perhaps that the eagle's "great power

---

*A third use of language is as an instrument of persuasion. This is the use we find in advertisements, propaganda bulletins, sermons, and political speeches. These three uses of language – the practical, the literary, and the hortatory – are not sharply divided. They may be thought of as three points of a triangle; most actual specimens of written language fall somewhere within the triangle. Most poetry conveys some information, and some poetry has a design on the reader. But language becomes *literature* when the desire to communicate experience predominates.

of vision, the vast height to which it soars in the sky, the wild grandeur of its abode, have . . . commended it to the poets of all nations."*

But unless we are interested in this information only for practical purposes, we are likely to feel a little disappointed, as though we had grasped the feathers of the eagle but not its soul. True, we have learned many facts about the eagle, but we have missed somehow its lonely majesty, its power, and the "wild grandeur" of its surroundings that would make the eagle something living rather than a mere museum specimen. For the living eagle we must turn to literature.

THE EAGLE

> He clasps the crag with crooked hands;
> Close to the sun in lonely lands,
> Ringed with the azure world, he stands.
>
> The wrinkled sea beneath him crawls;
> He watches from his mountain walls,
> And like a thunderbolt he falls.

Alfred, Lord Tennyson (1809–1892)

QUESTIONS

1. What is peculiarly effective about the expressions "crooked hands," "close to the sun," "ringed with the azure world," "wrinkled," "crawls," and "like a thunderbolt"?
2. Notice the formal pattern of the poem, particularly the contrast of "he stands" in the first stanza and "he falls" in the second. Is there any other contrast between the two stanzas?

If the preceding poem has been read well, the reader will feel that he has enjoyed a significant experience and understands eagles better, though in a different way, than he did from the encyclopedia article alone. For if the article *analyzes* man's experience with eagles, the poem in some sense *synthesizes* such an experience. Indeed, the two approaches to experience – the scientific and the literary – may be said to complement each other. And it may be contended that the kind of understanding one gets from the second is at least as valuable as the kind he gets from the first.

Encyclopedia Americana, IX, 473–74.

Literature, then, exists to communicate significant experience – significant because concentrated and organized. Its function is not to tell us *about* experience but to allow us imaginatively to *participate* in it. It is a means of allowing us, through the imagination, to live more fully, more deeply, more richly, and with greater awareness. It can do this in two ways: by *broadening* our experience – that is, by making us acquainted with a range of experience with which, in the ordinary course of events, we might have no contact – or by *deepening* our experience – that is, by making us feel more poignantly and more understandingly the everyday experiences all of us have.

Two false approaches often taken to poetry can be avoided if we keep this conception of literature firmly in mind. The first approach always looks for a lesson or a bit of moral instruction. The second expects to find poetry always beautiful. Let us consider a song from Shakespeare:

WINTER

When icicles hang by the wall,
    And Dick the shepherd blows his nail,
And Tom bears logs into the hall,
    And milk comes frozen home in pail,
When blood is nipped and ways be foul,   5
Then nightly sings the staring owl,
        "Tu-whit, tu-who!"
A merry note,
While greasy Joan doth keel° the pot.   skim

When all aloud the wind doth blow,   10
    And coughing drowns the parson's saw,
And birds sit brooding in the snow,
    And Marian's nose looks red and raw,
When roasted crabs° hiss in the bowl,   crab apples
Then nightly sings the staring owl,   15
        "Tu-whit, tu-who!"
A merry note,
While greasy Joan doth keel the pot.

William Shakespeare (1564–1616)

1. What are the meanings of "nail" (2) and "saw" (11)?
2. Is the owl's cry really a "merry" note? How are this adjective and the verb "sings" employed?
3. In what way does the owl's cry contrast with the other details of the poem?

In the poem "Winter" Shakespeare is attempting to communicate the quality of winter life around a sixteenth-century English country house. But instead of telling us flatly that winter in such surroundings is cold and in many respects unpleasant, though with some pleasant features too (the adjectives *cold, unpleasant,* and *pleasant* are not even used in the poem), he gives us a series of concrete homely details that suggest these qualities and enable us, imaginatively, to experience this winter life ourselves. The shepherd lad blows on his fingernails to warm his hands; the milk freezes in the pail between the cowshed and the kitchen; the roads are muddy; the folk listening to the parson have colds; the birds "sit brooding in the snow"; and the servant girl's nose is raw from cold. But pleasant things are in prospect. Logs are being brought in for a fire, hot cider or ale is being prepared, and the kitchen maid is making a hot soup or stew. In contrast to all these homely, familiar details of country life comes in the mournful, haunting, and eerie note of the owl.

Obviously the poem contains no moral. Readers who always look in poetry for some lesson, message, or noble truth about life are bound to be disappointed. Moral-hunters see poetry as a kind of sugar-coated pill – a wholesome truth or lesson made palatable by being put into pretty words. What they are really after is a sermon – not a poem, but something inspirational. Yet "Winter," which has appealed to readers now for nearly four centuries, is not inspirational and contains no moral preachment.

Neither is the poem "Winter" beautiful. Though it is appealing in its way and contains elements of beauty, there is little that is really beautiful in red raw noses, coughing in chapel, nipped blood, foul roads, and greasy kitchen maids. Yet some readers think that poetry deals exclusively with beauty – with sunsets, flowers, butterflies, love, God – and that the one appropriate response to any poem is, after a moment of awed silence, "Isn't that beautiful!" For such readers poetry is a precious affair, the enjoyment only of delicate souls, removed from the heat and sweat of ordinary life. But theirs is too narrow an approach to poetry. The function of poetry is sometimes to be ugly rather than beautiful. And poetry may deal with common colds and greasy kitchen maids as legitimately as with sunsets and flowers. Consider another example:

DULCE ET DECORUM EST

Bent double, like old beggars under sacks,
Knock-kneed, coughing like hags, we cursed through sludge,
Till on the haunting flares we turned our backs,
And towards our distant rest began to trudge.
Men marched asleep. Many had lost their boots,   5
But limped on, blood-shod. All went lame, all blind;
Drunk with fatigue; deaf even to the hoots
Of gas-shells dropping softly behind.

Gas! GAS! Quick, boys! – An ecstasy of fumbling,
Fitting the clumsy helmets just in time,   10
But someone still was yelling out and stumbling
And flound'ring like a man in fire or lime. –
Dim through the misty panes and thick green light,
As under a green sea, I saw him drowning.

In all my dreams before my helpless sight   15
He plunges at me, guttering, choking, drowning.

If in some smothering dreams, you too could pace
Behind the wagon that we flung him in,
And watch the white eyes writhing in his face,
His hanging face, like a devil's sick of sin,   20
If you could hear, at every jolt, the blood
Come gargling from the froth-corrupted lungs
Bitter as the cud
Of vile, incurable sores on innocent tongues, –
My friend, you would not tell with such high zest   25
To children ardent for some desperate glory,
The old lie: *Dulce et decorum est*
Pro patria mori.

Wilfred Owen (1893–1918)

QUESTIONS

1. The Latin quotation, from the Roman poet Horace, means "It is sweet and becoming to die for one's country." (Wilfred Owen died fighting for

England in World War I, a week before the armistice.) What is the poem's comment on this statement?

2. List the elements of the poem that to you seem not beautiful and therefore unpoetic. Are there any elements of beauty in the poem?
3. How do the comparisons in lines 1, 14, 20, and 23–24 contribute to the effectiveness of the poem?

Poetry takes all life as its province. Its primary concern is not with beauty, not with philosophical truth, not with persuasion, but with experience. Beauty and philosophical truth are aspects of experience, and the poet is often engaged with them. But poetry as a whole is concerned with all kinds of experience – beautiful or ugly, strange or common, noble or ignoble, actual or imaginary. One of the paradoxes of human existence is that all experience – even painful experience – when transmitted through the medium of art is, for the good reader, enjoyable. In real life, death and pain and suffering are not pleasurable, but in poetry they may be. In real life, getting soaked in a rainstorm is not pleasurable, but in poetry it can be. In actual life, if we cry, usually we are unhappy; but if we cry in a movie, we are manifestly enjoying it. We do not ordinarily like to be terrified in real life, but we sometimes seek movies or books that will terrify us. We find some value in all intense living. To be intensely alive is the opposite of being dead. To be dull, to be bored, to be imperceptive is in one sense to be dead. Poetry comes to us bringing life and therefore pleasure. Moreover, art focuses and so organizes experience as to give us a better understanding of it. And to understand life is partly to be master of it.

Between poetry and other forms of imaginative literature there is no sharp distinction. You may have been taught to believe that poetry can be recognized by the arrangement of its lines on the page or by its use of rime and meter. Such superficial tests are almost worthless. The Book of Job in the Bible and Melville's *Moby Dick* are highly poetical, but the familiar verse that begins: "Thirty days hath September, / April, June, and November . . ." is not. The difference between poetry and other literature is one only of degree. Poetry is the most condensed and concentrated form of literature, saying most in the fewest number of words. It is language whose individual lines, either because of their own brilliance or because they focus so powerfully what has gone before, have a higher voltage than most language has. It is language that grows frequently incandescent, giving off both light and heat.

Ultimately, therefore, poetry can be recognized only by the response made to it by a good reader. But there is a catch here. We are not all good readers. If we were, there would be no purpose for this book. And if you are a poor reader, much of what has been said about poetry so far must have seemed nonsensical. "How," you may ask, "can poetry be described as moving or exciting, when I have found it dull and boring? Poetry is just a fancy way of writing something that could be said more simply." So might a colorblind man deny that there is such a thing as color.

The act of communication involved in reading poetry is like the act of communication involved in receiving a message by radio. Two factors are involved: a transmitting station and a receiving set. The completeness of the communication depends on both the power and clarity of the transmitter and the sensitivity and tuning of the receiver. When a person reads a poem and no experience is transmitted, either the poem is not a good poem or the reader is a poor reader or not properly tuned. With new poetry, we cannot always be sure which is at fault. With older poetry, if it has acquired critical acceptance – has been enjoyed by generations of good readers – we may assume that the receiving set is at fault. Fortunately, the fault is not irremediable. Though we cannot all become expert readers, we can become good enough to find both pleasure and value in much good poetry, or we can increase the amount of pleasure we already find in poetry and the number of kinds of poetry we find it in. To help you increase your sensitivity and range as a receiving set is the purpose of this book.

Poetry, finally, is a kind of multidimensional language. Ordinary language – the kind that we use to communicate information – is one-dimensional. It is directed at only part of the listener, his understanding. Its one dimension is intellectual. Poetry, which is language used to communicate experience, has at least four dimensions. If it is to communicate experience, it must be directed at the *whole* man, not just at his understanding. It must involve not only his intelligence but also his senses, emotions, and imagination. Poetry, to the intellectual dimension, adds a sensuous dimension, an emotional dimension, and an imaginative dimension.

Poetry achieves its extra dimensions – its greater pressure per word and it greater tension per poem – by drawing more fully and more consistently than does ordinary language on a number of language resources, none of which is peculiar to poetry. These various resources form the subjects of a number of the following chapters. Among them are connotation, imagery, metaphor, symbol, paradox, irony, allusion, sound repetition, rhythm, and pattern. Using these resources and the materials of life, the poet shapes and makes his poem. Successful poetry is never effusive language. If it is to come alive it must be as cunningly put together and as efficiently organized as a tree. It must be an organism whose every part serves a useful purpose and cooperates with every other part to preserve and express the life that is within it.

*   *   *   *   *

SPRING

When daisies pied and violets blue,
    And lady-smocks all silver-white,
And cuckoo-buds of yellow hue
    Do paint the meadows with delight,
The cuckoo then, on every tree,   5
Mocks married men; for thus sings he,
            "Cuckoo!
Cuckoo, cuckoo!" O word of fear,
Unpleasing to a married ear!

When shepherds pipe on oaten straws,   10
    And merry larks are ploughmen's clocks,
When turtles tread, and rooks, and daws,
    And maidens bleach their summer smocks,
The cuckoo then, on every tree,
Mocks married men; for thus sings he,   15
            "Cuckoo!
Cuckoo, cuckoo!" O word of fear,
Unpleasing to a married ear!

William Shakespeare (1564–1616)

QUESTIONS

1. Vocabulary: *pied* (1), *lady-smocks* (2), *oaten straws* (10), *turtles* (12), *tread* (12), *daws* (12).
2. This song is a companion piece to "Winter." In what respects are the two poems similar? How do they contrast? What details show that this poem, like "Winter," was written by a realist, not simply by a man carried away with the beauty of spring?
3. The word "cuckoo" is "unpleasing to a married ear" because it sounds like *cuckold*. Cuckolds were a frequent butt of humor in earlier English literature. If you do not know the meaning of the word, look it up.
4. Is the tone of this poem solemn or light and semihumorous?

SIR PATRICK SPENS

The king sits in Dumferling toune,
    Drinking the blude-reid wine:
"O whar will I get guid sailor
    To sail this schip of mine?"

Up and spak an eldern knicht,°   knight
    Sat at the kings richt kne: 6
"Sir Patrick Spence is the best sailor
    That sails upon the se."

The king has written a braid° letter,   open, official
    And signd it wi his hand,   10
And sent it to Sir Patrick Spence,
    Was walking on the sand.

The first line that Sir Patrick red,
    A loud lauch lauched he;
The next line that Sir Patrick red,   15
    The teir blinded his ee.°   eye

"O wha is this has don this deid,
    This ill deid don to me,
To send me out this time o' the yeir,
    To sail upon the se!   20

"Mak hast, mak haste, my mirry men all,
    Our guid schip sails the morn."
"O say na sae,° my master deir,   say not so
    For I feir a deadlie storme.

"Late, late yestreen I saw the new moone,   25
    Wi the auld moone in hir arme,
And I feir, I feir, my deir master,
    That we will cum to harme."

O our Scots nobles wer richt laith°   loath
    To weet° their cork-heild schoone;° wet; cork-heeled shoes
Bot lang owre° a' the play wer playd,   ere
    Thair hats they swam aboone.°   their hats swam
                                   above them

O lang, lang may their ladies sit,
    Wi thair fans into their hand,
Or eir they se Sir Patrick Spence   35
    Cum sailing to the land.

O lang, lang may the ladies stand,
    Wi thair gold kems° in their hair,   *combs*
Waiting for thair ain deir lords,
    For they'll se thame na mair.   40

Haf owre, haf owre° to Aberdour,°   *half-over; Aberdeen*
    It's fiftie fadom deip,
And thair lies guid Sir Patrick Spence,
    Wi the Scots lords at his feit.

Anonymous

QUESTIONS

1. The term BALLAD refers usually to a relatively short or middle-length narrative poem written in stanzaic form. A FOLK BALLAD, of which this is one, is a ballad composed by an unknown author (but presumably of the common people) and designed to be sung (hence the stanzaic form). The folk ballads were transmitted orally over a period of time before being written down; hence they often exist in a number of versions. "Sir Patrick Spens," composed probably about the fifteenth century, was not written down until the eighteenth; of several versions this one is the shortest and usually considered the best. Its language and spelling, preserving the Scottish dialect of its origin, may prove an initial obstacle to the reader. Does it also provide a special flavor? Try to explain.

2. Like many of the folk ballads, this one is told, not in a continuous narrative tale, but in a series of scenes with abrupt transitions between them. How many such scenes do you count? What important scene is entirely omitted? Where do we finally learn what happened? Can you justify this method of narration?

3. Again as in most folk ballads, the story is told objectively. Considerable use is made of dialogue, and the narrator makes no explicit comments expressing his feelings or judgments about the events recounted. Does this method prevent the poem from implying feelings and judgments? What do Sir Patrick's reactions and actions tell us about his character? What contrasts are implied between Sir Patrick and his king? What contrasts are implied between Sir Patrick and the Scots nobles? Does the last line imply any comparative judgments on their characters?

4. Because so many (though far from all) folk ballads have been written in it, the

stanzaic form of this ballad has come to be known as *ballad stanza*. Can you describe it? How many lines are in each stanza? How many "beats" or accents do the respective lines contain? Which lines rime?

BALLAD OF BIRMINGHAM

(On the bombing of a church in Birmingham, Alabama, 1963)

"Mother dear, may I go downtown
Instead of out to play,
And march the streets of Birmingham
In a Freedom March today?"

"No, baby, no, you may not go,   5
For the dogs are fierce and wild,
And clubs and hoses, guns and jails
Aren't good for a little child."

"But, mother, I won't be alone,
Other children will go with me,   10
And march the streets of Birmingham
To make our country free."

"No, baby, no, you may not go,
For I fear those guns will fire.
But you may go to church instead   15
And sing in the children's choir."

She has combed and brushed her night-dark hair.
And bathed rose petal sweet,
And drawn white gloves on her small brown hands,
And white shoes on her feet.   20

The mother smiled to know her child
Was in the sacred place,
But that smile was the last smile
To come upon her face.

For when she heard the explosion,   25
Her eyes grew wet and wild.
She raced through the streets of Birmingham
Calling for her child.

She clawed through bits of glass and brick,
Then lifted out a shoe.   30
"O, here's the shoe my baby wore,
But, baby, where are you?"

Dudley Randall (b. 1914)

QUESTIONS

1. This poem is based on a historical incident. On Sunday, September 15, 1963, a dynamite bomb exploded in a black church in Birmingham, killing four children. How does the poem differ from the typical newspaper account of the incident?
2. What characteristics does this poem share with "Sir Patrick Spens"? Why do you think this twentieth-century poet chose to write in this traditional form?
3. What purpose does the poem have beyond simply telling a story? How is that purpose achieved?
4. On what central irony (see page 108) does the poem pivot?

THE PASTURE

I'm going out to clean the pasture spring;
I'll only stop to rake the leaves away
(And wait to watch the water clear, I may):
I shan't be gone long. – You come too.

I'm going out to fetch the little calf
That's standing by the mother. It's so young
It totters when she licks it with her tongue.
I shan't be gone long. – You come too.

Robert Frost (1874–1963)

QUESTIONS

1. Who is the speaker and to whom is he speaking?
2. Frost, as a poet, characteristically strove to capture the speech rhythms and language of the actual human voice in poems retaining a metrical form. In what lines is he particularly successful at this?
3. Originally the initial poem in Frost's second volume of verse, "The Pasture" was retained by Frost as the initial poem in collections of his verse. What additional meaning does the poem acquire from this position? Are poets usually concerned, would you guess, with the *arrangement* of poems in their books? Why or why not?

THIS IS MY LETTER

> This is my letter to the world
> That never wrote to me –
> The simple news that Nature told
> With tender majesty.
>
> Her message is committed
> To hands I cannot see;
> For love of her, sweet countrymen,
> Judge tenderly of me.

Emily Dickinson (1830–1886)

QUESTIONS

1. Only seven of the more than seventeen hundred poems written by Emily Dickinson were published during her lifetime, but the editors of her first slim volume, published four years after her death, placed this poem first. Was it a wise choice? To what does "This" (1) refer?
2. To whom does "her" (7) refer? What role does "Nature" (3) play in the poem?

TERENCE, THIS IS STUPID STUFF

> "Terence, this is stupid stuff:
> You eat your victuals fast enough;
> There can't be much amiss, 'tis clear,
> To see the rate you drink your beer.
> But oh, good Lord, the verse you make,   5
> It gives a chap the belly-ache.
> The cow, the old cow, she is dead;
> It sleeps well, the horned head:
> We poor lads, 'tis our turn now
> To hear such tunes as killed the cow.   10
> Pretty friendship 'tis to rhyme
> Your friends to death before their time
> Moping melancholy mad:
> Come, pipe a tune to dance to, lad."
>
> Why, if 'tis dancing you would be,   15
> There's brisker pipes than poetry.
> Say, for what were hop-yards meant,

Or why was Burton built on Trent?
Oh many a peer of England brews
Livelier liquor than the Muse,   20
And malt does more than Milton can
To justify God's ways to man.
Ale, man, ale's the stuff to drink
For fellows whom it hurts to think:
Look into the pewter pot   25
To see the world as the world's not.
And faith, 'tis pleasant till 'tis past:
The mischief is that 'twill not last.
Oh I have been to Ludlow fair
And left my necktie god knows where,   30
And carried half-way home, or near,
Pints and quarts of Ludlow beer:
Then the world seemed none so bad,
And I myself a sterling lad;
And down in lovely muck I've lain,   35
Happy till I woke again.
Then I saw the morning sky:
Heigho, the tale was all a lie;
The world, it was the old world yet,
I was I, my things were wet,   40
And nothing now remained to do
But begin the game anew.

Therefore, since the world has still
Much good, but much less good than ill,
And while the sun and moon endure   45
Luck's a chance, but trouble's sure,
I'd face it as a wise man would,
And train for ill and not for good.
'Tis true, the stuff I bring for sale
Is not so brisk a brew as ale: 50
Out of a stem that scored the hand
I wrung it in a weary land.
But take it: if the smack is sour,
The better for the embittered hour;
It should do good to heart and head   55
When your soul is in my soul's stead;

And I will friend you, if I may,
In the dark and cloudy day.

    There was a king reigned in the East:
There, when kings will sit to feast,   60
They get their fill before they think
With poisoned meat and poisoned drink.
He gathered all that springs to birth
From the many-venomed earth;
First a little, thence to more,   65
He sampled all her killing store;
And easy, smiling, seasoned sound,
Sate the king when healths went round.
They put arsenic in his meat
And stared aghast to watch him eat;   70
They poured strychnine in his cup
And shook to see him drink it up:
They shook, they stared as white's their shirt:
Them it was their poison hurt.
—I tell the tale that I heard told.   75
Mithridates, he died old.

A. E. Housman (1859–1936)

QUESTIONS

1. "Terence" (1) is Housman's poetic name for himself. Housman's poetry is largely pessimistic or sad; and this poem, placed near the end of his volume *A Shropshire Lad,* is his defense of the kind of poetry he wrote. Who is the speaker in the first fourteen lines? Who is the speaker in the rest of the poem? What is "the stuff I bring for sale" (49)?

2. "Hops" (17) and "malt" (21) are principal ingredients of beer and ale. "Burton-upon-Trent" (18) is an English city famous for its breweries. "Milton" (21), in the invocation of his epic poem *Paradise Lost,* declares that his purpose is to "justify the ways of God to men." What, in Housman's eyes, is the efficacy of liquor in helping one live a difficult life?

3. What six lines of the poem most explicitly sum up the poet's philosophy? Most people like reading material that is cheerful and optimistic (on the argument that "there's enough suffering and unhappiness in the world already"). What for Housman is the value of pessimistic and tragic literature?

4. "Mithridates" (76) was a king of Pontus and contemporary of Julius Caesar; his "tale" is told in Pliny's *Natural History.* What is the connection of this last verse paragraph with the rest of the poem?

2 Reading the Poem

The primary purpose of this book is to develop your ability to understand and appreciate poetry. Here are some preliminary suggestions:

1. Read a poem more than once. A good poem will no more yield its full meaning on a single reading than will a Beethoven symphony on a single hearing. Two readings may be necessary simply to let you get your bearings. And if the poem is a work of art, it will repay repeated and prolonged examination. One does not listen to a good piece of music once and forget it; one does not look at a good painting once and throw it away. A poem is not like a newspaper, to be hastily read and cast into the wastebasket. It is to be hung on the wall of one's mind.

2. Keep a dictionary by you and use it. It is futile to try to understand poetry without troubling to learn the meanings of the words of which it is composed. One might as well attempt to play tennis without a ball. One of your primary purposes while in college should be to build a good vocabulary, and the study of poetry gives you an excellent opportunity. A few other reference books will also be invaluable. Particularly desirable are a good book on mythology (your instructor can recommend one) and a Bible.

3. Read so as to hear the sounds of the words in your mind. Poetry is written to be heard: its meanings are conveyed through sound as well as through print. Every word is therefore important. The best way to read a poem is just the opposite of the best way to read a newspaper. One reads a

newspaper as rapidly as possible; one should read a poem as slowly as possible. When you cannot read a poem aloud, lip-read it: form the words with your tongue and mouth though you do not utter them. With ordinary reading material, lip reading is a bad habit; with poetry it is a good habit.

4. Always pay careful attention to what the poem is saying. Though one should be conscious of the sounds of the poem, he should never be so exclusively conscious of them that he pays no attention to what the poem means. For some readers reading a poem is like getting on board a rhythmical roller coaster. The car starts, and off they go, up and down, paying no attention to the landscape flashing past them, arriving at the end of the poem breathless, with no idea of what it has been about.* This is the wrong way to read a poem. One should make the utmost effort to follow the thought continuously and to grasp the full implications and suggestions. Because a poem says so much, several readings may be necessary, but on the very first reading one should determine which noun goes with which verb.

5. Practice reading poems aloud. When you find one you especially like, make your roommate or a friend listen to it. Try to read it to him in such a way that he will like it too. (a) Read it affectionately, but not affectedly. The two extremes oral readers often fall into are equally deadly. One is to read as if one were reading a tax report or a railroad timetable, unexpressively, in a monotone. The other is to elocute, with artificial flourishes and vocal histrionics. It is not necessary to put emotion into reading a poem. The emotion is already there. It only wants a fair chance to get out. It will express *itself* if the poem is read naturally and sensitively. (b) Of the two extremes, reading too fast offers greater danger than reading too slow. Read slowly enough that each word is clear and distinct and that the meaning has time to sink in. Remember that your roommate does not have the advantage, as you do, of having the text before him. Your ordinary rate of reading will probably be too fast. (c) Read the poem so that the rhythmical pattern is felt but not exaggerated. Remember that poetry is written in sentences, just as prose is, and that punctuation is a signal as to how it should be read. Give all grammatical pauses their full due. Do not distort the natural pronunciation of words or a normal accentuation of the sentence to fit into what you have decided is its metrical pattern. One of the worst ways to read a poem is to read it ta-*dum* ta-*dum* ta-*dum* with an exaggerated emphasis on every other syllable. On the other

*Some poems encourage this type of reading. When this is so, usually the poet has not made the best use of his rhythm to support his sense.

hand, it should not be read as if it were prose. An important test of your reading will be how you handle the end of a line when there is no punctuation there. A frequent mistake of the beginning reader is to treat each line as if it were a complete thought, whether grammatically complete or not, and to drop his voice at the end of it. A frequent mistake of the sophisticated reader is to take a running start upon approaching the end of a line and fly over it as if it were not there. The line is a rhythmical unit, and its end should be observed whether there is punctuation or not. If there is no punctuation, one observes it ordinarily by the slightest of pauses or by holding onto the last word in the line just a little longer than usual. One should not drop his voice. In line 12 of the following poem, one should hold onto the word "although" longer than if it occurred elsewhere in the line. But one should not lower his voice on it: it is part of the clause that follows in the next stanza.

THE MAN HE KILLED

Had he and I but met
By some old ancient inn,
We should have sat us down to wet
Right many a nipperkin!°   half-pint cup

But ranged as infantry,   5
And staring face to face,
I shot at him as he at me,
And killed him in his place.

I shot him dead because —
Because he was my foe,   10
Just so: my foe of course he was;
That's clear enough; although

He thought he'd 'list, perhaps,
Off-hand-like — just as I —
Was out of work — had sold his traps —   15
No other reason why.

Yes; quaint and curious war is!
You shoot a fellow down
You'd treat, if met where any bar is,
Or help to half-a-crown.   20

Thomas Hardy (1840–1928)

1. Vocabulary: *traps* (15).
2. In informational prose the repetition of a word like "because" (9–10) would be an error. What purpose does the repetition serve here? Why does the speaker repeat to himself his "clear" reason for killing a man (10–11)? The word "although" (12) gets more emphasis than it ordinarily would because it comes not only at the end of a line but at the end of a stanza. What purpose does this emphasis serve? Can the redundancy of "old ancient" (2) be poetically justified?
3. Someone has defined poetry as "the expression of elevated thought in elevated language." Comment on the adequacy of this definition in the light of Hardy's poem.

To aid us in the understanding of a poem, we may ask ourselves a number of questions about it. One of the most important is *Who is the speaker and what is the occasion?* A cardinal error of beginning readers is to assume always that the speaker is the poet himself. A far safer course is to assume always that the speaker is someone other than the poet himself. For even when the poet does speak directly and express his own thoughts and emotions, he does so ordinarily as a representative human being rather than as an individual who lives at a particular address, dislikes dill pickles, and favors blue neckties. We must always be cautious about identifying anything in a poem with the biography of the poet. Like the novelist and the playwright, he is fully justified in changing actual details of his own experience to make the experience of the poem more universal. We may well think of every poem, therefore, as being to some degree *dramatic,* that is, the utterance of a fictional character rather than of the poet himself. Many poems are expressly dramatic.

In "The Man He Killed" the speaker is a soldier; the occasion is his having been in battle and killed a man – obviously for the first time in his life. We can tell a good deal about him. He is not a career soldier: he enlisted only because he was out of work. He is a workingman: he speaks a simple and colloquial language ("nipperkin," "'list," "off-hand-like," "traps"), and he has sold the tools of his trade – he may have been a tinker or plumber. He is a friendly, kindly sort who enjoys a neighborly drink of ale in a bar and will gladly lend a friend a half crown when he has it. He has known what it is to be poor. In any other circumstances he would have been horrified at taking a human life. He has been given pause as it is. He is trying to figure it out. But he is not a deep thinker and thinks he has supplied a reason when he has only supplied a name: "I killed the man . . . because he was my foe." The critical question, of course, is *Why was the man his "foe"?* Even the speaker is left unsatisfied by his answer, though he is not analytical enough to know what is wrong with it. Obviously this poem is expressly dramatic. We need know nothing about Thomas Hardy's life (he was never a soldier and never killed a man) to realize that the poem is dramatic. The internal evidence of the poem tells us so.

A second important question that we should ask ourselves upon reading any poem is *What is the central purpose of the poem?** The purpose may be to tell a story, to reveal human character, to impart a vivid impression of a scene, to express a mood or an emotion, or to convey to us vividly some idea or attitude. Whatever the purpose is, we must determine it for ourselves and define it mentally as precisely as possible. Only then can we fully understand the function and meaning of the various details in the poem, by relating them to this central purpose. Only then can we begin to assess the value of the poem and determine whether it is a good one or a poor one. In "The Man He Killed" the central purpose is quite clear: it is to make us realize more keenly the irrationality of war. The puzzlement of the speaker may be our puzzlement. But even if we are able to give a more sophisticated answer than his as to why men kill each other, we ought still to have a greater awareness, after reading the poem, of the fundamental irrationality in war that makes men kill who have no grudge against each other and who might under different circumstances show each other considerable kindness.

IS MY TEAM PLOUGHING

"Is my team ploughing,
    That I was used to drive
And hear the harness jingle
    When I was man alive?"

---

*Our only reliable evidence of the poem's purpose, of course, is the poem itself. External evidence, when it exists, though often helpful, may also be misleading. Some critics have objected to the use of such terms as "purpose" and "intention" altogether; we cannot know, they maintain, what was *attempted* in the poem; we can know only what was *done*. Philosophically this position is impeccable. Yet it is possible to make inferences about what was attempted, and such inferences furnish a convenient and helpful way of talking about poetry.

Aye, the horses trample,   5
    The harness jingles now;
No change though you lie under
    The land you used to plough.

"Is football playing
    Along the river shore,   10
With lads to chase the leather,
    Now I stand up no more?"

Aye, the ball is flying,
    The lads play heart and soul;
The goal stands up, the keeper   15
    Stands up to keep the goal.

"Is my girl happy,
    That I thought hard to leave,
And has she tired of weeping
    As she lies down at eve?"   20

Aye, she lies down lightly,
    She lies not down to weep:
Your girl is well contented.
    Be still, my lad, and sleep.

"Is my friend hearty,   25
    Now I am thin and pine;
And has he found to sleep in
    A better bed than mine?"

Yes, lad, I lie easy,
    I lie as lads would choose;   30
I cheer a dead man's sweetheart,
    Never ask me whose.

A. E. Housman (1859–1936)

QUESTIONS

1. What is meant by "whose" in line 32?
2. Is Housman cynical in his observation of human nature and human life?
3. The word "sleep" in the concluding stanzas suggests three different meanings. What are they? How many meanings are suggested by the word "bed"?

Once we have answered the question *What is the central purpose of the poem?* we can consider another question, equally important to full understanding: *By what means is that purpose achieved?* It is important to distinguish means from ends. A student on an examination once used the poem "Is my team ploughing" as evidence that A. E. Housman believed in immortality, because in it a man speaks from the grave. This is as naive as to say that Thomas Hardy in "The Man He Killed" joined the army because he was out of work. The purpose of Housman's poem is to communicate poignantly a certain truth about human life: life goes on after our deaths pretty much as it did before – our dying does not disturb the universe. This purpose is achieved by means of a fanciful dramatic framework in which a dead man converses with his still-living friend. The framework tells us nothing about whether Housman believed in immortality (as a matter of fact, he did not). It is simply an effective means by which we *can* learn how Housman felt a man's death affected the life he left behind. The question *By what means is the purpose of the poem achieved?* is partially answered by describing the poem's dramatic framework, if it has any. The complete answer requires an accounting of various resources of communication that we will discuss in the rest of this book.

The most important preliminary advice we can give for reading poetry is to maintain always, while reading it, the utmost mental alertness. The most harmful idea one can get about poetry is that its purpose is to soothe and relax and that the best place to read it is lying in a hammock with a cool drink beside one and low music in the background. One *can* read poetry lying in a hammock but only if he refuses to put his mind in the same attitude as his body. Its purpose is not to soothe and relax but to arouse and awake, to shock one into life, to make one more alive. Poetry is not a substitute for a sedative.

An analogy can be drawn between reading poetry and playing tennis. Both offer great enjoyment if the game is played hard. A good tennis player must be constantly on the tip of his toes, concentrating on his opponent's every move. He must be ready for a drive to the right or a drive to the left, a lob overhead or a drop shot barely over the net. He must be ready for top spin or underspin, a ball that bounces crazily to the left or crazily to the right. He must jump for the high ones and run for the far ones. He will enjoy the game almost exactly in proportion to the effort he puts into it. The same is true of poetry. Great enjoyment is there, but this enjoyment demands a mental effort equivalent to the physical effort one puts into tennis.

The reader of poetry has one advantage over the tennis player. The poet is not trying to win a match. He may expect the reader to stretch for his shots, but he *wants* the reader to return them.

EXERCISE

1. Most of the poems in this book are accompanied by study questions that are by no means exhaustive. Following is a list of questions that you may apply to any poem or that your instructor may wish to use, in whole or in part, to supplement the questions to any particular poem. You will not be able to answer many of them until you have read further into the book.

   a. Who is the speaker? What kind of person is he?

   b. To whom is he speaking? What kind of person is he?

   c. What is the occasion?

   d. What is the setting in time (time of day, season, century, etc.)?

   e. What is the setting in place (indoors or out, city or country, nation, etc.)?

   f. What is the central purpose of the poem?

   g. State the central idea or theme of the poem in a sentence.

   h. Discuss the tone of the poem. How is it achieved?

   i. a. Outline the poem so as to show its structure and development, or
      b. Summarize the events of the poem.

   j. Paraphrase the poem.

   k. Discuss the diction of the poem. Point out words that are particularly well chosen and explain why.

   l. Discuss the imagery of the poem. What kinds of imagery are used?

   m. Point out examples of metaphor, simile, personification, and metonymy and explain their appropriateness.

   n. Point out and explain any symbols. If the poem is allegorical, explain the allegory.

   o. Point out and explain examples of paradox, overstatement, understatement, and irony. What is their function?

   p. Point out and explain any allusions. What is their function?

   q. Point out significant examples of sound repetition and explain their function.

   r. a. What is the meter of the poem?
      b. Copy the poem and mark its scansion.

   s. Discuss the adaptation of sound to sense.

   t. Describe the form or pattern of the poem.

   u. Criticize and evaluate the poem.

*   *   *   *   *

I GAVE MYSELF TO HIM

I gave myself to him,
And took himself for pay.
The solemn contract of a life
Was ratified this way.

The wealth might disappoint,   5
Myself a poorer prove
Than this great purchaser suspect,
The daily own of love

Depreciate the vision;
But till the merchant buy,   10
Still fable in the Isles of Spice
The subtle cargoes lie.

At least 'tis mutual risk,
Some found it mutual gain:
Sweet debt of life, each night to owe,   15
Insolvent every noon.

Emily Dickinson (1830–1886)

QUESTIONS

1. Your instructor may occasionally ask you, as a test of your understanding of a poem at its lowest level, or as a means of clearing up misunderstanding, to paraphrase its content. To PARAPHRASE a poem means to restate it in different language, so as to make its prose sense as plain as possible. The paraphrase may be longer or shorter than the poem, but it should contain as far as possible all the ideas in the poem in such a way as to make them clear to a puzzled reader. Figurative language should be reduced when possible to literal language; metaphors should be turned into similes. Though it is neither necessary nor possible to avoid using some words occurring in the original, you should in general use your own language.

    The central idea of the above poem is approximately this: Marriage is a relationship which may prove disappointing to both parties; but unless the risk is taken, the possibility of a very rich and satisfying reward is forfeited. The poem may be paraphrased as follows:

> I gave myself to him (in marriage), and took him as payment. In this way the solemn contract of our lives was entered into and affirmed. He (the payment) might prove disappointing to me (too little for what

I gave). I might prove to be a poorer bargain than he (the purchaser) had anticipated. The daily possession of love (of each other) might decrease the value that each of us had foreseen in it. But until a purchaser decides to buy, he can never know what he has gained or missed. At least the risk of disappointment in marriage is mutual; some have found marriage mutual gain. It is a "sweet debt" to owe love every night and then (having given it) to owe it again every noon.

2. A paraphrase is useful only if you understand that it is the barest, most inadequate expression of what the poem really says and is no more equivalent to the poem than a corpse is to a man. Once having made the paraphrase, you should endeavor to see how far short of the poem it falls and why. If the above paraphrase clarifies the poem for you in any respect, does it falsify the poem in any way? What features make the poem more appealing, more forceful, and more memorable than the paraphrase? At what points particularly does the paraphrase fall far short of the poem in imaginative vigor? Why do you think the paraphraser gave up on trying to put the phrase "sweet debt" into his own words?

3. The poem is imaginatively unified by an extended metaphor in which a marriage contract is compared to a sales contract (or the entering into a love relationship is compared to a commercial transaction). The woman is both the seller and the merchandise, the man both the purchaser and the payment. In what ways is this comparison effective and appropriate? Why, nevertheless, does the poem begin "I gave myself to him" rather than "I sold myself to him"? Is this slight departure from the central metaphor a flaw in the poem?

4. May the speaker of the poem be identified with the poet?

BEDTIME STORY

Long long ago when the world was a wild place
Planted with bushes and peopled by apes, our
Mission Brigade was at work in the jungle.
    Hard by the Congo

Once, when a foraging detail was active   5
Scouting for green-fly, it came on a grey man, the
Last living man, in the branch of a baobab
    Stalking a monkey.

Earlier men had disposed of, for pleasure,
Creatures whose names we scarcely remember –   10
Zebra, rhinoceros, elephants, wart-hog,
    Lion, rats, deer. But

After the wars had extinguished the cities
Only the wild ones were left, half-naked
Near the Equator: and here was the last one,   15
    Starved for a monkey.

By then the Mission Brigade had encountered
Hundreds of such men: and their procedure,
History tells us, was only to feed them:
    Find them and feed them;   20

Those were the orders. And this was the last one.
Nobody knew that he was, but he was. Mud
Caked on his flat grey flanks. He was crouched, half-
    Armed with a shaved spear

Glinting beneath broad leaves. When their jaws cut   25
Swathes through the bark and he saw fine teeth shine,
Round eyes roll round and forked arms waver
    Huge as the rough trunks

Over his head, he was frightened. Our workers
Marched through the Congo before he was born, but   30
This was the first time perhaps that he'd seen one.
    Staring in hot still

Silence, he crouched there: then jumped. With a long swing
Down from his branch, he had angled his spear too
Quickly, before they could hold him, and hurled it   35
    Hard at the soldier

Leading the detail. How could he know Queen's
Orders were only to help him? The soldier
Winced when the tipped spear pricked him. Unsheathing his
    Sting was a reflex.   40

Later the Queen was informed. There were no more
Men. An impetuous soldier had killed off,
Purely by chance, the <u>penultimate</u> primate.
    When she was certain,   ⌐next to the last

Squadrons of workers were fanned through the Congo   45
Detailed to bring back the man's picked bones to be
Sealed in the archives in amber. I'm quite sure
    Nobody found them

After the most industrious search, though.
Where had the bones gone? Over the earth, dear,   50
Ground by the teeth of the termites, blown by the
    Wind, like the dodo's.

George MacBeth (b. 1932)

QUESTIONS

1. Vocabulary: *green-fly* (6), *penultimate* (43), *primate* (43), *amber* (47).
2. Who is speaking? Describe him. To whom is he speaking? When?
3. What comments does the poem suggest about the nature, history, and destiny of the human species? Are contrasts implied between the human species and the speaker's species?
4. What is the force of the final comparison to the dodo (52)?
5. How would you read the first two stanzas aloud? The last three?

WHEN IN ROME

Marrie dear
the box is full . . .
take
whatever you like
to eat . . .   5

      (an egg
      or soup
      . . . there ain't no meat.)

there's endive there
and   10
cottage cheese . . .
      (whew! if I had some
      black-eyed peas . . .)

there's sardines
on the shelves   15
and such . . .
but
don't
get my anchovies . . .
they cost   20
too much!

(me get the
anchovies indeed!
what she think, she got —
a bird to feed?)   25

there's plenty in there
to fill you up . . .

(yes'm. just the
sight's
enough!   30

Hope I lives till I get
home
I'm tired of eatin'
what they eats in Rome . . .)

Mari Evans

QUESTIONS

1. Who are the two speakers? What is the situation? Why are the second speaker's words enclosed in parentheses?
2. What are the attitudes of the two speakers toward one another?
3. What implications have the title and the last two lines?

MIRROR

I am silver and exact. I have no preconceptions.
Whatever I see I swallow immediately
Just as it is, unmisted by love or dislike.
I am not cruel, only truthful —
The eye of a little god, four-cornered.   5
Most of the time I meditate on the opposite wall.
It is pink, with speckles. I have looked at it so long
I think it is a part of my heart. But it flickers.
Faces and darkness separate us over and over.

Now I am a lake. A woman bends over me,   10
Searching my reaches for what she really is.
Then she turns to those liars, the candles or the moon.
I see her back, and reflect it faithfully.
She rewards me with tears and an agitation of hands.

I am important to her. She comes and goes. 15
Each morning it is her face that replaces the darkness.
In me she has drowned a young girl, and in me an old woman
Rises toward her day after day, like a terrible fish.

Sylvia Plath (1932–1963)

QUESTIONS

1. Who is the speaker? Distinguish means from ends.
2. In what ways is the mirror like and unlike a person (stanza 1)? In what ways is it like a lake (stanza 2)?
3. What is the meaning of the last two lines?

BREAK OF DAY

'Tis true, 'tis day; what though it be?
Oh, wilt thou therefore rise from me?
Why should we rise because 'tis light?
Did we lie down because 'twas night?
Love which in spite of darkness brought us hither 5
Should, in despite of light, keep us together.

Light hath no tongue, but is all eye;
If it could speak as well as spy,
This were the worst that it could say:
That, being well, I fain would stay, 10
And that I loved my heart and honor so,
That I would not from him that had them go.

Must business thee from hence remove?
Oh, that's the worst disease of love;
The poor, the foul, the false, love can 15
Admit, but not the busied man.
He which hath business and makes love, doth do
Such wrong as when a married man doth woo.

John Donne (1573–1631)

QUESTIONS

1. Who is the speaker? Who is addressed? What is the situation? Can the speaker be identified with the poet?
2. Explain the metaphor in line 7. To whom does "I" (10–12) refer? Is "love" (15) the subject or object of "can admit"?

3. Summarize the arguments used by the speaker to keep the person addressed from leaving. What is the speaker's scale of value?
4. Are the two persons married or unmarried? Justify your answer.

THERE'S BEEN A DEATH IN THE OPPOSITE HOUSE

There's been a death in the opposite house
As lately as today.
I know it by the numb look
Such houses have alway.

The neighbors rustle in and out,   5
The doctor drives away.
A window opens like a pod,
Abrupt, mechanically;

Somebody flings a mattress out, —
The children hurry by;   10
They wonder if it died on that, —
I used to when a boy.

The minister goes stiffly in
As if the house were his,
And he owned all the mourners now,   15
And little boys besides;

And then the milliner, and the man
Of the appalling trade,   *[mortician, also the pall, the*
To take the measure of the house.   *cover for the coffin (pall*
There'll be that dark parade   20   *bearer)]*

Of tassels and of coaches soon;
It's easy as a sign, —
The intuition of the news
In just a country town.

Emily Dickinson (1830–1886)

QUESTIONS

1. What can we know about the speaker in the poem?
2. By what signs does he recognize that a death has occurred? Explain them stanza by stanza.
3. Comment on the words "appalling" (18) and "dark" (20).
4. What is the speaker's attitude toward death?

A STUDY OF READING HABITS

When getting my nose in a book
Cured most things short of school,
It was worth ruining my eyes
To know I could still keep cool,
And deal out the old right hook   5
To dirty dogs twice my size.

Later, with inch-thick specs,
Evil was just my lark:
Me and my cloak and fangs
Had ripping times in the dark.   10
The women I clubbed with sex!
I broke them up like meringues.

Don't read much now: the dude
Who lets the girl down before
The hero arrives, the chap   15
Who's yellow and keeps the store,
Seem far too familiar. Get stewed:
Books are a load of crap.

Philip Larkin (b. 1922)

QUESTIONS

1. The three stanzas delineate three stages in the speaker's life. Describe each.
2. What kind of person is the speaker? What kind of books does he read? May he
   be identified with the poet?
3. Contrast the advice given by the speaker in stanza 3 with the advice given by
   Terence in "Terence, this is stupid stuff" (page 16). Are A. E. Housman
   and Philip Larkin at odds in their attitudes toward drinking and reading?
   Discuss.

ENGRAVED ON THE COLLAR OF A DOG WHICH I GAVE
TO HIS ROYAL HIGHNESS

I am his Highness' dog at Kew;
Pray tell me, sir, whose dog are you?

Alexander Pope (1688–1744)

3 Denotation and Connotation

A primary distinction between the practical use of language and the literary use is that in literature, especially in poetry, a *fuller* use is made of individual words. To understand this, we need to examine the composition of a word.

The average word has three component parts: sound, denotation, and connotation. It begins as a combination of tones and noises, uttered by the lips, tongue, and throat, for which the written word is a notation. But it differs from a musical tone or a noise in that it has a meaning attached to it. The basic part of this meaning is its DENOTATION or denotations: that is, the dictionary meaning or meanings of the word. Beyond its denotations, a word may also have connotations. The CONNOTATIONS are what it suggests beyond what it expresses: its overtones of meaning. It acquires these connotations by its past history and associations, by the way and the circumstances in which it has been used. The word *home,* for instance, by denotation means only a place where one lives, but by connotation it suggests security, love, comfort, and family. The words *childlike* and *childish* both mean "characteristic of a child," but *childlike* suggests meekness, innocence, and wide-eyed wonder, while *childish* suggests pettiness, willfulness, and temper tantrums. If we name over a series of coins: *nickel, peso, lira, shilling, sen, doubloon,* the word *doubloon,* to four out of five readers, will immediately suggest pirates, though one will find nothing about pirates in looking up its meaning in the dictionary. Pirates are part of its connotation.

Connotation is very important to the poet, for it is one of the means by which he can concentrate or enrich his meaning – say more in fewer words. Consider, for instance, the following short poem:

THERE IS NO FRIGATE LIKE A BOOK

There is no frigate like a book
To take us lands away,
Nor any coursers like a page
Of prancing poetry:
This traverse may the poorest take
Without oppress of toll;
How frugal is the chariot
That bears the human soul!

Emily Dickinson (1830–1886)

In this poem Emily Dickinson is considering the power of a book or of poetry to carry us away, to let us escape from our immediate surroundings into a world of the imagination. To do this she has compared literature to various means of transportation: a boat, a team of horses, a wheeled land vehicle. But she has been careful to choose kinds of transportation and names for them that have romantic connotations. "Frigate" suggests exploration and adventure; "coursers," beauty, spirit, and speed; "chariot," speed and the ability to go through the air as well as on land. (Compare "Swing Low, Sweet Chariot" and the myth of Phaethon, who tried to drive the chariot of Apollo, and the famous painting of Aurora with her horses, once hung in almost every school.) How much of the meaning of the poem comes from this selection of vehicles and words is apparent if we try to substitute for them, say, *steamship, horses,* and *streetcar.*

QUESTIONS

1. What is lost if *miles* is substituted for "lands" (2) or *cheap* for "frugal" (7)?
2. How is "prancing" (4) peculiarly appropriate to poetry as well as to coursers? Could the poet have without loss compared a book to coursers and poetry to a frigate?
3. Is this account appropriate to all kinds of poetry or just to certain kinds? That is, was the poet thinking of poems like Wilfred Owen's "Dulce et Decorum Est" (page 8) or of poems like Coleridge's "Kubla Khan" (page 297) and Walter de la Mare's "The Listeners" (page 299)?

Just as a word has a variety of connotations, so also it may have more than one denotation. If we look up the word *spring* in the dictionary, for instance, we will find that it has between twenty-five and thirty distinguishable meanings: It may mean (1) a pounce or leap, (2) a season of the year, (3) a natural source of water, (4) a coiled elastic wire, etc. This variety of denotation, complicated by additional tones of connotation, makes language confusing and difficult to use. Any person using words must be careful to define by context precisely the meanings that he wishes. But the difference between the writer using language to communicate information and the poet is this: the practical writer will always attempt to confine his words to one meaning at a time; the poet will often take advantage of the fact that the word has more than one meaning by using it to mean more than one thing at the same time. Thus when Edith Sitwell in one of her poems writes, "This is the time of the wild spring and the mating of tigers," she uses the word *spring* to denote both a season of the year and a sudden leap and she uses *tigers* rather than *lambs* or *birds* because it has a connotation of fierceness and wildness that the other two lack.

WHEN MY LOVE SWEARS THAT SHE IS MADE OF TRUTH

> When my love swears that she is made of truth,
> I do believe her, though I know she lies,
> That she might think me some untutored youth,
> Unlearnèd in the world's false subtleties.
> Thus vainly thinking that she thinks me young,   5
> Although she knows my days are past the best,
> Simply I credit her false-speaking tongue;
> On both sides thus is simple truth supprest.
> But wherefore says she not she is unjust?°   unfaithful
> And wherefore say not I that I am old?   10
> Oh, love's best habit is in seeming trust,
> And age in love loves not to have years told:
> Therefore I lie with her and she with me,
> And in our faults by lies we flattered be.

William Shakespeare (1564–1616)

QUESTIONS

1. How old is the speaker in the poem? How old is his beloved? What is the nature of their relationship?

2. How is the contradiction in line 2 to be resolved? How is the one in lines 5–6 to be resolved? Who is lying to whom?
3. How do "simply" (7) and "simple" (8) differ in meaning? The words "vainly" (5), "habit" (11), "told" (12), and "lie" (13) all have double meanings. What are they?
4. What is the tone of the poem – i.e. the attitude of the speaker toward his situation? Should line 11 be taken as an expression of (a) wisdom, (b) conscious rationalization, or (c) unconscious self-deception? In answering these questions, consider both the situation and the connotations of all the important words beginning with "swears" (1) and ending with "flattered" (14).

A frequent misconception of poetic language is that the poet seeks always the most beautiful or noble-sounding words. What he really seeks are the most *meaningful* words, and these vary from one context to another. Language has many levels and varieties, and the poet may choose from them all. His words may be grandiose or humble, fanciful or matter of fact, romantic or realistic, archaic or modern, technical or everyday, monosyllabic or polysyllabic. Usually his poem will be pitched pretty much in one key. The words in Emily Dickinson's "There is no frigate like a book" and those in Thomas Hardy's "The Man He Killed" (page 21) are chosen from quite different areas of language, but each poet has chosen the words most meaningful for his own poetic context. Sometimes a poet may import a word from one level or area of language into a poem composed mostly of words from a different level or area. If he does this clumsily, the result will be incongruous and sloppy. If he does it skillfully, the result will be a shock of surprise and an increment of meaning for the reader. In fact, the many varieties of language open to the poet provide his richest resource. His task is one of constant exploration and discovery. He searches always for the secret affinities of words that allow them to be brought together with soft explosions of meaning.

THE NAKED AND THE NUDE

> For me, the naked and the nude
> (By lexicographers construed
> As synonyms that should express
> The same deficiency of dress
> Or shelter) stand as wide apart   5
> As love from lies, or truth from art.

Lovers without reproach will gaze
On bodies naked and ablaze;
The hippocratic eye will see
In nakedness, anatomy;   10
And naked shines the Goddess when
She mounts her lion among men.

The nude are bold, the nude are sly
To hold each treasonable eye.
While draping by a showman's trick   15
Their dishabille in rhetoric,
They grin a mock-religious grin
Of scorn at those of naked skin.

The naked, therefore, who compete
Against the nude may know defeat;   20
Yet when they both together tread
The briary pastures of the dead,
By Gorgons with long whips pursued,
How naked go the sometime nude!

*sometime
nude)*   *Robert Graves (b. 1895)*

QUESTIONS

1. Vocabulary: *lexicographers* (2), *construed* (2), *hippocratic* (9), *dishabille* (16), *Gorgons* (23).
2. What kind of language is used in lines 2–5? Why? (For example, why is "deficiency" used in preference to *lack?* Purely because of meter?)
3. What is meant by "rhetoric" (16)? Why is the word "dishabille" used in this line instead of some less fancy word?
4. Explain why the poet chose his wording instead of the following alternatives: *brave* for "bold" (13), *clever* for "sly" (13), *clothing* for "draping" (15), *smile* for "grin" (17).
5. What, for the poet, is the difference in connotation between "naked" and "nude"? Try to explain reasons for the difference. If your own sense of the two words differs from that of Graves, state the difference and give reasons to support your sense of them.
6. Explain the reversal in the last line.

The person using language to convey information is largely indifferent to the sound of his words and is hampered by their connotations and multiple denotations. He tries to confine each word to a single exact meaning. He uses, one might say, a fraction of the word and throws the rest away. The poet, on the other hand, tries to use as much of the word as he can. He is interested in sound and uses it to reinforce meaning (see chapter 13). He is interested in connotation and uses it to enrich and convey meaning. And he may use more than one denotation.

The purest form of practical language is scientific language. The scientist needs a precise language for conveying information precisely. The fact that words have multiple denotations and various overtones of meaning is a hindrance to him in accomplishing his purpose. His ideal language would be a language with a one-to-one correspondence between word and meaning; that is, every word would have one meaning only, and for every meaning there would be only one word. Since ordinary language does not fulfill these conditions, he has invented one that does. A statement in his language looks something like this:

$$SO_2 + H_2O = H_2SO_3$$

In such a statement the symbols are entirely unambiguous; they have been stripped of all connotation and of all denotations but one. The word *sulfurous,* if it occurred in poetry, might have all kinds of connotations: fire, smoke, brimstone, hell, damnation. But H_2SO_3 means one thing and one thing only: sulfurous acid.

The ambiguity and multiplicity of meanings possessed by words are an obstacle to the scientist but a resource to the poet. Where the scientist wants singleness of meaning, the poet wants richness of meaning. Where the scientist requires and has invented a strictly one-dimensional language, in which every word is confined to one denotation, the poet needs a multidimensional language, and he creates it partly by using a multidimensional vocabulary, in which to the dimension of denotation he adds the dimensions of connotation and sound.

The poet, we may say, plays on a many-stringed instrument. And he sounds more than one note at a time.

The first problem in reading poetry, therefore, or in reading any kind of literature, is to develop a sense of language, a feeling for words. One needs to become acquainted with their shape, their color, and their flavor. There are two ways of doing this: extensive use of the dictionary and extensive reading.

EXERCISES

1. Robert Frost has said that "Poetry is what evaporates from all translations." On the basis of this chapter, can you explain why this statement is true? How much of a word can be translated?

2. Which of the following words have the most "romantic" connotations?
   a. horse (   ) steed (   ) equine quadruped (   )
   b. China (   ) Cathay (   )
   Which of the following is the most emotionally connotative?
   c. mother (   ) female parent (   ) dam (   )
   Which of the following have the more favorable connotations?
   d. average (   ) mediocre (   )
   e. secret agent (   ) spy (   )
   f. adventurer (   ) adventuress (   )

3. Fill each blank with the word richest in meaning in the given context. Explain.
   a. I still had hopes, my latest hours to crown,
      Amidst these humble bowers to lay me down;
      To husband out life's _____taper_____ at the close,   *candle, taper*
      And keep the flame from wasting by repose.

                                           Goldsmith

   b. She was a _____phantom_____ of delight   *ghost, phantom,*
      When first she gleamed upon my sight.   *spectre, spook*

                                  Wordsworth

   c. His sumptuous watch-case, though concealed it lies,
      Like a good conscience, _____solid_____ joy supplies.   *perfect, solid,*

                               Edward Young   *thorough*

   d. Charmed magic _____casements_____ opening on the foam   *casements, windows*
      Of _____perilous_____ seas, in faery lands forlorn.   *dangerous, perilous*

                                              Keats

   e. Thou _____still_____ unravished bride of quietness.   *still, yet*

                                              Keats

   f. I'll _____lug_____ the guts into the neighbor room.   *bear, carry, convey,*

                                     Shakespeare   *lug*

   g. The iron tongue of midnight hath _____told_____   *said, struck, told*
      twelve.

                                     Shakespeare

h. In poetry each word reverberates like the note of a
well-tuned ___lyre___ and always leaves   *banjo, guitar, lyre*
behind it a multitude of vibrations.

Joubert

i. I think that with this ___sacred___ new alliance   *holy, sacred*
I may ensure the public, and defy
All other magazines of art or science.

Byron

j. Care on the maiden brow shall put
A wreath of wrinkles, and thy foot
Be shod with pain: not silken dress
But toil shall ___clothe___ thy loveliness.   *clothe, tire, weary*

C. Day Lewis

4. Ezra Pound has defined great literature as being "simply language charged
with meaning to the utmost possible degree." Would this be a good definition of poetry? The word "charged" is roughly equivalent to *filled*. Why is
"charged" a better word in Pound's definition? What do its associations with
storage batteries, guns, and dynamite suggest about poetry?

*   *   *   *   *

RICHARD CORY

Whenever Richard Cory went down town,
We people on the pavement looked at him:
He was a gentleman from sole to crown,
Clean favored, and imperially slim.

And he was always quietly arrayed,   5
And he was always human when he talked;
But still he fluttered pulses when he said,
"Good-morning," and he glittered when he walked.

And he was rich – yes, richer than a king –
And admirably schooled in every grace: 10
In fine, we thought that he was everything
To make us wish that we were in his place.

So on we worked, and waited for the light,
And went without the meat, and cursed the bread;
And Richard Cory, one calm summer night,   15
Went home and put a bullet through his head.

Edwin Arlington Robinson (1869–1935)

QUESTIONS

1. In how many senses is Richard Cory a gentleman?
2. The word "crown" (3), meaning the top of the head, is familiar to you from "Jack and Jill," but why does Robinson use the unusual phrase "from sole to crown" instead of the common *from head to foot* or *from top to toe?*
3. List the words that express or suggest the idea of aristocracy or royalty.
4. Try to explain why the poet chose his wording rather than the following alternatives: *sidewalk* for "pavement" (2), *good-looking* for "Clean favored" (4), *thin* for "slim" (4), *dressed* for "arrayed" (5), *courteous* for "human" (6), *wonderfully* for "admirably" (10), *trained* for "schooled" (10), *manners* for "every grace" (10), *in short* for "in fine" (11). What other examples of effective diction do you find in the poem?
5. Why is "Richard Cory" a good name for the character in this poem?
6. This poem is a good example of how ironic contrast (see chapter 7) generates meaning. The poem makes no direct statement about life; it simply relates an incident. What larger meanings about life does it suggest?
7. A leading American critic has said of this poem: "In 'Richard Cory' . . . we have a superficially neat portrait of the elegant man of mystery; the poem builds up deliberately to a very cheap surprise ending; but all surprise endings are cheap in poetry, if not, indeed, elsewhere, for poetry is written to be read not once but many times."* Do you agree with this evaluation? Discuss.

WHEN GREEN BUDS HANG IN THE ELM

When green buds hang in the elm like dust
    And sprinkle the lime like rain,
Forth I wander, forth I must,
    And drink of life again.

Forth I must by hedgerow bowers
    To look at the leaves uncurled,
And stand in the fields where cuckoo flowers
    Are lying about the world.

A. E. Housman (1859–1936)

*Yvor Winters, *Edwin Arlington Robinson* (Norfolk, Conn.: New Directions, 1946), p. 52.

1. The "lime" (2), also called the linden, is a common English shade tree (not to be confused with the fruit tree). Why is the verb "sprinkle" (2) chosen over *dapple, powder,* or *speckle?* "Cuckoo flowers" (7) are spring-blooming wildflowers. Why does the poet select them over some other variety? What two meanings has "lying" (8)?
2. Why does the speaker repeat the words "forth I must" (3, 5)? What impulses are at conflict in him? What is his attitude toward the world?

NAMING OF PARTS

To-day we have naming of parts. Yesterday,
We had daily cleaning. And to-morrow morning,
We shall have what to do after firing. But to-day,
To-day we have naming of parts. Japonica
Glistens like coral in all of the neighboring gardens,   5
     And to-day we have naming of parts.

This is the lower sling swivel. And this
Is the upper sling swivel, whose use you will see,
When you are given your slings. And this is the piling swivel,
Which in your case you have not got. The branches   10
Hold in the gardens their silent, eloquent gestures,
     Which in our case we have not got.

This is the safety-catch, which is always released
With an easy flick of the thumb. And please do not let me
See anyone using his finger. You can do it quite easy   15
If you have any strength in your thumb. The blossoms
Are fragile and motionless, never letting anyone see
     Any of them using their finger.

And this you can see is the bolt. The purpose of this
Is to open the breech, as you see. We can slide it   20
Rapidly backwards and forwards: we call this
Easing the spring. And rapidly backwards and forwards
The early bees are assaulting and fumbling the flowers:
     They call it easing the Spring.

They call it easing the Spring: it is perfectly easy   25
If you have any strength in your thumb: like the bolt,
And the breech, and the cocking-piece, and the point of balance,

Which in our case we have not got; and the almond-blossom
Silent in all of the gardens and the bees going backwards and forwards,
For to-day we have naming of parts.   30

Henry Reed (b. 1914)

QUESTIONS

1. Who is the speaker (or who are the speakers) in the poem, and what is the situation?
2. What basic contrasts are represented by the trainees and by the gardens?
3. What is it that the trainees "have not got" (28)? How many meanings have the phrases "easing the Spring" (22) and "point of balance" (27)?
4. What differences in language and rhythm do you find between the lines concerning "naming of parts" and those describing the gardens?
5. Does the repetition of certain phrases throughout the poem have any special function or is it done only to create a kind of refrain?
6. What statement does the poem make about war as it affects men and their lives?

JUDGING DISTANCES

Not only how far away, but the way that you say it
Is very important. Perhaps you may never get
The knack of judging a distance, but at least you know
How to report on a landscape: the central sector,
The right of arc and that, which we had last Tuesday,   5
        And at least you know

That maps are of time, not place, so far as the army
Happens to be concerned – the reason being,
Is one which need not delay us. Again, you know
There are three kinds of tree, three only, the fir and the poplar,   10
And those which have bushy tops to; and lastly
        That things only seem to be things.

A barn is not called a barn, to put it more plainly,
Or a field in the distance, where sheep may be safely grazing.
You must never be over-sure. You must say, when reporting: 15
At five o'clock in the central sector is a dozen
Of what appear to be animals; whatever you do,
Don't call the bleeders *sheep*.

I am sure that's quite clear; and suppose, for the sake of example,
The one at the end, asleep, endeavors to tell us   20
What he sees over there to the west, and how far away,
After first having come to attention. There to the west,
On the fields of summer the sun and the shadows bestow
    Vestments of purple and gold.

The still white dwellings are like a mirage in the heat,   25
And under the swaying elms a man and a woman
Lie gently together. Which is, perhaps, only to say
That there is a row of houses to the left of arc,
And that under some poplars a pair of what appear to be humans
    Appear to be loving.   30

Well that, for an answer, is what we might rightly call
Moderately satisfactory only, the reason being,
Is that two things have been omitted, and those are important.
The human beings, now: in what direction are they,
And how far away, would you say? And do not forget   35
    There may be dead ground in between.

There may be dead ground in between; and I may not have got
The knack of judging a distance; I will only venture
A guess that perhaps between me and the apparent lovers,
(Who, incidentally, appear by now to have finished,)   40
At seven o'clock from the houses, is roughly a distance
    Of about one year and a half.

Henry Reed (b. 1914)

QUESTIONS

1. In what respect are maps "of time, not place" (7) in the army?
2. Though they may be construed as belonging to the same speaker, there are
   two speaking voices in this poem. Identify each and put quotation marks
   around the lines spoken by the second voice.
3. Two kinds of language are used in this poem – army "officialese" and the
   language of human experience. What are the characteristics of each? What is
   the purpose of each? Which is more precise?
4. The word "bleeders" (18) – i.e., "bloody creatures" – is British profanity. To
   which of the two kinds of language does it belong? Or is it perhaps a third
   kind of language?
5. As in "Naming of Parts" (these two poems are part of a series of three with
   the general title "Lessons of War") the two kinds of language used might

possibly be called "unpoetic" and "poetic." Is the "unpoetic" language *really* unpoetic? In other words, is its use inappropriate in these two poems? Explain.

6. The phrase "dead ground" (36) takes on symbolic meaning in the last stanza. What is its literal meaning? What is its symbolic meaning? What does the second speaker mean by saying that the distance between himself and the lovers is "about one year and a half" (42)? In what respect is the contrast between the recruits and the lovers similar to that between the recruits and the gardens in "Naming of Parts"? What meanings are generated by the former contrast?

ELEGY FOR YARDS, POUNDS, AND GALLONS

An unduly elected body of our elders
Is turning you out of office and schoolroom
Through ten long years, is phasing you
Out of our mouths and lives forever.

Words have been lost before: some hounded   5
Nearly to death, and some transplanted
With roots dead set against stone,
And some let slide into obscure senescence,

Some even murdered beyond recall like extinct animals —
(It would be cruel to rehearse their names: 10
They might stir from sleep on the dusty shelves
In pain for a moment).

Yet you, old emblems of distance and heaviness,
Solid and liquid companions, our good measures,
When have so many been forced to languish   15
For years through a deliberate deathwatch?

How can we name your colorless replacements
Or let them tell us for our time being
How much we weigh, how short we are,
Or how little we have left to drink?   20

Goodbye to Pounds by the Ton and all their Ounces,
To Gallons, Quarts, and Pints,
To Yards whose Feet are inching their last Mile,
Weighed down, poured out, written off,

And drifting slowly away from us   25
Like drams, like chains and gills,
To become as quaint as leagues and palms
In an old poem.

David Wagoner (b. 1926)

QUESTIONS

1. Vocabulary: *Elegy* (title); *senescence* (8). *Drams* and *gills* (26) are obsolescent
   liquid measures; *chains, leagues,* and *palms* (26–27) are obsolescent measures of
   length.
2. On August 18, 1972, the U.S. Senate approved a Metric Conversion Act (S.
   2483) which, if approved also by the House and the President, would provide
   for a supervised ten-year changeover from our present system of old English
   measures to the metric system. The metric system is demonstrably more
   logical and efficient because (a) its units fit into each other in multiples of ten,
   (b) its nomenclature uses only one basic term for each kind of measurement
   plus uniform prefixes for other units (e.g., centimeter, meter, kilometer;
   centigram, gram, kilogram); and (c) the other most important nations in the
   world (including England) have already adopted it. Why, then, does the poet
   lament the passing of the old measures? What will have been lost?
3. Comment on the poet's use of language in lines 1, 2, 7, 14, 19–20, and 23–24.
   Would it be possible to express the meanings of line 23 with the new terms?
   Why or why not?

CROSS

My old man's a white old man
And my old mother's black.
If ever I cursed my white old man
I take my curses back.

If ever I cursed my black old mother   5
And wished she were in hell,
I'm sorry for that evil wish
And now I wish her well.

My old man died in a fine big house.
My ma died in a shack.   10
I wonder where I'm gonna die,
Being neither white nor black?

Langston Hughes (1902–1967)

1. What different denotations does the title have? Explain.
2. The language in this poem, such as "old man" (1, 3, 9), "ma" (10), and "gonna" (11), is plain, and even colloquial. Is it appropriate to the subject? Why?

BASE DETAILS

> If I were fierce, and bald, and short of breath,
>   I'd live with scarlet Majors at the Base,
> And speed glum heroes up the line to death.
>   You'd see me with my puffy petulant face,
> Guzzling and gulping in the best hotel,   5
>   Reading the Roll of Honor. "Poor young chap,"
> I'd say – "I used to know his father well;
>   Yes, we've lost heavily in this last scrap."
> And when the war is done and youth stone dead,
> I'd toddle safely home and die – in bed.   10

Siegfried Sassoon (1886–1967)

QUESTIONS

1. Vocabulary: *petulant* (4).
2. In what two ways may the title be interpreted? (Both words have two pertinent meanings.) What applications has "scarlet" (2)? What is the force of "fierce" (1)? Try to explain why the poet chose his wording rather than the following alternatives: *fleshy* for "puffy" (4), *eating and drinking* for "guzzling and gulping" (5), *battle* for "scrap" (8), *totter* for "toddle" (10).
3. Who evidently is the speaker? (The poet, a British captain in World War I, was decorated for bravery on the battlefield.) Does he mean what he says? What is the purpose of the poem?

INSPIRATION ON PERSPIRATION

> Here's a little proverb you surely ought to know;
> Horses sweat and men perspire but ladies only glow.

Anonymous

4 Imagery

Experience comes to us largely through the senses. My experience of a spring day, for instance, may consist partly of certain emotions I feel and partly of certain thoughts I think, but most of it will be a cluster of sense impressions. It will consist of *seeing* blue sky and white clouds, budding leaves and daffodils; of *hearing* robins and bluebirds singing in the early morning; of *smelling* damp earth and blossoming hyacinths; and of *feeling* a fresh wind against my cheek. The poet seeking to express his experience of a spring day must therefore provide a selection of the sense impressions he has. Like Shakespeare (page 11), he must give the reader "daisies pied" and "lady-smocks all silver-white" and "merry larks" and the song of the cuckoo and maidens bleaching their summer smocks. Without doing so he will probably fail to evoke the emotions that accompanied his sensations. His language, therefore, must be more *sensuous* than ordinary language. It must be more full of imagery.

IMAGERY may be defined as the representation through language of sense experience. Poetry appeals directly to our senses, of course, through its music and rhythms, which we actually hear when it is read aloud. But indirectly it appeals to our senses through imagery, the representation to the imagination of sense experience. The word *image* perhaps most often suggests a mental picture, something seen in the mind's eye – and *visual* imagery is the most frequently occurring kind of imagery in poetry. But an image may also represent a sound; a smell; a taste; a tactile experience, such as hardness, wetness, or cold; an internal sensation, such as hunger, thirst, or nausea; or movement or tension in the muscles or joints. If we wished to be scientific, we could extend this list further, for psychologists no longer confine themselves to five or even six senses, but for purposes of discussing poetry the above classification should ordinarily be sufficient.

MEETING AT NIGHT

The gray sea and the long black land;
And the yellow half-moon large and low;
And the startled little waves that leap
In fiery ringlets from their sleep,
As I gain the cove with pushing prow,   5
And quench its speed i' the slushy sand.

Then a mile of warm sea-scented beach;
Three fields to cross till a farm appears;
A tap at the pane, the quick sharp scratch
And blue spurt of a lighted match,   10
And a voice less loud, through its joys and fears,
Than the two hearts beating each to each!

Robert Browning (1812–1889)

"Meeting at Night" is a poem about love. It makes, one might say, a number of statements about love: being in love is a sweet and exciting experience; when one is in love everything seems beautiful to him, and the most trivial things become significant; when one is in love his sweetheart seems the most important object in the world. But the poet actually *tells* us none of these things directly. He does not even use the word *love* in his poem. His business is to communicate experience, not information. He does this largely in two ways. First, he presents us with a specific situation, in which a lover goes to meet his sweetheart. Second, he describes the lover's journey so vividly in terms of sense impressions that the reader not only sees and hears what the lover saw and heard but also shares his anticipation and excitement.

Every line in the poem contains some image, some appeal to the senses: the gray sea, the long black land, the yellow half-moon, the startled little waves with their fiery ringlets, the blue spurt of the lighted match – all appeal to our sense of sight and convey not only shape but also color and motion. The warm sea-scented beach appeals to the senses of both smell and touch. The pushing prow of the boat on the slushy sand, the tap at the pane, the quick scratch of the match, the low speech of the lovers, and the sound of their hearts beating – all appeal to the sense of hearing.

PARTING AT MORNING

> Round the cape of a sudden came the sea,
> And the sun looked over the mountain's rim:
> And straight was a path of gold for him,
> And the need of a world of men for me.

Robert Browning (1812–1889)

QUESTIONS

1. This poem is a sequel to "Meeting at Night." "Him" (3) refers to the sun. Does the last line mean that the lover needs the world of men or that the world of men needs the lover? Or both?
2. Does the sea *actually* come suddenly around the cape or *appear* to? Why does Browning mention the *effect* before its *cause* (the sun looking over the mountain's rim)?
3. Do these two poems, taken together, suggest any larger truths about love? Browning, in answer to a question, said that the second part is the man's confession of "how fleeting is the belief (implied in the first part) that such raptures are self-sufficient and enduring – as for the time they appear."

The sharpness and vividness of any image will ordinarily depend on how specific it is and on the poet's use of effective detail. The word *hummingbird,* for instance, conveys a more definite image than does *bird,* and *ruby-throated hummingbird* is sharper and more specific still. It is not necessary, however, that for a vivid representation something be completely described. One or two especially sharp and representative details will ordinarily serve the alert reader, allowing his imagination to fill in the rest. Tennyson in "The Eagle" (page 5) gives only one detail about the eagle itself – that he clasps the crag with "crooked hands" – but this detail is an effective and memorable one. Robinson tells us that Richard Cory (page 42) was "clean favored," "slim," and "quietly arrayed," but the detail that really brings Cory before us is that he "glittered when he walked." Browning, in "Meeting at Night," calls up a whole scene with "A tap at the pane, the quick sharp scratch/And blue spurt of a lighted match."

Since imagery is a peculiarly effective way of evoking vivid experience, and since it may be used by the poet to convey emotion and suggest ideas as well as to cause a mental reproduction of sensations, it is an invaluable resource of the poet. In general, he will seek concrete or image-bearing words in preference to abstract or non-image-bearing words. We cannot evaluate a poem, however, by the amount or quality of its imagery alone. Sense impression is only one of the elements of experience. A poet may attain his ends by other means. We must never judge any single element of a poem except in reference to the total intention of that poem.

*   *   *   *   *

A LATE AUBADE

You could be sitting now in a carrel
Turning some liver-spotted page,
Or rising in an elevator-cage
Toward Ladies' Apparel.

You could be planting a raucous bed   5
Of salvia, in rubber gloves,
Or lunching through a screed of someone's loves
With pitying head,

Or making some unhappy setter
Heel, or listening to a bleak   10
Lecture on Schoenberg's serial technique.
Isn't this better?   (musical theory)

Think of all the time you are not
Wasting, and would not care to waste,
Such things, thank God, not being to your taste.   15
Think what a lot

Of time, by woman's reckoning,
You've saved, and so may spend on this,
You who had rather lie in bed and kiss
Than anything.   20

It's almost noon, you say? If so,
Time flies, and I need not rehearse
The rosebuds-theme of centuries of verse.
If you *must* go,

Wait for a while, then slip downstairs   25
And bring us up some chilled white wine,
And some blue cheese, and crackers, and some fine
Ruddy-skinned pears.

Richard Wilbur (b. 1921)

QUESTIONS

1. Vocabulary: *Aubade* (title), *carrel* (1), *screed* (7), *Schoenberg* (11).
2. Who is the speaker? What is the situation? What plea is the speaker making?
3. As lines 22–23 suggest, this poem treats an age-old theme of poetry. What
   is it? In what respects is this an original treatment of it? Though line 23 is
   general in reference, it alludes specifically to a famous poem by Robert Herrick (see page 88). In what respects are these two poems similar? In what
   respects are they different?
4. What clues are there in the poem as to the characters and personalities of the
   two people involved?
5. How does the last stanza provide a fitting conclusion to the poem?

ON MOONLIT HEATH AND LONESOME BANK

On moonlit heath and lonesome bank
    The sheep beside me graze;
And yon the gallows used to clank
    Fast by the four cross ways.

A careless shepherd once would keep   5
    The flocks by moonlight there,
And high amongst the glimmering sheep
    The dead man stood on air.

They hang us now in Shrewsbury jail:
    The whistles blow forlorn,   10
And trains all night groan on the rail
    To men that die at morn.

There sleeps in Shrewsbury jail to-night,
    Or wakes, as may betide,
A better lad, if things went right,   15
    Than most that sleep outside.

And naked to the hangman's noose
    The morning clocks will ring
A neck God made for other use
    Than strangling in a string.   20

And sharp the link of life will snap,
    And dead on air will stand
Heels that held up as straight a chap
    As treads upon the land.

So here I'll watch the night and wait   25
    To see the morning shine,
When he will hear the stroke of eight
    And not the stroke of nine;

And wish my friend as sound a sleep
    As lads' I did not know,   30
That shepherded the moonlit sheep
    A hundred years ago.

A. E. Housman (1859–1936)

QUESTIONS

1. Vocabulary: *heath* (1).
2. Housman explains in a note to lines 5–6 that "Hanging in chains was called keeping sheep by moonlight." Where is this idea repeated?
3. What is the speaker's attitude toward his friend? Toward other young men who have died by hanging? What is the purpose of the reference to the young men hanged "a hundred years ago"?
4. Discuss the kinds of imagery present in the poem and their role in the development of the dramatic situation.
5. Discuss the use of language in stanza 5.

A NARROW FELLOW IN THE GRASS

A narrow fellow in the grass
Occasionally rides;
You may have met him – did you not?
His notice sudden is.

The grass divides as with a comb,   5
A spotted shaft is seen,
And then it closes at your feet
And opens further on.

He likes a boggy acre,
A floor too cool for corn,   10
Yet when a boy, and barefoot,
I more than once at noon

Have passed, I thought, a whip-lash
Unbraiding in the sun,
When, stooping to secure it,   15
It wrinkled, and was gone.

Several of nature's people
I know, and they know me;
I feel for them a transport
Of cordiality;   20

But never met this fellow,
Attended or alone,
Without a tighter breathing
And zero at the bone.

Emily Dickinson (1830–1886)

QUESTIONS

1. The subject of this poem is never named. What is it? How does the imagery
   identify it?
2. The last two lines might be paraphrased as "without being frightened." Why
   is Dickinson's wording more effective?
3. Who is the speaker?

LIVING IN SIN

She had thought the studio would keep itself;
no dust upon the furniture of love.
Half heresy, to wish the taps less vocal,
the panes relieved of grime. A plate of pears,
a piano with a Persian shawl, a cat   5
stalking the picturesque amusing mouse
had risen at his urging.

Not that at five each separate stair would writhe
under the milkman's tramp; that morning light
so coldly would delineate the scraps   10
of last night's cheese and three sepulchral bottles;
that on the kitchen shelf among the saucers
a pair of beetle-eyes would fix her own –
envoy from some village in the moldings . . .
Meanwhile, he, with a yawn,   15
sounded a dozen notes upon the keyboard,
declared it out of tune, shrugged at the mirror,
rubbed at his beard, went out for cigarettes;
while she, jeered by the minor demons,
pulled back the sheets and made the bed and found   20
a towel to dust the table-top,
and let the coffee-pot boil over on the stove.
By evening she was back in love again,
though not so wholly but throughout the night
she woke sometimes to feel the daylight coming   25
like a relentless milkman up the stairs.

Adrienne Rich (b. 1929)

QUESTIONS

1. Explain the grammatical structure and meaning of the sentence in lines 4–7.
   What are its subject and verb? To whom or what does "his" (8) refer? What
   kind of life do its images conjure up?
2. On what central contrast is the poem based? What is its central mood or
   emotion?
3. Discuss the various kinds of imagery used and their function in conveying the
   experience of the poem.

THOSE WINTER DAYS

Sundays too my father got up early
and put his clothes on in the blueblack cold,
then with cracked hands that ached
from labor in the weekday weather made
banked fires blaze. No one ever thanked him.   5
I'd wake and hear the cold splintering, breaking.
When the rooms were warm, he'd call,
and slowly I would rise and dress,
fearing the chronic angers of that house,

Speaking indifferently to him,   10
who had driven out the cold
and polished my good shoes as well.
What did I know, what did I know
of love's austere and lonely offices?

Robert Hayden (b. 1913)

QUESTIONS

1. Vocabulary: *offices* (14).
2. What kind of imagery is central to the poem? How is this imagery related to the emotional concerns of the poem?
3. How do the subsidiary images relate to the central images?
4. From what point in time does the speaker view the subject matter of the poem? What has happened to him in the interval?

TO AUTUMN

Season of mists and mellow fruitfulness,
    Close bosom-friend of the maturing sun;
Conspiring with him how to load and bless
    With fruit the vines that round the thatch-eves run;
To bend with apples the mossed cottage-trees,   5
    And fill all fruit with ripeness to the core;
        To swell the gourd, and plump the hazel shells
With a sweet kernel; to set budding more,
    And still more, later flowers for the bees,
    Until they think warm days will never cease,   10
        For summer has o'er-brimmed their clammy cells.

Who hath not seen thee oft amid thy store?
    Sometimes whoever seeks abroad may find
Thee sitting careless on a granary floor,
    Thy hair soft-lifted by the winnowing wind;   15
Or on a half-reaped furrow sound asleep,
    Drowsed with the fume of poppies, while thy hook
        Spares the next swath and all its twinèd flowers:
And sometimes like a gleaner thou dost keep
    Steady thy laden head across a brook;   20
    Or by a cider-press, with patient look,
        Thou watchest the last oozings hours by hours.

Where are the songs of Spring? Ay, where are they?
    Think not of them, thou hast thy music too,—
While barred clouds bloom the soft-dying day,   25
    And touch the stubble-plains with rosy hue;
Then in a wailful choir the small gnats mourn
    Among the river sallows, borne aloft
        Or sinking as the light wind lives or dies;
And full-grown lambs loud bleat from hilly bourn;   30
    Hedge-crickets sing; and now with treble soft
    The red-breast whistles from a garden-croft;
        And gathering swallows twitter in the skies.

John Keats (1795–1821)

QUESTIONS

1. Vocabulary: *hook* (17), *barred* (25), *sallows* (28), *bourn* (30), *croft* (32).
2. How many kinds of imagery do you find in the poem? Give examples of each.
3. Are the images arranged haphazardly or are they carefully organized? In answering this question, consider: (a) With what aspect of autumn is each stanza particularly concerned? (b) What kind of imagery is dominant in each stanza? (c) What time of the season is presented in each stanza? (d) Is there any progression in time of day?
4. What is Autumn personified as in stanza 2? Is there any suggestion of personification in the other two stanzas?
5. Although the poem is primarily descriptive, what attitude toward transience and passing beauty is implicit in it?

OF PHYLLIS

In petticoat of green,
Her hair about her eyne,°   eyes
Phyllis beneath an oak
Sat milking her fair flock:
Among that sweet-strained moisture, rare delight,
Her hand seemed milk in milk, it was so white.

William Drummond (1585–1649)

5 Figurative Language 1

Metaphor, Personification, Metonymy

*Poetry provides the one permissible way
of saying one thing and meaning another.*

ROBERT FROST

Let us assume that your roommate has just come in out of a rainstorm and you say to him, "Well, you're a pretty sight! Got slightly wet, didn't you?" And he replies, "Wet? I'm drowned! It's raining cats and dogs outside, and my raincoat's just like a sieve!"

It is likely that you and your roommate understand each other well enough, and yet if you examine this conversation literally, that is to say unimaginatively, you will find that you have been speaking nonsense. Actually you have been speaking figuratively. You have been saying less than what you mean, or more than what you mean, or the opposite of what you mean, or something else than what you mean. You did not mean that your roommate was a pretty sight but that he was a wretched sight. You did not mean that he got slightly wet but that he got very wet. Your roommate did not mean that he got drowned but that he got drenched. It was not raining cats and dogs; it was raining water. And your roommate's raincoat is so unlike a sieve that not even a baby would confuse them.

If you are familiar with Molière's play *Le Bourgeois Gentilhomme,* you will remember how delighted M. Jourdain was to discover that he had been speaking prose all his life. You may be equally surprised to discover that you have been speaking a kind of subpoetry all your life. The difference between your figures of speech and the poet's is that yours are probably worn and trite, the poet's fresh and original.

On first examination, it might seem absurd to say one thing and mean another. But we all do it and with good reason. We do it because we can say what we want to say more vividly and forcefully by figures than we can by saying it directly. And we can say more by figurative statement than we can by literal statement. Figures of speech are another way of adding extra dimensions to language. We shall examine their usefulness more particularly later in this chapter.

Broadly defined, a FIGURE OF SPEECH is any way of saying something other than the ordinary way, and some rhetoricians have classified as many as 250 separate figures. For our purposes, however, a figure of speech is more narrowly definable as a way of saying one thing and meaning another, and we need be concerned with no more than a dozen. FIGURATIVE LANGUAGE – language using figures of speech – is language that cannot be taken literally.

METAPHOR and SIMILE are both used as a means of comparing things that are essentially unlike. The only distinction between them is that in simile the comparison is *expressed* by the use of some word or phrase, such as *like, as, than, similar to, resembles,* or *seems;* in metaphor the comparison is *implied* – that is, the figurative term is *substituted for* or *identified with* the literal term.

THE GUITARIST TUNES UP

> With what attentive courtesy he bent
> Over his instrument;
> Not as a lordly conquerer who could
> Command both wire and wood,
> But as a man with a loved woman might,
> Inquiring with delight
> What slight essential things she had to say
> Before they started, he and she, to play.

> *Frances Cornford (1886–1960)*

QUESTION

1. Explore the comparison. Does it principally illuminate the guitarist or the lovers or both? What one word brings its two terms together?

THE HOUND

Life the hound
Equivocal
Comes at a bound
Either to rend me
Or to befriend me.   5
I cannot tell
The hound's intent
Till he has sprung
At my bare hand
With teeth or tongue.   10
Meanwhile I stand
And wait the event.

Robert Francis (b. 1901)

QUESTION

1. What does "equivocal" (2) mean? Show how this is the key word in the poem. What is the effect of placing it on a line by itself?

Metaphors may take one of four forms, depending on whether the literal and figurative terms are respectively *named* or *implied*. In the first form of metaphor, as in simile, both the literal and figurative terms are named. In Francis's poem, for example, the literal term is "life" and the figurative term is "hound." In the second form, the literal term is *named* and the figurative term is *implied*.

BEREFT

Where had I heard this wind before
Change like this to a deeper roar?
What would it take my standing there for,
Holding open a restive door,
Looking downhill to a frothy shore?   5
Summer was past and day was past.
Somber clouds in the west were massed.
Out in the porch's sagging floor
Leaves got up in a coil and hissed,
Blindly struck at my knee and missed.   10

Something sinister in the tone
Told me my secret must be known:
Word I was in the house alone
Somehow must have gotten abroad,
Word I was in my life alone,   15
Word I had no one left but God.

Robert Frost (1874–1963)

QUESTIONS

1. Describe the situation precisely. What time of day and year is it? Where is the
   speaker? What is happening to the weather?
2. To what are the leaves in lines 9–10 compared?
3. The word "hissed" (9) is onomatopoetic (see page 200). How is its effect
   reinforced in the lines following?
4. Though lines 9–10 present the clearest example of the second form of
   metaphor, there are others. To what is the wind ("it") compared in line 3?
   Why is the door (4) "restive" and what does this do (figuratively) to the
   door? To what is the speaker's "life" compared (15)?
5. What is the tone of the poem? How reassuring is the last line?

In the third form of metaphor, the literal term is *implied* and the figurative
term is *named*. In the fourth form, both the literal *and* figurative terms are
implied. The following poem exemplifies both types:

IT SIFTS FROM LEADEN SIEVES

It sifts from leaden sieves,
It powders all the wood.
It fills with alabaster wool
The wrinkles of the road.

It makes an even face   5
Of mountain and of plain –
Unbroken forehead from the east
Unto the east again.

It reaches to the fence,
It wraps it rail by rail   10
Till it is lost in fleeces;
It deals celestial veil

To stump and stack and stem –
A summer's empty room –
Acres of joints where harvests were,   15
Recordless°, but for them.   unrecorded

It ruffles wrists of posts
As ankles of a queen,
Then stills its artisans like ghosts,
Denying they have been.   20

Emily Dickinson (1830–1886)

QUESTIONS

1. This poem consists essentially of a series of metaphors having the same literal term, identified only as "It." What is "It"?
2. In several of these metaphors the figurative term is named – "alabaster wool" (3), "fleeces" (11), "celestial veil" (12). In two of them, however, the figurative term as well as the literal term is left unnamed. To what is "It" compared in lines 1–2? In lines 17–18?
3. Comment on the additional metaphorical expressions or complications contained in "leaden sieves" (1), "alabaster wool" (3), "even face" (5), "unbroken forehead" (7), "a summer's empty room" (14), "artisans" (19).

Metaphors of the fourth form, as one might guess, are comparatively rare. An extended example, however, is provided by Dickinson's "I like to see it lap the miles" (page 209).

PERSONIFICATION consists in giving the attributes of a human being to an animal, an object, or a concept. It is really a subtype of metaphor, an implied comparison in which the figurative term of the comparison is always a human being. When Sylvia Plath makes a mirror speak and think (page 31), she is personifying an object. When Keats describes autumn as a harvester "sitting careless on a granary floor" or "on a half-reaped furrow sound asleep" (page 58), he is personifying a concept. Personifications differ in the degree to which they ask the reader actually to visualize the literal term in human form. In Keats's comparison we are asked to make a complete identification of autumn with a human being. In Sylvia Plath's, though the mirror speaks and thinks, we continue to visualize it as a mirror; similarly, in Frost's "Bereft" (page 62), the "restive" door remains in appearance a door tugged by the wind. In Browning's reference to "the startled little waves" (page 51), a personification is barely suggested; we would make a mistake if we tried to visualize the waves in human form or even, really, to think of them as having human emotions.*

Closely related to personification is APOSTROPHE, which consists in addressing someone absent or something nonhuman as if it were alive and present and could reply to what is being said. When the speaker in James Joyce's poem (page 175) cries out, "My love, my love, my love, why have you left me alone?" he is apostrophizing his departed sweetheart. The speaker in Shakespeare's "Fear no more the heat o' the sun" (page 338) is apostrophizing the body of a dead boy. William Blake apostrophizes the tiger throughout his famous poem (page 285) but does not otherwise personify it. Keats apostrophizes as well as personifies autumn (page 58), and David Wagoner both apostrophizes and personifies the old English measures in his elegy (page 47). Personification and apostrophe are both ways of giving life and immediacy to one's language, but since neither requires great imaginative power on the part of the poet – apostrophe especially does not – they may degenerate into mere mannerisms and are to be found as often in bad and mediocre poetry as in good. We need to distinguish between their effective use and their merely conventional use.

DR. SIGMUND FREUD DISCOVERS THE SEA SHELL

> Science, that simple saint, cannot be bothered
> Figuring what anything is for:
> Enough for her devotions that things are
> And can be contemplated soon as gathered.
>
> She knows how every living thing was fathered,   5
> She calculates the climate of each star,
> She counts the fish at sea, but cannot care
> Why any one of them exists, fish, fire or feathered.

---

*The various figures of speech blend into each other, and it is sometimes difficult to classify a specific example as definitely metaphor or symbol, symbolism or allegory, understatement or irony, irony or paradox. Often a given example may exemplify two or more figures at once. When Donne's speaker in "Break of Day" (page 32) says "Light hath no tongue, but is all eye" and then imagines light speaking as well as spying, she is not only personifying light but is metaphorically comparing the sun to an eye and is metonymically identifying light and the sun. In the poem "A White Rose" (page 82), beginning "The red rose whispers of passion," the red rose is personified by the verb *whispers* but is at the same time a symbol. The important consideration in reading poetry is not that we classify figures definitively but that we construe them correctly.

Why should she? Her religion is to tell
By rote her rosary of perfect answers.   10
Metaphysics she can leave to man:
She never wakes at night in heaven or hell

Staring at darkness. In her holy cell
There is no darkness ever: the pure candle
Burns, the beads drop briskly from her hand.   15

Who dares to offer Her the curled sea shell!
She will not touch it! – knows the world she sees
Is all the world there is! Her faith is perfect!

And still he offers the sea shell . . .
                                     What surf
Of what far sea upon what unknown ground   20
Troubles forever with that asking sound?
What surge is this whose question never ceases?

Archibald MacLeish (b. 1892)

QUESTIONS

1. Vocabulary: *metaphysics* (11).
2. This poem employs an extended personification. List the ways in which
   science is appropriately compared to a saint. In what way is its faith "perfect"
   (18)?
3. Who is "he" in line 19?
4. Who was Sigmund Freud, and what discoveries did he make about human
   nature?
5. What does the sea shell represent?

TO DAFFODILS

                Fair Daffodils, we weep to see
                    You haste away so soon;
                As yet the early-rising sun
                    Has not attained his noon.
                        Stay, stay,   5
                    Until the hasting day
                        Has run
                    But to the evensong;
                And having prayed together, we
                    Will go with you along.   10

We have short time to stay as you;
　　We have as short a spring;
　As quick a growth to meet decay
　　As you, or anything.
　　　We die   15
　　As your hours do, and dry
　　　Away
　Like to the summer's rain;
Or as the pearls of morning's dew
　Ne'er to be found again.   20

Robert Herrick (1591–1674)

QUESTIONS

1. Vocabulary: *evensong* (8). evening prayer, whom its sung
2. Try rewriting this poem without the apostrophe. For instance, lines 1–2 might be rendered as "We weep to see fair daffodils / Hasten away so soon" and line 5 as "If they'd but stay," with third person pronouns substituted for second person pronouns throughout the rest of the poem. How does the revision compare with the original in effectiveness? Why?
3. Is the statement made in line 11 literally true? What is the poem about? What do the daffodils and "the hasting day" (6) symbolize?
4. What other figures of speech are used in the poem? What form of metaphor is contained within the simile in line 19?

SYNECDOCHE (the use of the part for the whole) and METONYMY (the use of something closely related for the thing actually meant) are alike in that both substitute some significant detail or aspect of an experience for the experience itself. Thus, Shakespeare uses synecdoche when he says that the cuckoo's song is unpleasing to a "married ear" (page 11), for he means a married *man*. Robert Graves uses synecdoche in "The Naked and the Nude" (page 38) when he refers to a doctor as a "hippocratic eye," and T. S. Eliot uses it in "The Love Song of J. Alfred Prufrock" when he refers to a crab or lobster as "a pair of ragged claws" (page 262). Shakespeare uses metonymy when he says that the yellow cuckoo-buds "paint the meadows with delight" (page 11), for he means with bright color, which produces delight. Robert Frost uses metonymy in "Out, Out—" (page 124) when he describes an injured boy holding up his cut hand "as if to keep / The life from spilling," for literally he means to keep the blood from spilling. In each case, however, there is a gain in vividness and meaning. Eliot, by substituting for the crab that part which seizes its prey, tells us something important about the crab and makes us see it more vividly. Shakespeare, by referring to bright color as "delight" evokes not only the visual effect but the emotional response it arouses. Frost tells us both that the boy's hand is bleeding and that his life is in danger.

Many synecdoches and metonymies, of course, like many metaphors, have become so much a part of the language that they no longer strike us as figurative; such is the case with *redskin* for Indian, *paleface* for white man, and *salt* and *tar* for sailor. Such figures are referred to as dead metaphors or dead figures. Synecdoche and metonymy are so much alike that it is hardly worth while to distinguish between them, and the latter term is increasingly coming to be used for both. In this book metonymy will be used for both figures – that is, for any figure in which a part or something closely related is substituted for the thing literally meant.

SHE SIGHTS A BIRD

> She sights a bird, she chuckles,
> She flattens, then she crawls,
> She runs without the look of feet,
> Her eyes increase to balls,
>
> Her jaws stir, twitching, hungry,   5
> Her teeth can hardly stand,
> She leaps – but robin leaped the first!
> Ah, pussy of the sand,
>
> The hopes so juicy ripening
> You almost bathed your tongue   10
> When bliss disclosed a hundred wings
> And fled with every one!

Emily Dickinson (1830–1886)

QUESTIONS

1. Identify the metonymy in line 11. Why is it effective? How is it prepared for in the poem?
2. What other figures of speech does the poem make use of?

We said at the beginning of this chapter that figurative language often provides a more effective means of saying what we mean than does direct statement. What are some of the reasons for that effectiveness?

First, figurative language affords us imaginative pleasure. Imagination might be described in one sense as that faculty or ability of the mind that proceeds by sudden leaps from one point to another, that goes up a stair by leaping in one jump from the bottom to the top rather than by climbing up one step at a time.* The mind takes delight in these sudden leaps, in seeing likenesses between unlike things. We have probably all taken pleasure in staring into a fire and seeing castles and cities and armies in it, or in looking into the clouds and shaping them into animals or faces, or in seeing a man in the moon. We name our plants and flowers after fancied resemblances; jack-in-the-pulpit, babies'-breath, Queen Anne's lace. Figures of speech are therefore satisfying in themselves, providing us with a source of pleasure in the exercise of the imagination.

Second, figures of speech are a way of bringing additional imagery into verse, of making the abstract concrete, of making poetry more sensuous. When MacLeish personifies science (page 65), he gives body and form to what had previously been only a concept. When Emily Dickinson compares poetry to "prancing coursers" (page 36), she objectifies imaginative and rhythmical qualities by presenting them in visual terms. When Robert Browning compares the crisping waves to "fiery ringlets" (page 51), he starts with one image and transforms it into three. Figurative language is a way of multiplying the sense appeal of poetry.

Third, figures of speech are a way of adding emotional intensity to otherwise merely informative statements and of conveying attitudes along with information. If we say, "So-and-so is a rat" or "My feet are killing me," our meaning is as much emotional as informative. When Thomas Hardy compares "tangled bine-stems" to "strings of broken lyres" (page 312), he not only draws an exact visual comparison but also conjures up a feeling of despondency through the suggestion of discarded instruments no longer capable of making music. When Wilfred Owen compares a soldier caught in a gas attack to a man drowning under a green sea (page 8), he conveys a feeling of despair and suffocation as well as a visual image.

Fourth, figures of speech are a means of concentration, a way of saying much in brief compass. Like words, they may be multidimensional. Consider, for instance, the merits of comparing life to a candle, as Shakespeare does in a passage from *Macbeth* (page 125). Life is like a candle in that it begins and ends in darkness; in that while it burns, it gives

---

*It is also the faculty of mind that is able to "picture" or "image" absent objects as if they were present. It was with imagination in this sense that we were concerned in the chapter on imagery.

off light and energy, is active and colorful; in that it gradually consumes itself, gets shorter and shorter; in that it can be snuffed out at any moment; in that it is brief at best, burns only for a short duration. Possibly your imagination can suggest other similarities. But at any rate, Macbeth's compact metaphorical description of life as a "brief candle" suggests certain truths about life that would require dozens of words to state in literal language. At the same time it makes the abstract concrete, provides imaginative pleasure, and adds a degree of emotional intensity.

Obviously one of the necessary abilities for reading poetry is the ability to interpret figurative language. Every use of figurative language involves a risk of misinterpretation, though the risk is well worth taking. For the person who can translate the figure, the dividends are immense. Fortunately all people have imagination to some degree, and imagination can be cultivated. By practice one's ability to interpret figures of speech can be increased.

EXERCISE

1. Identify each of the following quotations as literal or figurative. If figurative, explain what is being compared to what and explain the appropriateness of the comparison. EXAMPLE: "Talent is a cistern; genius is a fountain." ANSWER: A metaphor. Talent = cistern; genius = fountain. Talent exists in finite supply; it can be used up. Genius is inexhaustible, ever renewing.

   a. O tenderly the haughty day
      Fills his blue urn with fire.   *Emerson*

   b. It is with words as with sunbeams – the more they are condensed, the
      deeper they burn.   *Robert Southey*

   c. Joy and Temperance and Repose
      Slam the door on the doctor's nose.   *Anonymous*

   d. The pen is mightier than the sword.   *Edward Bulwer-Lytton*

   e. The strongest oaths are straw
      To the fire i' the blood.   *Shakespeare*

   f. The Cambridge ladies . . . live in furnished souls.   *e. e. cummings*

   g. The green lizard and the golden snake,
      Like unimprisoned flames, out of their trance awake.   *Shelley*

   h. Dorothy's eyes, with their long brown lashes, looked very much like her
      mother's.   *Laetitia Johnson*

   i. Is this the face that launched a thousand ships?   *Marlowe*

j. What should such fellows as I do crawling between earth and heaven?

                 Shakespeare

k. Love's feeling is more soft and sensible
 Than are the tender horns of cockled snails.   *Shakespeare*

l. The tawny-hided desert crouches watching her.   *Francis Thompson*

m. . . . Let us sit upon the ground
 And tell sad stories of the death of kings.   *Shakespeare*

n. See, from his [Christ's, on the cross] head, his hands, his side
 Sorrow and love flow mingled down.   *Isaac Watts*

o. Now half [of the departing guests] to the setting moon are gone,
 And half to the rising day.   *Tennyson*

p. I do not know whether my present poems are better than the earlier ones.
 But this is certain: they are much sadder and sweeter, like pain dipped in
 honey.   *Heinrich Heine*

q. . . . clouds. . . . Shepherded by the slow, unwilling wind. *Shelley*

r. Let us eat and drink, for tomorrow we shall die.   *Isaiah 22:13*

s. Let us eat and drink, for tomorrow we may die.
          Common misquotation of the above

     * * * * *

THE SILKEN TENT

   She is as in a field a silken tent
   At midday when a sunny summer breeze
   Has dried the dew and all its ropes relent,
   So that in guys it gently sways at ease,
   And its supporting central cedar pole,   5
   That is its pinnacle to heavenward
   And signifies the sureness of the soul,
   Seems to owe naught to any single cord,
   But strictly held by none, is loosely bound
   By countless silken ties of love and thought   10
   To everything on earth the compass round,
   And only by one's going slightly taut
   In the capriciousness of summer air
   Is of the slightest bondage made aware.

           Robert Frost (1874–1963)

1. A poet may use a variety of metaphors and similes in developing his subject or may, as Frost does here, develop a single figure at length (this poem is an excellent example of EXTENDED or SUSTAINED SIMILE). What are the advantages of each type of development?
2. Explore the similarities between the two things compared.

METAPHORS

I'm a riddle in nine syllables,
An elephant, a ponderous house,
A melon strolling on two tendrils.
O red fruit, ivory, fine timbers!
This loaf's big with its yeasty rising.
Money's new-minted in this fat purse.
I'm a means, a stage, a cow in calf.
I've eaten a bag of green apples,
Boarded the train there's no getting off.

Sylvia Plath (1932–1963)

QUESTIONS

1. Like its first metaphor, this poem is a riddle to be solved by identifying the literal terms of its metaphors. After you have identified the speaker ("riddle," "elephant," "house," "melon," "stage," "cow"), identify the literal meanings of the related metaphors ("syllables," "tendrils," "fruit," "ivory," "timbers," "loaf," "yeasty rising," "money," "purse," "train"). How is line 8 to be interpreted?
2. How does the form of the poem relate to its content?

TOADS

Why should I let the toad *work*
   Squat on my life?
Can't I use my wit as a pitchfork
   And drive the brute off?

Six days of the week it soils   5
   With its sickening poison –
Just for paying a few bills!
   That's out of proportion.

Lots of folk live on their wits:
   Lecturers, lispers,   10
Losels,° loblolly-men,° louts –   scoundrels; bumpkins
   They don't end as paupers;

Lot of folk live up lanes
   With fires in a bucket,
Eat windfalls and tinned sardines –   15
   They seem to like it.

Their nippers° have got bare feet,   children
   Their unspeakable wives
Are skinny as whippets – and yet
   No one actually *starves.*   20

Ah, were I courageous enough
   To shout *Stuff your pension!*
But I know, all too well, that's the stuff
   That dreams are made on;

For something sufficiently toad-like   25
   Squats in me, too;
Its hunkers° are heavy as hard luck,   haunches
   And cold as snow,

And will never allow me to blarney
   My way to getting   30
The fame and the girl and the money
   All at one sitting.

I don't say, one bodies the other
   One's spiritual truth;
But I do say it's hard to lose either,   35
   When you have both.

Philip Larkin (b. 1922)

QUESTIONS

1. How many "toads" are described in the poem? Where is each located? How are they described? What are the antecedents of the pronouns "one" and "the other / one" (33–34) respectively?
2. What characteristics have the people mentioned in stanza 3 in common? Those mentioned in stanzas 4–5?
3. Explain the pun in stanza 6 and the literary allusion it leads into. (If you don't recognize it, check Shakespeare's *Tempest,* Act IV, Scene 1, line 146.)

4. The first "toad" is explicitly identified as "work" (1). The literal term for the second "toad" is not named. Why not? What do you take it to be?
5. What kind of person is the speaker? What are his attitudes toward work?

A VALEDICTION: FORBIDDING MOURNING

As virtuous men pass mildly away,
    And whisper to their souls to go,
While some of their sad friends do say,
    The breath goes now, and some say, no:

So let us melt, and make no noise,   5
    No tear-floods, nor sigh-tempests move,
'Twere profanation of our joys
    To tell the laity our love.

Moving of th' earth brings harms and fears,
    Men reckon what it did and meant,   10
But trepidation of the spheres,
    Though greater far, is innocent.

Dull sublunary lovers' love
    (Whose soul is sense) cannot admit
Absence, because it doth remove   15
    Those things which elemented it.

But we by a love so much refined,
    That ourselves know not what it is,
Inter-assurèd of the mind,
    Care less, eyes, lips, and hands to miss.   20

Our two souls therefore, which are one,
    Though I must go, endure not yet
A breach, but an expansion,
    Like gold to airy thinness beat.

If they be two, they are two so   25
    As stiff twin compasses are two,
Thy soul the fixed foot, makes no show
    To move, but doth, if th' other do.

[handwritten margin note: In the astronomy of the time, anything under the moon's sphere is subject to change & imperfection]

And though it in the center sit,
 Yet when the other far doth roam,
It leans, and hearkens after it,
 And grows erect, as that comes home.   30

Such wilt thou be to me, who must
 Like th' other foot, obliquely run;
Thy firmness makes my circle just,   35
 And makes me end, where I begun.

John Donne (1572–1631)

QUESTIONS

written while is wife when he left = she was pregnant —
exploration of leaving, but with idea of returning

1. Vocabulary: *valediction* (title), *profanation* (7), *laity* (8), *trepidation* (11), *innocent* (12), *sublunary* (13), *elemented* (16). Line 11 is a reference to the spheres of the Ptolemaic cosmology, whose movements caused no such disturbance as does a movement of the earth – that is, an earthquake.
2. Is the speaker in the poem about to die? Or about to leave on a journey?
3. The poem is organized around a contrast of two kinds of lovers: the "laity" (8) and, as their implied opposite, the priesthood. Are these terms literal or metaphorical? What two major contrasts are drawn between these two kinds of lovers?
4. Find and explain three similes and one metaphor used to describe the parting of true lovers. The figure in the last three stanzas is one of the most famous in English literature. Demonstrate its appropriateness by obtaining a drawing compass or by using two pencils to imitate the two legs.
5. What kind of language is used in the poem? Is the language consonant with the figures of speech?

TO HIS COY MISTRESS

Had we but world enough, and time,
This coyness, lady, were no crime.
We would sit down, and think which way
To walk, and pass our long love's day.
Thou by the Indian Ganges' side   5
Shouldst rubies find; I by the tide
Of Humber would complain. I would
Love you ten years before the Flood,
And you should, if you please, refuse
Till the conversion of the Jews.   10
My vegetable love should grow

Vaster than empires, and more slow;
An hundred years should go to praise
Thine eyes, and on thy forehead gaze;
Two hundred to adore each breast,   15
But thirty thousand to the rest;
An age at least to every part,
And the last age should show your heart.
For, lady, you deserve this state,
Nor would I love at lower rate.   20
  But at my back I always hear
Time's wingèd chariot hurrying near;
And yonder all before us lie
Deserts of vast eternity.
Thy beauty shall no more be found,   25
Nor, in thy marble vault, shall sound
My echoing song; then worms shall try
That long-preserved virginity,
And your quaint honor turn to dust,
And into ashes all my lust: 30
The grave's a fine and private place,
But none, I think, do there embrace.
  Now therefore, while the youthful hue
Sits on thy skin like morning dew,
And while thy willing soul transpires   35
At every pore with instant fires,
Now let us sport us while we may,
And now, like amorous birds of prey,
Rather at once our time devour
Than languish in his slow-chapped power.   40
Let us roll all our strength and all
Our sweetness up into one ball,
And tear our pleasures with rough strife
Thorough° the iron gates of life.   through
Thus, though we cannot make our sun   45
Stand still, yet we will make him run.

Andrew Marvell (1621–1678)

QUESTIONS

1. Vocabulary: *mistress* (title), *Humber* (7), *transpires* (35), *chapped* (40).
2. Outline the speaker's argument in three sentences, beginning with *If, But,* and *Therefore.* Is the speaker urging his mistress to marry him?

3. Explain the appropriateness of "vegetable love" (11). What simile in the third section contrasts with it and how? What image in the third section contrasts with the distance between the Ganges and the Humber in section one?
4. Explain the figures in lines 22, 24, and 40 and their implications.
5. Explain the last two lines. For what is "sun" a metonymy?
6. Is this poem principally about love or about time? If the latter, what might making love represent? What philosophy is the poet advancing here?

LOVELIEST OF TREES

Loveliest of trees, the cherry now
Is hung with bloom along the bough,
And stands about the woodland ride
Wearing white for Eastertide.

Now, of my threescore years and ten,   5
Twenty will not come again,
And take from seventy springs a score,
It only leaves me fifty more.

And since to look at things in bloom
Fifty springs are little room,   10
About the woodlands I will go
To see the cherry hung with snow.

A. E. Housman (1859–1936)

QUESTIONS
another carpe diem poem, w/o love interest
1. Very briefly, this poem presents a philosophy of life. In a sentence, what is it?
2. How old is the speaker? Why does he assume that his life will be seventy years in length? What is surprising about the words "only" (8) and "little" (10)?
3. A good deal of ink has been spilt over whether "snow" (12) is literal or figurative. What do you say? Justify your answer.

TO A FRIEND WHOSE WORK HAS COME TO NOTHING

Now all the truth is out,
Be secret and take defeat
From any brazen throat,
For how can you compete,
Being honor bred, with one   5

Who, were it proved he lies,
Were neither shamed in his own
Nor in his neighbors' eyes?
Bred to a harder thing
Than Triumph, turn away   10
And like a laughing string
Whereon mad fingers play
Amid a place of stone,
Be secret and exult,
Because of all things known   15
That is most difficult.

William Butler Yeats (1865–1939)

QUESTIONS

1. The specific occasion for this poem was the defeat of Yeats's friend and patroness, Lady Augusta Gregory, in a bitter political contest to bring a magnificent collection of French Impressionist paintings to Dublin. The city officials, provincial, complacent, and ignorant, instituted a campaign of vilification and misrepresentation against Lady Gregory and her associates. The person referred to in Lines 5–8 was a powerful Dublin journalist. How does Yeats raise a purely local and ephemeral dispute into a matter of lasting and universal significance?
2. Discuss the major contrasts on which the poem rests. What essentially is the poet's advice to his friend? Is this primarily a poem of advice or tribute?
3. Identify and discuss the figures of speech involved in line 3.
4. Discuss the meaning of the simile in lines 11–14 and the importance of its contribution to the poem.

DREAM DEFERRED

What happens to a dream deferred?

Does it dry up
like a raisin in the sun?
Or fester like a sore –
And then run?
Does it stink like rotten meat?   5
Or crust and sugar over –
like a syrupy sweet?

Maybe it just sags
like a heavy load.

Or does it explode?   10

Langston Hughes (1902–1967)

QUESTIONS

1. Of the six images, five are similes. Which is a metaphor? Comment on its
   position and its effectiveness.
2. Since the dream could be any dream, the poem is general in its implication.
   What happens to your understanding of it on learning that its author was a
   black American?

ON HIS SEVENTY-FIFTH BIRTHDAY

I strove with none, for none was worth my strife;
   Nature I loved, and next to Nature, Art;
I warmed both hands before the fire of Life;
   It sinks; and I am ready to depart.

Walter Savage Landor (1775–1864)

QUESTIONS

1. What has been the speaker's attitude toward life? What is his attitude toward
   approaching death? Why?
2. What does the metaphor contribute to the meaning of the poem?

ON A CLERGYMAN'S HORSE BITING HIM

The steed bit his master;
   How came this to pass?
He heard the good pastor
   Cry, "All flesh is grass."

Anonymous

6 Figurative Language 2

Symbol, Allegory

THE ROAD NOT TAKEN

Two roads diverged in a yellow wood,
And sorry I could not travel both
And be one traveler, long I stood
And looked down one as far as I could
To where it bent in the undergrowth;   5

Then took the other, as just as fair,
And having perhaps the better claim,
Because it was grassy and wanted wear;
Though as for that the passing there
Had worn them really about the same,   10

And both that morning equally lay
In leaves no step had trodden black.
Oh, I kept the first for another day!
Yet knowing how way leads on to way,
I doubted if I should ever come back.   15

I shall be telling this with a sigh
Somewhere ages and ages hence:
Two roads diverged in a wood, and I —
I took the one less traveled by,
And that has made all the difference.   20

Robert Frost (1874–1963)

1. Does the speaker feel that he made the wrong choice in taking the road "less traveled by"? If not, why does he sigh? What does he regret?
2. Why does the choice between two roads that seem very much alike make such a big difference many years later?

A SYMBOL may be roughly defined as something that means *more* than what it is. "The Road Not Taken," for instance, concerns a choice made between two roads by a person out walking in the woods. He would like to explore both roads. He tells himself that he will explore one and then come back and explore the other, but he knows that he shall probably be unable to do so. By the last stanza, however, we realize that the poet is talking about something more than the choice of paths in a wood, for such a choice would be relatively unimportant, while this choice is one that will make a great difference in the speaker's life and that he will remember with a sigh "ages and ages hence." We must interpret his choice of a road as a symbol for any choice in life between alternatives that appear almost equally attractive but will result through the years in a large difference in the kind of experience one knows.

Image, metaphor, and symbol shade into each other and are sometimes difficult to distinguish. In general, however, an image means only what it is; a metaphor means something other than what it is; and a symbol means what it is and something more too.* If I say that a shaggy brown dog was rubbing its back against a white picket fence, I am talking about nothing but a dog (and a picket fence) and am therefore presenting an image. If I say, "Some dirty dog stole my wallet at the party," I am not talking about a dog at all and am therefore using a metaphor. But if I say, "You can't teach an old dog new tricks," I am talking not only about dogs but about living creatures of any species and am therefore speaking symbolically. Images, of course, do not cease to be images when they become incorporated in metaphors or symbols. If we are discussing the sensuous qualities of "The Road Not Taken" we should refer to the two leaf-strewn roads in the yellow wood as an image; if we are discussing the significance of the poem, we talk about them as symbols.

Symbols vary in the degree of identification and definition given them by their authors. Frost in this poem forces us to interpret the choice of

---

*This account does not hold for nonliterary symbols such as the letters of the alphabet and algebraic signs (the symbol ∞ for infinity or $=$ for equals). Here, the symbol is meaningless except as it stands for something else, and the connection between the sign and what it stands for is purely arbitrary.

roads symbolically by the degree of importance he gives it in the last stanza. Sometimes poets are much more specific in identifying their symbols. Sometimes they do not identify them at all. Consider, for instance, the following poems.

A WHITE ROSE

> The red rose whispers of passion,
>> And the white rose breathes of love;
> Oh, the red rose is a falcon,
>> And the white rose is a dove.
>
> But I send you a cream-white rosebud,
>> With a flush on its petal tips;
> For the love that is purest and sweetest
>> Has a kiss of desire on the lips.

John Boyle O'Reilly (1844–1890)

QUESTIONS

1. Could the poet have made the white rose a symbol of passion and the red rose a symbol of love? Why not?
2. In the second stanza, why does the speaker send a rosebud rather than a rose?

MY STAR

> All that I know
>> Of a certain star
> Is, it can throw
>> (Like the angled spar)
> Now a dart of red,   5
>> Now a dart of blue;
> Till my friends have said
>> They would fain see, too,
> My star that dartles the red and the blue!
> Then it stops like a bird; like a flower, hangs furled: 10
>> They must solace themselves with the Saturn above it.
> What matter to me if their star is a world?
>> Mine has opened its soul to me; therefore I love it.

Robert Browning (1812–1889)

In his first two lines O'Reilly indicates so clearly that his red rose is a symbol of physical desire and his white rose a symbol of spiritual attachment that when we get to the metaphor in the third line, we unconsciously substitute passion for the red rose in our minds, knowing without thinking that what O'Reilly is really likening is falcons and passion, not falcons and roses. Similarly in the second stanza, the symbolism of the white rosebud with pink tips is specifically indicated in the last two lines, although, as a matter of fact, it would have been clear from the first stanza. In Browning's poem, on the other hand, there is nothing specific to tell us that Browning is talking about anything other than just a star, and it is only the star's importance to him that makes us suspect that he is talking about something more.

The symbol is the richest and at the same time the most difficult of the poetical figures. Both its richness and its difficulty result from its imprecision. Although the poet may pin down the meaning of his symbol to something fairly definite and precise, as O'Reilly does in "A White Rose," more often the symbol is so general in its meaning that it is able to suggest a great variety of more specific meanings. It is like an opal that flashes out different colors when slowly turned in the light. The choice in "The Road Not Taken," for instance, concerns some choice in life, but what choice? Was it a choice of profession? (Frost took the road "less traveled by" in deciding to become a poet.) A choice of hobby? A choice of wife? It might be any or all or none of these. We cannot determine what particular choice the poet had in mind, if any, and it is not important that we do so. The general meaning of the poem is clear enough. It is an expression of regret that the possibilities of life-experience are so sharply limited. One must live with one wife, have one native country, follow one profession. The speaker in the poem would have liked to explore both roads, but he could explore only one. The person with a craving for life, however satisfied with his own choice, will always long for the realms of experience that had to be passed by. Because the symbol is a rich one, the poem suggests other meanings too. It affirms a belief in the possibility of choice and says something of the nature of choice – how each choice limits the range of possible future choices, so that we make our lives as we go, both freely choosing and being determined by past choices. Though not primarily a philosophical poem, it obliquely comments on the issue of free will versus determinism and indicates the poet's own position. It is able to do all these things, concretely and compactly, by its use of an effective symbol.

"My Star," if we interpret it symbolically, likewise suggests a variety of meanings. It has been most often interpreted as a tribute to Browning's wife, Elizabeth Barrett Browning. As one critic writes, "She shone upon his life like a star of various colors; but the moment the world attempted to pry into the secret of her genius, she shut off the light altogether."* The poem has also been taken to refer to Browning's own peculiar genius, "his gift for seeing in events and things a significance hidden from other men."† A third suggestion is that Browning was thinking of his own peculiar poetic style. He loved harsh, jagged sounds and rhythms and grotesque images; most people of his time found beauty only in the smoother-flowing, melodic rhythms and more conventionally poetic images of his contemporary Tennyson's style, which could be symbolized by Saturn in the poem. The point is not that any one of these interpretations is right or necessarily wrong. We cannot say what the poet had specifically in mind. Literally, the poem is an expression of affection for a particular star in the sky that has a unique beauty and fascination for the poet but in which no one else can see the qualities that the poet sees. If we interpret the poem symbolically, the star is a symbol for anything in life that has unique meanings and value for an individual, which other people cannot see. Beyond this, the meaning is "open." And because the meaning is open, the reader is justified in bringing his own experience to its interpretation. Browning's cherished star might remind him of, for instance, an old rag doll he particularly loved as a child, though its button eyes were off and its stuffing coming out and it had none of the crisp bright beauty of waxen dolls with real hair admired by other children.

Between the extremes represented by "The White Rose" and "My Star" a poem may exercise all degrees of control over the range and meaning of its symbolism. Consider another example.

YOU, ANDREW MARVELL

And here face down beneath the sun
And here upon earth's noonward height
To feel the always coming on
The always rising of the night:

*William Lyon Phelps, *Robert Browning: How to Know Him* (Indianapolis: Bobbs-Merrill, 1932), p. 165.
†Quoted from William Clyde DeVane, *A Browning Handbook* (New York: Crofts, 1935), p. 202.

To feel creep up the curving east   5
The earthly chill of dusk and slow
Upon those under lands the vast
And ever-climbing shadow grow

And strange at Ecbatan the trees
Take leaf by leaf the evening strange   10
The flooding dark about their knees
The mountains over Persia change

And now at Kermanshah the gate
Dark empty and the withered grass
And through the twilight now the late   15
Few travelers in the westward pass

And Baghdad darken and the bridge
Across the silent river gone
And through Arabia the edge
Of evening widen and steal on   20

And deepen on Palmyra's street
The wheel rut in the ruined stone
And Lebanon fade out and Crete
High through the clouds and overblown

And over Sicily the air   25
Still flashing with the landward gulls
And loom and slowly disappear
The sails above the shadowy hulls

And Spain go under and the shore
Of Africa the gilded sand   30
And evening vanish and no more
The low pale light across that land

Nor now the long light on the sea:
And here face downward in the sun
To feel how swift how secretly   35
The shadow of the night comes on . . .

                                   Archibald MacLeish (b. 1892)

1. We ordinarily speak of *nightfall.* Why does MacLeish speak of the "rising" of the night? What implicit metaphorical comparison is suggested by phrases like "rising of the night" (4), "the flooding dark" (11), "the bridge/Across the silent river gone" (17–18), "deepen on Palmyra's street" (21), "Spain go under" (29), and so on?
2. Does the comparative lack of punctuation serve any function? What is the effect of the repetition of "and" throughout the poem?
3. Ecbatan was founded in 700 B.C. and is associated in history with Cyrus the Great, founder of the Persian Empire, and with Alexander the Great. Kermanshah was another ancient city of Persia. Where are Baghdad, Palmyra, Lebanon, Crete?

On the literal level, "You, Andrew Marvell" is about the coming on of night. The poet, lying at noon full length in the sun somewhere in the United States,* pictures in his mind the earth's shadow, halfway around the world, moving silently westward over Persia, Syria, Crete, Sicily, Spain, Africa, and finally the Atlantic – approaching swiftly, in fact, the place where he himself lies. But the title of the poem tells us that, though particularly concerned with the passage of a day, it is more generally concerned with the swift passage of time; for the title is an allusion to a famous poem on this subject by Andrew Marvell ("To His Coy Mistress," page 75) and especially to two lines of that poem:

> But at my back I always hear
> Time's wingèd chariot hurrying near.

Once we are aware of this larger concern of the poem, two symbolical levels of interpretation open to us. Marvell's poem is primarily concerned with the swift passing of man's life; and the word *night,* we know, if we have had any experience with other literature, is a natural and traditional metaphor or symbol for death. The poet, then, is thinking not only about the passing of a day but about the passing of his life. He is at present "upon earth's noonward height" – in the full flush of manhood – but he is acutely conscious of the declining years ahead and of "how swift how secretly" his death comes on.

If we are to account fully for all the data of the poem, however, a third level of interpretation is necessary. What has dictated the poet's choice of

---

*MacLeish has identified the fixed location of the poem as Illinois on the shore of Lake Michigan.

geographical references? The places named, of course, progress from east to west; but they have a further linking characteristic. Ecbatan, Kermanshah, Baghdad, and Palmyra are all ancient or ruined cities, the relics of past empires and crumbled civilizations. Lebanon, Crete, Sicily, Spain, and North Africa are places where civilization once flourished more vigorously than it does at present. On a third level, then, the poet is concerned, not with the passage of a day nor with the passage of a lifetime, but with the passage of historical epochs. The poet's own country – the United States – now shines "upon the earth's noonward height" as a favored nation in the sun of history, but its civilization, too, will pass.

Meanings ray out from a symbol, like the corona around the sun or like connotations around a richly suggestive word. But the very fact that a symbol may be so rich in its meanings makes it necessary that we use the greatest tact in its interpretation. Though Browning's "My Star" might, if memory and reason be stretched, make us think of a rag doll, still we should not go around telling people that in this poem Browning uses the star to symbolize a rag doll, for this interpretation is private, idiosyncratic, and narrow. The poem allows it but does not itself suggest it. Moreover, we should never assume that because the meaning of a symbol is more or less open, we may make it mean anything we choose. We would be wrong, for instance, in interpreting the choice in "The Road Not Taken" as some choice between good and evil, for the poem tells us that the two roads are much alike and that both lie "in leaves no step had trodden black." Whatever the choice is, it is a choice between two goods. Whatever our interpretation of a symbolical poem, it must be tied firmly to the facts of the poem. We must not let loose of the string and let our imaginations go ballooning up among the clouds. Because the symbol is capable of adding so many dimensions to a poem, it is a peculiarly effective resource of the poet, but it is also peculiarly susceptible of misinterpretation by the untrained or incautious reader.

Accurate interpretation of the symbol requires delicacy, tact, and good sense. The reader must keep his balance while walking a tightrope between too little and too much – between underinterpretation and overinterpretation. If he falls off, however, it is much more desirable that he fall off on the side of too little. The reader who reads "The Road Not Taken" as being only about a choice between two roads in a wood has at least gotten part of the experience that the poem communicates, but the reader who reads into it anything he chooses might as well discard the poem and simply daydream.

Above all, we should avoid the disease of seeing symbols everywhere, like a man with hallucinations, whether there are symbols there or not. It is better to miss a symbol now and then than to walk constantly among shadows and mirages.

TO THE VIRGINS, TO MAKE MUCH OF TIME

Gather ye rosebuds while ye may,
    Old Time is still a-flying;
And this same flower that smiles today
    Tomorrow will be dying.

The glorious lamp of heaven, the Sun,   5
    The higher he's a-getting,
The sooner will his race be run,
    And nearer he's to setting.

That age is best which is the first,
    When youth and blood are warmer;   10
But being spent, the worse, and worst
    Times still succeed the former.

Then be not coy, but use your time;
    And while ye may, go marry;
For having lost but once your prime,   15
    You may forever tarry.

Robert Herrick (1591–1674)

QUESTIONS

1. The first two stanzas might be interpreted literally if the third and fourth stanzas did not force us to interpret them symbolically. What do the rosebuds symbolize (stanza 1)? What does the course of a day symbolize (stanza 2)? Does the poet fix the meaning of the rosebud symbol in the last stanza or merely name *one* of its specific meanings?
2. How does the title help us interpret the meaning of the symbol? Why did Herrick use "virgins" instead of *maidens?*
3. Why is such haste necessary in gathering the rosebuds? True, the blossoms die quickly, but they are replaced by others. Who *really* is dying?
4. What are the "worse, and worst" times (11)? Why?
5. Why did the poet use his wording rather than the following alternatives: *blooms* for "smiles" (3), *course* for "race" (7), *used* for "spent" (11), *spend* for "use" (13)?

ALLEGORY is a narrative or description that has a second meaning beneath the surface one. Although the surface story or description may have its own interest, the author's major interest is in the ulterior meaning. When Pharaoh in the Bible, for instance, has a dream in which seven fat kine are devoured by seven lean kine, the story does not really become significant until Joseph interprets its allegorical meaning: that Egypt is to enjoy seven years of fruitfulness and prosperity followed by seven years of famine. Allegory has been defined sometimes as an extended metaphor and sometimes as a series of related symbols. But it is usually distinguishable from both of these. It is unlike extended metaphor in that it involves a *system* of related comparisons rather than one comparison drawn out. It differs from symbolism in that it puts less emphasis on the images for their own sake and more on their ulterior meanings. Also, these meanings are more fixed. In allegory usually there is a one-to-one correspondence between the details and a single set of ulterior meanings. In complex allegories the details may have more than one meaning, but these meanings tend to be definite. Meanings do not ray out from allegory as they do from a symbol.

Allegory is less popular in modern literature than it was in medieval and Renaissance writing, and it is much less often found in short poems than in long works such as *The Faerie Queene, Everyman,* and *Pilgrim's Progress.* It has sometimes, especially with political allegory, been used to conceal meaning rather than reveal it (or, rather, to conceal it from some people while revealing it to others). Though less rich than the symbol, allegory is an effective way of making the abstract concrete and has occasionally been used effectively even in fairly short poems.

PEACE

Sweet Peace, where dost thou dwell? I humbly crave,
　　　　Let me once know.
　　I sought thee in a <u>secret cave</u>,
　　　　And asked, if Peace were there.
A hollow wind did seem to answer, No,　　　　　　　5
　　　　Go seek elsewhere.

I did; and going did a rainbow note.
　　　　Surely, thought I,
　　This is the lace of Peace's coat:
　　　　I will search out the matter.　　　　　　　10
But while I looked the clouds immediately
　　　　Did break and scatter.

Then went I to a garden and did spy
                    A gallant flower,
        The crown imperial. Sure, said I,   15
                    Peace at the root must dwell.
But when I digged, I saw a worm devour
                    What showed so well.

At length I met a rev'rend good old man,
                    Whom when for Peace   20
        I did demand, he thus began:
                    There was a Prince of old Christ
At Salem° dwelt, who lived with good increase   Jerusalem
                    Of flock and fold.

He sweetly lived; yet sweetness did not save   25
                    His life from foes.
        But after death out of his grave
                    There sprang twelve stalks of wheat;
Which many wond'ring at, got some of those
                    To plant and set.   30

It prospered strangely, and did soon disperse
                    Through all the earth:
        For they that taste it do rehearse,
                    That virtue lies therein,
A secret virtue, bringing peace and mirth   35
                    By flight of sin.

Take of this grain, which in my garden grows,
                    And grows for you;
        Make bread of it: and that repose
                    And peace which ev'rywhere   40
With so much earnestness you do pursue,
                    Is only there.

George Herbert (1593–1633)

QUESTIONS

1. Identify the Prince (22), his flock and fold (24), the twelve stalks of wheat
   (28), the grain (37), and the bread (39).

2. Should the secret cave (stanza 1), the rainbow (stanza 2), and the garden (stanza 3) be taken merely in the sense of "I searched everywhere" or should they be assigned more precise meanings?

3. Who is the "rev'rend good old man" (19), and what is *his* garden (37)?

EXERCISE

1. Determine whether "sleep," in the following poems, is literal, metaphorical, symbolical, or other. In each case explain and justify your answer.

   a. "On moonlit heath and lonesome bank," page 54, line 13.
   b. "On moonlit heath and lonesome bank," line 29.
   c. "Stopping by Woods on a Snowy Evening," page 138.
   d. "The Chimney Sweeper," page 107.
   e. "Is my team ploughing," page 23.
   f. "Ulysses," page 92, line 5.
   g. "The Toys," page 252.
   h. "Elegy for Yards, Pounds, and Gallons," page 47.
   i. "My Sweetest Lesbia," page 140.
   j. "Nature the gentlest mother is," page 141.

$$* \qquad * \qquad * \qquad * \qquad *$$

OTHERS, I AM NOT THE FIRST

Others, I am not the first,
Have willed more mischief than they durst:
If in the breathless night I too
Shiver now, 'tis nothing new.

More than I, if truth were told,   5
Have stood and sweated hot and cold,
And through their reins in ice and fire
Fear contended with desire.

Agued once like me were they,
But I like them shall win my way   10
Lastly to the bed of mold
Where there's neither heat nor cold.

But from my grave across my brow
Plays no wind of healing now,
And fire and ice within me fight   15
Beneath the suffocating night.

A. E. Housman (1859–1936)

1. Vocabulary: *reins* (7), *agued* (9).
2. In what condition or predicament does the speaker see himself? With what reflections does he try to console himself? How successfully?
3. How does the speaker view human life? Of what is "night" (3, 16) a symbol? Of what are "heat" and "cold" (12) symbols?

FIRE AND ICE

Some say the world will end in fire,
Some say in ice.
From what I've tasted of desire
I hold with those who favor fire.
But if it had to perish twice,
I think I know enough of hate
To say that for destruction ice
Is also great
And would suffice.

Robert Frost (1874–1963)

QUESTIONS

1. Who are "Some"? To what two theories do lines 1–2 refer?
2. Do "fire" and "ice," in this and in the preceding poem, have the same or different meanings? In which poem are the terms metaphorical? In which, symbolical? Explain.
3. Frost's poem ends with an example of *understatement* (see next chapter). How does it affect the tone of the poem? In what state of mind is the speaker in Frost's poem as compared with the speaker in Housman's?

ULYSSES (read)

It little profits that an idle king,
By this still hearth, among these barren crags,
Matched with an agèd wife, I mete and dole
Unequal laws unto a savage race,
That hoard, and sleep, and feed, and know not me.   5
I cannot rest from travel; I will drink
Life to the lees. All times I have enjoyed
Greatly, have suffered greatly, both with those
That loved me, and alone; on shore, and when

Through scudding drifts the rainy Hyades 10
Vext the dim sea. I am become a name;
For always roaming with a hungry heart
Much have I seen and known, – cities of men
And manners, climates, councils, governments,
Myself not least, but honored of them all; 15
And drunk delight of battle with my peers,
Far on the ringing plains of windy Troy.
I am a part of all that I have met;
Yet all experience is an arch wherethrough
Gleams that untraveled world, whose margin fades 20
For ever and for ever when I move.
How dull it is to pause, to make an end,
To rust unburnished, not to shine in use!
As though to breathe were life! Life piled on life
Were all too little, and of one to me 25
Little remains; but every hour is saved
From that eternal silence, something more,
A bringer of new things; and vile it were
For some three suns to store and hoard myself,
And this grey spirit yearning in desire 30
To follow knowledge like a sinking star,
Beyond the utmost bound of human thought.

This is my son, mine own Telemachus,
To whom I leave the scepter and the isle –
Well-loved of me, discerning to fulfil 35
This labor, by slow prudence to make mild
A rugged people, and through soft degrees
Subdue them to the useful and the good.
Most blameless is he, centered in the sphere
Of common duties, decent not to fail 40
In offices of tenderness, and pay
Meet adoration to my household gods,
When I am gone. He works his work, I mine.

There lies the port; the vessel puffs her sail:
There gloom the dark, broad seas. My mariners, 45
Souls that have toiled, and wrought, and thought with me –
That ever with a frolic welcome took
The thunder and the sunshine, and opposed

Free hearts, free foreheads – you and I are old;
Old age hath yet his honor and his toil. 50
Death closes all; but something ere the end,
Some work of noble note, may yet be done,
Not unbecoming men that strove with Gods.
The lights begin to twinkle from the rocks;
The long day wanes; the slow moon climbs; the deep 55
Moans round with many voices. Come, my friends,
'Tis not too late to seek a newer world.
Push off, and sitting well in order smite
The sounding furrows; for my purpose holds
To sail beyond the sunset, and the baths 60
Of all the western stars, until I die.
It may be that the gulfs will wash us down;
It may be we shall touch the Happy Isles,
And see the great Achilles, whom we knew.
Though much is taken, much abides; and though 65
We are not now that strength which in old days
Moved earth and heaven, that which we are, we are:
One equal temper of heroic hearts,
Made weak by time and fate, but strong in will
To strive, to seek, to find, and not to yield. 70

Alfred, Lord Tennyson (1809–1892)

QUESTIONS

1. Vocabulary: *Hyades* (10), *meet* (42).
2. Ulysses, king of Ithaca, is a legendary Greek hero, a major figure in Homer's *Iliad,* the hero of Homer's *Odyssey,* and a minor figure in Dante's *Divine Comedy.* After ten years at the siege of Troy, Ulysses set sail for home but, having incurred the wrath of the god of the sea, he was subjected to storms and vicissitudes and was forced to wander for another ten years, having many adventures and seeing most of the Mediterranean world before again reaching Ithaca, his wife, and his son. Once back home, according to Dante, he still wished to travel and "to follow virtue and knowledge." In Tennyson's poem, Ulysses is represented as about to set sail on a final voyage from which he will not return. Where is Ulysses standing during his speech? Whom is he addressing? Locate Ithaca on a map. Where exactly, in geographical terms, does Ulysses intend to sail (59–64)? (The Happy Isles were the Elysian fields, or Greek paradise; Achilles was another Greek prince, the hero of the *Iliad,* who was killed at the siege of Troy.)

3. Characterize Ulysses. What kind of person is he as Tennyson represents him?
4. What does Ulysses symbolize? What way of life is being recommended?
5. Find as many evidences as you can that Ulysses's desire for travel represents something more than mere wanderlust and wish for adventure.
6. Give two reasons why Tennyson might have Ulysses travel westward.
7. Interpret lines 18–21 and 26–29. What is symbolized by "the thunder and the sunshine" (48)? What do the two metonymies in line 49 stand for? What metaphor is implied in line 23?

CURIOSITY

   may have killed the cat; more likely
   the cat was just unlucky, or else curious
   to see what death was like, having no cause
   to go on licking paws, or fathering
   litter on litter of kittens, predictably.   5

   Nevertheless, to be curious
   is dangerous enough. To distrust
   what is always said, what seems,
   to ask old questions, interfere in dreams,
   leave home, smell rats, have hunches   10
   do not endear cats to those doggy circles
   where well-smelt baskets, suitable wives, good lunches
   are the order of things, and where prevails
   much wagging of incurious heads and tails.

   Face it. Curiosity   15
   will not cause us to die –
   only lack of it will.
   Never to want to see
   the other side of the hill
   or that improbable country   20
   where living is an idyll
   (although a probable hell)
   would kill us all.
   Only the curious
   have, if they live, a tale   25
   worth telling at all.

   Dogs say cats love too much, are irresponsible,
   are changeable, marry too many wives,

desert their children, chill all dinner tables
with tales of their nine lives.   30
Well, they are lucky. Let them be
nine-lived and contradictory,
curious enough to change, prepared to pay
the cat price, which is to die
and die again and again,   35
each time with no less pain.
A cat minority of one
is all that can be counted on
to tell the truth. And what cats have to tell
on each return from hell   40
is this: that dying is what the living do,
that dying is what the loving do,
and that dead dogs are those who do not know
that dying is what, to live, each has to do.

Alastair Reid (b. 1926)

QUESTIONS

1. On the surface this poem is a dissertation on cats. What deeper comments
   does it make? Of what are cats and dogs, in this poem, symbols?
2. In what different senses are the words "death," "die," and "dying" here used?
3. Compare and contrast this poem in meaning and manner with "Ulysses."

THE SEA-TURTLE AND THE SHARK

Strange but true is the story
of the sea-turtle and the shark –
the instinctive drive of the weak to survive
in the oceanic dark.
Driven,   5
riven
by hunger
from abyss to shoal,
sometimes the shark swallows
the sea-turtle whole.   10
The sly reptilian marine
withdraws,
into the shell
of his undersea craft,

his leathery head and the rapacious claws   15
                    that can rip
            a rhinoceros' hide
                    or strip
        a crocodile to fare-thee-well;
                        now,   20
                inside the shark,
    the sea-turtle begins the churning seesaws
        of his descent into pelagic hell;
                then . . . *then,*
                with ravenous jaws   25
        that can cut sheet steel scrap,
            the sea-turtle gnaws
. . . and gnaws . . . and gnaws . . .
        his way in a way that appalls —
                his way to freedom,   30
            beyond the vomiting dark,
            beyond the stomach walls
                of the shark.

                                    Melvin B. Tolson (1900–1966)

QUESTIONS

1. This poem is excerpted from the book *Harlem Gallery,* where it is presented as the composition of a fictional black poet Hideho Heights. What is its allegorical meaning? Why is "his" (30) italicized?
2. Comment on the meanings of "craft" (14), "pelagic" (23), "appalls" (29).

LOVE SONG: I AND THOU

Nothing is plumb, level or square:
        the studs are bowed, the joists
are shaky by nature, no piece fits
        any other piece without a gap
or pinch, and bent nails   5
        dance all over the surfacing
like maggots. By Christ
        I am no carpenter, I built
the roof for myself, the walls
        for myself, the floors   10
for myself, and got

hung up in it myself. I
danced with a purple thumb
   at this house-warming, drunk
with my prime whiskey: rage.   15
   Oh I spat rage's nails
into the frame-up of my work:
   it held. It settled plumb,
level, solid, square and true
   for that one moment. Then   20
it screamed and went on through
   skewing as wrong the other way.
God damned it. This is hell,
   but I planned it, I sawed it,
I nailed it, and I   25
   will live in it until it kills me.
I can nail my left palm
   to the left-hand cross-piece but
I can't do everything myself.
   I need a hand to nail the right,   30
a help, a love, a you, a wife.

Alan Dugan (b. 1923)

QUESTIONS

1. What clues are there that this house is not literal? What does it stand for?
2. Why does the speaker swear "By Christ" rather than *By God* (7)? Where else in the poem is Christ alluded to? What parallels and differences does the speaker see between himself and Christ?
3. "God damned it" (23) at first sounds like another curse, but the past tense makes its meaning more precise. What are the implications of lines 24–26? What implications are added in the phrase "by nature" (3)? What meanings has "prime" (15)?
4. What is the meaning of the last three lines?
5. Allegory, symbol, and extended metaphor are often difficult to tell apart, and perhaps have no fixed boundaries. (Some writers have defined allegory as extended metaphor.) Classification is unimportant so long as meanings are perceived. Nevertheless, how would you classify this?

EXERCISE

1. In what respects are the following poems alike? In what respects are they essentially different?

DUST OF SNOW

The way a crow
Shook down on me
The dust of snow
From a hemlock tree

Has given my heart
A change of mood
And saved some part
Of a day I had rued.

Robert Frost (1874–1963)

SOFT SNOW

I walked abroad in a snowy day;
I asked the soft snow with me to play;
She played and she melted in all her prime,
And the winter called it a dreadful crime.

William Blake (1757–1827)

EXERCISE

1. Which of the following poems are symbolical? Which are not?

EPIGRAM

Oh, God of dust and rainbows, help us see
That without dust the rainbow would not be.

Langston Hughes (1902–1967)

FOG

The fog comes
on little cat feet.

It sits looking
over harbor and city
on silent haunches
and then moves on.

Carl Sandburg (1878–1967)

ON SEEING WEATHER-BEATEN TREES

Is it as plainly in our living shown,
By slant and twist, which way the wind hath blown?

Adelaide Crapsey (1878–1914)

WIND AND SILVER

Greatly shining,
The Autumn moon floats in the thin sky;
And the fish-ponds shake their backs and flash their dragon scales
As she passes over them.

Amy Lowell (1874–1925)

PESSIMIST AND OPTIMIST

Two men look out through the same bars:
One sees the mud, and one the stars.

Frederick Langbridge (1849–1923)

THE SILVER SWAN

The silver swan, who living had no note,
When death approached, unlocked her silent throat;
Leaning her breast against the reedy shore,
Thus sung her first and last, and sung no more:
Farewell, all joys; O death, come close mine eyes;
More geese than swans now live, more fools than wise.

Anonymous (c. 1612)

7 Figurative Language 3

Paradox, Overstatement, Understatement, Irony

Aesop tells the tale of a traveler who sought refuge with a Satyr on a bitter winter night. On entering the Satyr's lodging, he blew on his fingers, and was asked by the Satyr what he did it for. "To warm them up," he explained. Later, on being served with a piping hot bowl of porridge, he blew also on it, and again was asked what he did it for. "To cool it off," he explained. The Satyr thereupon thrust him out of doors, for he would have nothing to do with a man who could blow hot and cold with the same breath.

A PARADOX is an apparent contradiction that is nevertheless somehow true. It may be either a situation or a statement. Aesop's tale of the traveler illustrates a paradoxical situation. As a figure of speech, paradox is a statement. When Alexander Pope wrote that a literary critic of his time would "damn with faint praise," he was using a verbal paradox, for how can a man damn by praising?

When we understand all the conditions and circumstances involved in a paradox, we find that what at first seemed impossible is actually entirely plausible and not strange at all. The paradox of the cold hands and hot porridge is not strange to a man who knows that a stream of air directed upon an object of different temperature will tend to bring that object closer to its own temperature. And Pope's paradox is not strange when we realize that *damn* is being used figuratively, and that Pope means only that a too reserved praise may damage an author with the public almost as much as adverse criticism. In a paradoxical statement the contradiction usually stems from one of the words being used figuratively or in more than one sense.

The value of paradox is its shock value. Its seeming impossibility startles the reader into attention and, thus, by the fact of its apparent absurdity, it underscores the truth of what is being said.

TO LUCASTA, GOING TO THE WARS

Tell me not, Sweet, I am unkind,
 That from the nunnery
Of thy chaste breast and quiet mind
 To war and arms I fly.

True, a new mistress now I chase,   5
 The first foe in the field;
And with a stronger faith embrace
 A sword, a horse, a shield.

Yet this inconstancy is such
 As you too shall adore;   10
I could not love thee, Dear, so much,
 Loved I not honor more.

Richard Lovelace (1618–1658)

QUESTIONS

1. State the basic paradox of the poem in a sentence. How is the paradox to be resolved?
2. Do you find any words in the poem used in more than one meaning?

Overstatement, understatement, and verbal irony form a continuous series, for they consist, respectively, of saying more, saying less, and saying the opposite of what one really means.

OVERSTATEMENT, or *hyperbole*, is simply exaggeration but exaggeration in the service of truth. It is not the same as a fish story. If you say, "I'm starved!" or "You could have knocked me over with a feather!" or "I'll die if I don't pass this course!" you do not expect to be believed; you are merely adding emphasis to what you really mean. (And if you say, "There were literally millions of people at the dance!" you are merely piling one overstatement on top of another, for you really mean that "There were figuratively millions of people at the dance," or, literally, "The dance hall was very crowded.") Like all figures of speech, overstatement may be used with a variety of effects. It may be humorous or grave, fanciful or restrained, convincing or unconvincing. When Tennyson says of his eagle (page 3) that it is "*Close* to the sun in lonely lands," he says what appears to be literally true, though we know from our study of astronomy that it is not. When Wordsworth reports of his daffodils in "I wandered lonely as a cloud" that they "stretched *in never-ending line*" along the margin of a bay, he too reports faithfully a visual appearance. When Frost says, at the conclusion of "The Road Not Taken" (page 80),

> I shall be saying this with a sigh
> Somewhere *ages and ages hence,*

we are scarcely aware of the overstatement, so quietly is the assertion made. Unskillfully used, however, overstatement may seem strained and ridiculous, leading us to react as Gertrude does to the player-queen's speeches in *Hamlet:* "The lady doth protest too much."

It is paradoxical that one can emphasize a truth either by overstating it or by understating it. UNDERSTATEMENT, or saying less than one means, may exist in what one says or merely in how one says it. If, for instance, upon sitting down to a loaded dinner plate, you say, "This looks like a good bite," you are actually stating less than the truth; but if you say, with Artemus Ward, that a man who holds his hand for half an hour in a lighted fire will experience "a sensation of excessive and disagreeable warmth," you are stating what is literally true but with a good deal less force than the situation might seem to warrant.

A RED, RED ROSE

O my luve is like a red, red rose,
   That's newly sprung in June.
O my luve is like the melodie
   That's sweetly played in tune.

As fair art thou, my bonnie lass,   5
   So deep in luve am I,
And I will luve thee still, my dear,
   Till a'° the seas gang° dry.   all; go

Till a' the seas gang dry, my dear,
   And the rocks melt wi' the sun!   10
And I will love thee still, my dear,
   While the sands o' life shall run.

And fare thee wel, my only luve,
          And fare thee wel awhile!
And I will come again, my luve,   15
          Though it were ten thousand mile!

Robert Burns (1759–1796)

THE ROSE FAMILY

The rose is a rose,
And was always a rose.
But the theory now goes
That the apple's a rose,
And the pear is, and so's   5
The plum, I suppose.
The dear only knows
What will next prove a rose.
You, of course, are a rose –
But were always a rose.   10

Robert Frost (1874–1963)

QUESTION

1. Burns and Frost use the same metaphor in paying tribute to their loved ones;
   otherwise their methods are opposed. Burns begins with a couple of
   conventionally poetic similes and proceeds to a series of overstatements. Frost
   begins with literal and scientific fact (the apple, pear, plum, and rose all
   belong to the same botanical family, the Rosaceae), and then slips in his
   metaphor so casually and quietly that the assertion has the effect of
   understatement. What is the function of "of course" and "but" in the last two
   lines?

Like paradox, *irony* has meanings that extend beyond its use merely as a
figure of speech.

VERBAL IRONY, saying the opposite of what one means, is often
confused with sarcasm and with satire, and for that reason it may be well to
look at the meanings of all three terms. SARCASM and SATIRE both imply
ridicule, one on the colloquial level, the other on the literary level. Sarcasm
is simply bitter or cutting speech, intended to wound the feelings (it
comes from a Greek word meaning to tear flesh). Satire is a more formal
term, usually applied to written literature rather than to speech and

ordinarily implying a higher motive: it is ridicule (either bitter or gentle) of human folly or vice, with the purpose of bringing about reform or at least of keeping other people from falling into similar folly or vice. Irony, on the other hand, is a literary device or figure that may be used in the service of sarcasm or ridicule or may not. It is popularly confused with sarcasm and satire because it is so often used as their tool: but irony may be used without either sarcastic or satirical intent, and sarcasm and satire may exist (though they do not usually) without irony. If, for instance, one of the members of your class raises his hand on the discussion of this point and says, "I don't understand," and your instructor replies, with a tone of heavy disgust in his voice, "Well, I wouldn't expect *you* to," he is being sarcastic but not ironical; he means exactly what he says. But if, after you have done particularly well on an examination, your instructor brings your test papers into the classroom saying, "Here's some *bad* news for you: you all got A's and B's!" he is being ironical but not sarcastic. Sarcasm, we may say, is cruel, as a bully is cruel: it intends to give hurt. Satire is both cruel and kind, as a surgeon is cruel and kind: it gives hurt in the interest of the patient or of society. Irony is neither cruel nor kind: it is simply a device, like a surgeon's scalpel, for performing any operation more skillfully.

Though verbal irony always implies the opposite of what is said, it has many gradations, and only in its simplest forms does it mean *only* the opposite of what is said. In more complex forms it means both what is said and the opposite of what is said, at once, though in different ways and with different degrees of emphasis. When Terence's critic, in "Terence, this is stupid stuff" (page 16) says, "*Pretty* friendship 'tis to rhyme / Your friends to death before their time" (11–12), we may substitute the literal *sorry* for "pretty" with little or no loss of meaning. When Terence speaks in reply, however, of the pleasure of drunkenness – "And down in *lovely* muck I've lain, / Happy till I woke again" (35–36) – we cannot substitute *loathsome* for "lovely" without considerable loss of meaning, for, while muck is actually extremely unpleasant to lie in, it may *seem* lovely to an intoxicated person. Thus two meanings – one the opposite of the other – operate at once.

Like all figures of speech, verbal irony runs the danger of being misunderstood. With irony the risks are perhaps greater than with other figures, for if metaphor is misunderstood, the result may be simply bewilderment; but if irony is misunderstood, the reader goes away with exactly the opposite idea from what the user meant to convey. The results of misunderstanding if, for instance, you ironically called someone a villain, might be calamitous. For this reason the user of irony must be very skillful in its use, conveying by an altered tone or by a wink of the eye or pen, that he is speaking ironically; and the reader of literature must be always alert to recognize the subtle signs that irony is intended.

No matter how broad or obvious the irony, there will always be in any large audience, a number who will misunderstand. The humorist Artemus Ward used to protect himself against these people by writing at the bottom of his newspaper column, "This is writ ironical." But irony is most delightful and most effective, for the good reader, when it is subtlest. It sets up a special understanding between writer and reader that may add either grace or force. If irony is too obvious, it sometimes seems merely crude. But if effectively used, it, like all figurative language, is capable of adding extra dimensions to meaning.

HEART: WE WILL FORGET HIM!

Heart! We will forget him!
You and I, tonight!
You may forget the warmth he gave,
I will forget the light!

When you have done, pray tell me
That I may straight begin!
Haste! lest while you're lagging
I remember him!

Emily Dickinson (1830–1886)

QUESTIONS

1. Who is the speaker? What can we infer about her relationship with "him"?
2. How far does the speaker mean what she is saying? To what extent is she ironical? How do we know?
3. What additional figures of speech are central in the poem?
4. Is this poem sarcastic? Satirical?

The term *irony* always implies some sort of discrepancy or incongruity. In verbal irony the discrepancy is between what is said and what is meant. In other forms the discrepancy may be between appearance and reality or between expectation and fulfillment. These other forms of irony are, on the whole, more important resources for the poet than is verbal irony. Two types, especially, are important for the beginning student to know.

In DRAMATIC IRONY* the discrepancy is not between what the speaker says and what he means but between what the speaker says and what the author means. The speaker's words may be perfectly straightforward, but the author, by putting these words in a particular speaker's mouth, may be indicating to the reader ideas or attitudes quite opposed to those the speaker is voicing. This form of irony is more complex than verbal irony and demands a more complex response from the reader. It may be used not only to convey attitudes but also to illuminate character, for the author who uses it is indirectly commenting not only upon the value of the ideas uttered but also upon the nature of the person who utters them. Such comment may be harsh, gently mocking, or sympathetic.

THE CHIMNEY SWEEPER

> When my mother died I was very young,
> And my father sold me while yet my tongue
> Could scarcely cry " 'weep! 'weep! 'weep! 'weep!"
> So your chimneys I sweep, and in soot I sleep.
>
> There's little Tom Dacre, who cried when his head,   5
> That curled like a lamb's back, was shaved; so I said,
> "Hush, Tom! never mind it, for, when your head's bare,
> You know that the soot cannot spoil your white hair."
>
> And so he was quiet, and that very night,
> As Tom was asleeping, he had such a sight!   10
> That thousands of sweepers, Dick, Joe, Ned, and Jack,
> Were all of them locked up in coffins of black.

---

*The term *dramatic irony*, which stems from Greek tragedy, often connotes something more specific and perhaps a little different from what I am developing here. It is used of a speech or an action in a story which has much greater significance to the audience than to the character who speaks or performs it, because of possession by the audience of knowledge the character does not have, as when the enemies of Ulysses, in the *Odyssey,* wish good luck and success to a man who the reader knows is Ulysses himself in disguise, or as when Oedipus, in the play by Sophocles, bends every effort to discover the murderer of Laius so that he may avenge the death, not knowing, as the audience does, that Laius is the man whom he himself once slew. I have appropriated the term for a perhaps slightly different situation, because no other suitable term exists. Both uses have the common characteristic – that the author conveys to the reader something different, or at least something more, than the character himself intends.

And by came an Angel who had a bright key,
And he opened the coffins and set them all free;
Then down a green plain leaping, laughing, they run,   15
And wash in a river, and shine in the sun.

Then naked and white, all their bags left behind,
They rise upon clouds and sport in the wind;
And the Angel told Tom, if he'd be a good boy,
He'd have God for his father, and never want joy.   20

And so Tom awoke, and we rose in the dark,
And got with our bags and our brushes to work.
Though the morning was cold, Tom was happy and warm;
So if all do their duty they need not fear harm.

William Blake (1757–1827)

QUESTIONS

1. In the eighteenth century small boys, sometimes no more than four or five years old, were employed to climb up the narrow chimney flues and clean them, collecting the soot in bags. Such boys, sometimes sold to the master sweepers by their parents, were miserably treated by their masters and often suffered disease and physical deformity. Characterize the boy who speaks in this poem. How do his and the poet's attitudes toward his lot in life differ? How, especially, are the meanings of the poet and the speaker different in lines 3, 7–8, and 24?

2. The dream in lines 11–20, besides being a happy dream, is capable of symbolic interpretations. Point out possible significances of the sweepers' being "locked up in coffins of black" and the Angel's releasing them with a bright key to play upon green plains.

A third type of irony is IRONY OF SITUATION. This occurs when there is a discrepancy between the actual circumstances and those that would seem appropriate or between what one anticipates and what actually comes to pass. If a man and his second wife, on the first night of their honeymoon, are accidentally seated at the theater next to the man's first wife, we should call the situation ironical. When, in O. Henry's famous short story "The Gift of the Magi" a poor young husband pawns his most prized possession, a gold watch, in order to buy his wife a set of combs for her hair for Christmas, and his wife sells her most prized possession, her long brown hair, in order to buy a fob for her husband's watch, we call the situation ironical. When King Midas, in the famous fable, is granted his fondest wish, that anything he touch turn to gold, and then finds that he cannot eat because even his food turns to gold, we call the situation ironical. When Coleridge's Ancient Mariner finds himself in the middle of the ocean with "Water, water, everywhere" but not a "drop to drink," we call the situation ironical. In each case the circumstances are not what would seem appropriate or what we would expect.

Dramatic irony and irony of situation are powerful devices for the poet, for, like symbol, they enable him to suggest meanings without stating them–to communicate a great deal more than he says. We have seen one effective use of irony of situation in "Richard Cory" (page 42). Another is in "Ozymandias," which follows.

Irony and paradox may be trivial or powerful devices, depending on their use. At their worst they may degenerate into mere mannerism and mental habit. At their best they may greatly extend the dimensions of meaning in a work of literature. Because irony and paradox are devices that demand an exercise of critical intelligence, they are particularly valuable as safeguards against sentimentality.

OZYMANDIAS

I met a traveller from an antique land
Who said: Two vast and trunkless legs of stone
Stand in the desert . . . Near them, on the sand,
Half sunk, a shattered visage lies, whose frown,
And wrinkled lip, and sneer of cold command,   5
Tell that its sculptor well those passions read
Which yet survive, stamped on these lifeless things,
The hand that mocked them, and the heart that fed:
And on the pedestal these words appear:
"My name is Ozymandias, king of kings: 10
Look on my works, ye Mighty, and despair!"
Nothing beside remains. Round the decay
Of that colossal wreck, boundless and bare
The lone and level sands stretch far away.

Percy Bysshe Shelley (1792–1822)

QUESTIONS

1. "Survive" (7) is a transitive verb with "hand" and "heart" as direct objects. Whose hand? Whose heart? What figure of speech is exemplified in "hand" and "heart"?
2. Characterize Ozymandias.

3. Ozymandias was an ancient Egyptian tyrant. This poem was first published in 1817. Of what is Ozymandias a *symbol?* What contemporary reference might the poem have had in Shelley's time?
4. What is the theme of the poem and how is it "stated"?

EXERCISE

1. Identify each of the following quotations as literal or figurative. If figurative, identify the figure as paradox, overstatement, understatement, or irony and explain the use to which it is put (emotional emphasis, humor, satire, etc.).

   a. Poetry is a language that tells us, through a more or less emotional reaction, something that cannot be said. *Edwin Arlington Robinson*

   b. Have not the Indians been kindly and justly treated? Have not the temporal things, the vain baubles and filthy lucre of this world, which were too apt to engage their worldly and selfish thoughts, been benevolently taken from them? And have they not instead thereof, been taught to set their affections on things above? *Washington Irving*

   c. A man who could make so vile a pun would not scruple to pick a pocket. *John Dennis*

   d. Last week I saw a woman flayed, and you will hardly believe how much it altered her person for the worse. *Swift*

   e. . . . Where ignorance is bliss,
   'Tis folly to be wise. *Thomas Gray*

   f. All night I made my bed to swim; with my tears I dissolved my couch. *Psalms 6:6*

   g. Believe him, he has known the world too long,
   And seen the death of much immortal song. *Pope*

   h. Give me my Romeo: and, when he shall die,
   Take him and cut him out in little stars,
   And he will make the face of heaven so fine
   That all the world will be in love with night,
   And pay no worship to the garish sun. *Juliet, in Shakespeare*

   i. Immortality will come to such as are fit for it; and he who would be a great soul in the future must be a great soul now. *Emerson*

   j. Whoe'er their crimes for interest only quit,
   Sin on in virtue, and good deeds *commit.* *Edward Young*

*   *   *   *   *

MY HEART LEAPS UP

My heart leaps up when I behold
A rainbow in the sky:
So was it when my life began;
So is it now I am a man;
So be it when I shall grow old,
        Or let me die!
The Child is father of the Man;
And I could wish my days to be
Bound each to each by natural piety.

William Wordsworth (1770–1850)

QUESTIONS

1. Why is line 7 paradoxical? Explain the paradox and comment on its significance.
2. What meanings has the word "natural" (9)? What does Wordsworth imply by linking it with "piety"?

BATTER MY HEART, THREE-PERSONED GOD

Batter my heart, three-personed God, for you
As yet but knock, breathe, shine, and seek to mend;
That I may rise and stand, o'erthrow me; and bend
Your force to break, blow, burn, and make me new.
I, like an usurped town, to another due,   5
Labor to admit you, but oh, to no end;
Reason, your viceroy in me, me should defend,
But is captived, and proves weak or untrue.
Yet dearly I love you and would be loved fain,°   gladly
But am betrothed unto your enemy;   10
Divorce me, untie or break that knot again,
Take me to you, imprison me, for I
Except° you enthrall me, never shall be free,   unless
Nor ever chaste, except you ravish me.

John Donne (1572–1631)

QUESTIONS

1. In this sonnet (No. 14 in a group called "Holy Sonnets") Donne addresses God in a series of metaphors and paradoxes. What is the paradox in the first

quatrain? To what is the "three-personed God" metaphorically compared? To what is Donne compared? Can the first three verbs of the parallel lines 2 and 4 be taken as addressed to specific "persons" of the Trinity (Father, Son, Holy Spirit)? If so, to which are "knock" and "break" addressed? "breathe" and "blow"? "shine" and "burn"? (What concealed pun helps in the attribution of the last pair? What etymological pun in the attribution of the second?)
2. To what does Donne compare himself in the second quatrain? To what is God compared? Who is the usurper? What role does Reason play in this political metaphor, and why is it a weak one?
3. To what does Donne compare himself in the sestet (lines 9–14)? To what does he compare God? Who is the "enemy" (10)? Resolve the paradox in lines 12–13 by explaining the double meaning of "enthrall." Resolve the paradox in line 14 by explaining the double meaning of "ravish."
4. Sum up the meaning of the poem in a sentence.

SCYLLA TOOTHLESS

Scylla is toothless; yet when she was young,
She had both tooth enough, and too much tongue:
What should I now of toothless Scylla say?
But that her tongue hath worn her teeth away.

Anonymous

QUESTIONS

1. In line 2 which noun is literal, which figurative? Identify and explain the figure.
2. What additional figure is added in line 4? Explain how the blend of literal and figurative in line 2 makes it possible.

INCIDENT

Once riding in old Baltimore
    Heart-filled, head-filled with glee,
I saw a Baltimorean
    Keep looking straight at me.

Now I was eight and very small,   5
    And he was no whit bigger,
And so I smiled, but he poked out
    His tongue, and called me, "Nigger."

I saw the whole of Baltimore
                From May until December;   10
Of all the things that happened there
                That's all that I remember.

                                        Countee Cullen (1903–1946)

QUESTION

1. What accounts for the effectiveness of the last stanza? Comment on the title.
   Is it in key with the meaning of the poem?

SOUTHERN COP

Let us forgive Ty Kendricks
The place was Darktown. He was young.
His nerves were jittery. The day was hot.
The Negro ran out of the alley.
And so Ty shot.   5

Let us understand Ty Kendricks
The Negro must have been dangerous,
Because he ran;
And here was a rookie with a chance
To prove himself man.   10

Let us condone Ty Kendricks
If we cannot decorate.
When he found what the Negro was running for,
It was all too late;
And all we can say for the Negro is   15
It was unfortunate.

Let us pity Ty Kendricks
He has been through enough,
Standing there, his big gun smoking,
Rabbit-scared, alone,   20
Having to hear the wenches wail
And the dying Negro moan.

                                        Sterling Brown (b. 1901)

1. Explain the poem in terms of irony and understatement. Is the irony verbal or dramatic?
2. What is the poem's purpose?

FORMAL APPLICATION

"The poets apparently want to rejoin the human race." TIME

I shall begin by learning to throw
the knife, first at trees, until it sticks
in the trunk and quivers every time;

next from a chair, using only wrist
and fingers, at a thing on the ground,   5
a fresh ant hill or a fallen leaf;

then at a moving object, perhaps
a pieplate swinging on twine, until
I pot it at least twice in three tries.

Meanwhile, I shall be teaching the birds   10
that the skinny fellow in sneakers
is a source of suet and bread crumbs,

first putting them on a shingle nailed
to a pine tree, next scattering them
on the needles, closer and closer   15

to my seat, until the proper bird,
a towhee, I think, in black and rust
and gray, takes tossed crumbs six feet away.

Finally, I shall coordinate
conditioned reflex and functional   20
form and qualify as Modern Man.

You see the splash of blood and feathers
and the blade pinning it to the tree?
It's called an "Audubon Crucifix."

The phrase has pleasing (even pious)   25
connotations, like *Arbeit Macht Frei,*
"Molotov Cocktail," and *Enola Gay.*

Donald W. Baker (b. 1923)

QUESTIONS

1. *Arbeit Macht Frei* (26) ("Labor liberates") was the slogan of the German Nazi Party. "Molotov Cocktail" (27), a homemade hand grenade named after Stalin's foreign minister, was widely used during the Spanish Civil War and World War II. *Enola Gay* (27) was the American plane that dropped the first atom bomb on Hiroshima. In what ways are the connotations of these phrases – and of "Audubon Crucifix" (24)–"pleasing"?
2. What different kinds of irony operate in this poem? Discuss.
3. What meanings has the title?

THE UNKNOWN CITIZEN

(To JS/07/M/378 This Marble Monument Is Erected by the State)

He was found by the Bureau of Statistics to be
One against whom there was no official complaint,
And all the reports on his conduct agree
That, in the modern sense of an old-fashioned word, he was a saint,
For in everything he did he served the Greater Community.   5
Except for the War till the day he retired
He worked in a factory and never got fired,
But satisfied his employers, Fudge Motors Inc.
Yet he wasn't a scab or odd in his views,
For his Union reports that he paid his dues,   10
(Our report on his Union shows it was sound)
And our Social Psychology workers found
That he was popular with his mates and liked a drink.
The Press are convinced that he bought a paper every day
And that his reactions to advertisements were normal in every way.   15
Policies taken out in his name prove that he was fully insured,
And his Health-card shows he was once in hospital but left it cured.
Both Producers Research and High-Grade Living declare
He was fully sensible to the advantages of the Installment Plan
And had everything necessary to the Modern Man,   20
A phonograph, a radio, a car and a frigidaire.
Our researchers into Public Opinion are content
That he held the proper opinions for the time of year;
When there was peace, he was for peace; when there was war, he went.
He was married and added five children to the population,   25
Which our Eugenist says was the right number for a parent of
    his generation,

And our teachers report that he never interfered with their education.
Was he free? Was he happy? The question is absurd:
Had anything been wrong, we should certainly have heard.

W. H. Auden (1907–1973)

QUESTIONS

1. Vocabulary: *scab* (9), *Eugenist* (26).
2. Explain the allusion and the irony in the title. Why was the citizen "unknown"?
3. This obituary of an unknown state "hero" was apparently prepared by a functionary of the state. Give an account of the citizen's life and character from Auden's own point of view.
4. What trends in modern life and social organization does the poem satirize?

DEPARTMENTAL

An ant on the tablecloth
Ran into a dormant moth
Of many times his size.
He showed not the least surprise.
His business wasn't with such.   5
He gave it scarcely a touch,
And was off on his duty run.
Yet if he encountered one
Of the hive's enquiry squad
Whose work is to find out God   10
And the nature of time and space,
He would put him onto the case.
Ants are a curious race;
One crossing with hurried tread
The body of one of their dead   15
Isn't given a moment's arrest —
Seems not even impressed.
But he no doubt reports to any
With whom he crosses antennae,
And they no doubt report   20
To the higher up at court.
Then word goes forth in Formic:
"Death's come to Jerry McCormic,
Our selfless forager Jerry.
Will the special Janizary   25

Whose office it is to bury
The dead of the commissary
Go bring him home to his people.
Lay him in state on a sepal.
Wrap him for shroud in a petal.   30
Embalm him with ichor of nettle.
This is the word of your Queen."
And presently on the scene
Appears a solemn mortician;
And taking formal position   35
With feelers calmly atwiddle,

Seizes the dead by the middle,
And heaving him high in air,
Carries him out of there.
No one stands round to stare.   40
It is nobody else's affair.

It couldn't be called ungentle.
But how thoroughly departmental.

Robert Frost (1874–1963)

QUESTIONS

1. Vocabulary: *dormant* (2), *Formic* (22), *Janizary* (25), *commissary* (27), *sepal* (29), *ichor* (31).
2. The poem is ostensibly about ants. Is it ultimately about ants? Give reasons to support your view that it is or is not.
3. What is the author's attitude toward the "departmental" organization of ant society? How is it indicated? Could this poem be described as "gently satiric"? If so, in what sense?
4. Compare and contrast this poem with "The Unknown Citizen" in content and manner.

MR. Z

Taught early that his mother's skin was the sign of error,
He dressed and spoke the perfect part of honor;
Won scholarships, attended the best schools,
Disclaimed kinship with jazz and spirituals;
Chose prudent, raceless views for each situation,   5
Or when he could not cleanly skirt dissension,
Faced up to the dilemma, firmly seized
Whatever ground was Anglo-Saxonized.

In diet, too, his practice was exemplary:
Of pork in its profane forms he was wary;   10
Expert in vintage wines, sauces and salads,
His palate shrank from cornbread, yams and collards.

He was as careful whom he chose to kiss:
His bride had somewhere lost her Jewishness,
But kept her blue eyes; an Episcopalian   15
Prelate proclaimed them matched chameleon.
Choosing the right addresses, here, abroad,
They shunned those places where they might be barred;
Even less anxious to be asked to dine
Where hosts catered to kosher accent or exotic skin.   20

And so he climbed, unclogged by ethnic weights,
An airborne plant, flourishing without roots.
Not one false note was struck – until he died:
His subtly grieving widow could have flayed
The obit writers, ringing crude changes on a clumsy phrase: 25
"One of the most distinguished members of his race."

M. Carl Holman (b. 1919)

QUESTIONS

1. Vocabulary: *profane* (10), *kosher* (20), *exotic* (20), *ethnic* (21), *obit* (25).
2. Explain Mr. Z's motivation and the strategies he used to achieve his goal.
3. What is the author's attitude toward Mr. Z? Is he satirizing him or the society that produced him? Why does he not give Mr. Z a name?
4. What judgments on Mr. Z are implied by the metaphors in lines 16 and 22? Explain them.
5. What kind of irony is operating in the last line? As you reread the poem, where else do you detect ironic overtones?
6. What is Mr. Z's color?

WHEN FIRST MY WAY TO FAIR I TOOK

When first my way to fair I took
Few pence in purse had I,
And long I used to stand and look
At things I could not buy.

Now times are altered: if I care   5
    To buy a thing, I can;
The pence are here and here's the fair,
    But where's the lost young man?

—To think that two and two are four
    And neither five nor three   10
The heart of man has long been sore
    And long 'tis like to be.

A. E. Housman (1859–1936)

1. Explain line 8. What kind of irony do the first two stanzas exhibit?
2. Of what are the mathematical statements in line 9–10 symbolic? Paraphrase these lines in words that express their symbolic meaning.

MY LAST DUCHESS

Ferrara

That's my last duchess painted on the wall,
Looking as if she were alive. I call
That piece a wonder, now; Fra Pandolf's hands
Worked busily a day, and there she stands.
Will't please you sit and look at her? I said   5
"Fra Pandolf" by design, for never read
Strangers like you that pictured countenance,
The depth and passion of its earnest glance,
But to myself they turned (since none puts by
The curtain I have drawn for you, but I)   10
And seemed as they would ask me, if they durst,
How such a glance came there; so, not the first
Are you to turn and ask thus. Sir, 'twas not
Her husband's presence only, called that spot
Of joy into the Duchess' cheek; perhaps   15
Fra Pandolf chanced to say, "Her mantle laps
Over my lady's wrist too much," or, "Paint
Must never hope to reproduce the faint
Half-blush that dies along her throat." Such stuff

Was courtesy, she thought, and cause enough 20
For calling up that spot of joy. She had
A heart – how shall I say? – too soon made glad,
Too easily impressed; she liked whate'er
She looked on, and her looks went everywhere.
Sir, 'twas all one! My favor at her breast, 25
The dropping of the daylight in the West,
The bough of cherries some officious fool
Broke in the orchard for her, the white mule
She rode with round the terrace – all and each
Would draw from her alike the approving speech, 30
Or blush, at least. She thanked men – good! but thanked
Somehow – I know not how – as if she ranked
My gift of a nine-hundred-years-old name
With anybody's gift. Who'd stoop to blame
This sort of trifling? Even had you skill 35
In speech – which I have not – to make your will
Quite clear to such an one, and say, "Just this
Or that in you disgusts me; here you miss,
Or there exceed the mark" – and if she let
Herself be lessoned so, nor plainly set 40
Her wits to yours, forsooth, and made excuse –
E'en then would be some stooping; and I choose
Never to stoop. Oh, sir, she smiled, no doubt,
Whene'er I passed her; but who passed without
Much the same smile? This grew; I gave commands; 45
Then all smiles stopped together. There she stands
As if alive. Will 't please you rise? We'll meet
The company below, then. I repeat,
The Count your master's known munificence
Is ample warrant that no just pretense 50
Of mine for dowry will be disallowed;
Though his fair daughter's self, as I avowed
At starting, is my object. Nay, we'll go
Together down, sir. Notice Neptune, though,
Taming a sea-horse, thought a rarity, 55
Which Claus of Innsbruck cast in bronze for me!

Robert Browning (1812–1889)

QUESTIONS

1. Vocabulary: *officious* (27), *munificence* (49).
2. Ferrara is in Italy. The time is during the Renaissance, probably the sixteenth century. To whom is the Duke speaking? What is the occasion? Are the Duke's remarks about his last Duchess a digression, or do they have some relation to the business at hand?
3. Characterize the Duke as fully as you can. How does your characterization differ from the Duke's opinion of himself? What kind of irony is this?
4. Why was the Duke dissatisfied with his last Duchess? Was it sexual jealousy? What opinion do you get of the Duchess's personality, and how does it differ from the Duke's opinion?
5. What characteristics of the Italian Renaissance appear in the poem (marriage customs, social classes, art)? What is the Duke's attitude toward art? Is it insincere?
6. What happened to the Duchess? Should we have been told?

EARTH

"A planet doesn't explode of itself," said drily
The Martian astronomer, gazing off into the air —
"That they were able to do it is proof that highly
Intelligent beings must have been living there."

John Hall Wheelock (b. 1886)

JACK AND HIS FATHER

"Jack," quoth his father, "how shall I ease take?
If I stand, my legs ache; and if I kneel
My knees ache; if I go, then my feet ache;
If I lie, my back aches; if I sit, I feel
My hips ache." "Sir,," quoth Jack, "pain to exile,
Since all these ease not, best ye hang awhile."

John Heywood (1497?–1580?)

8 Allusion

The famous English diplomat and letter writer Lord Chesterfield was once invited to a great dinner given by the Spanish ambassador. At the conclusion of the meal the host rose and proposed a toast to his master, the king of Spain, whom he compared to the sun. The French ambassador followed with a health to the king of France, whom he likened to the moon. It was then Lord Chesterfield's turn. "Your excellencies have taken from me," he said, "all the greatest luminaries of heaven, and the stars are too small for me to make a comparison of my royal master; I therefore beg leave to give your excellencies – Joshua!"*

For a reader familiar with the Bible – that is, for one who recognizes the Biblical allusion – Lord Chesterfield's story will come as a stunning revelation of his wit. For an ALLUSION – a reference to something in history or previous literature – is, like a richly connotative word or a symbol, a means of suggesting far more than it says. The one word "Joshua," in the context of Chesterfield's toast, calls up in the reader's mind the whole Biblical story of how the Israelite captain stopped the sun and the moon in order that the Israelites might finish a battle and conquer their enemies before nightfall.[†] The force of the toast lies in its extreme economy; it says

---

*Samuel Shellabarger, *Lord Chesterfield and His World* (Boston: Little, Brown, 1951), p. 132.

[†]Joshua 10:12–14.

so much in so little, and it exercises the mind of the reader to make the connection for himself.

The effect of Chesterfield's allusion is chiefly humorous or witty, but allusions may also have a powerful emotional effect. The essayist William Hazlitt writes of addressing a fashionable audience about the lexicographer Samuel Johnson. Speaking of Johnson's great heart and of his charity to the unfortunate, Hazlitt recounted how, finding a drunken prostitute lying in Fleet Street late at night, Johnson carried her on his broad back to the address she managed to give him. The audience, unable to face the picture of the famous dictionary-maker doing such a thing, broke out in titters and expostulations. Whereupon Hazlitt simply said: "I remind you, ladies and gentlemen, of the parable of the Good Samaritan." The audience was promptly silenced.*

Allusions are a means of reinforcing the emotion or the ideas of one's own work with the emotion or ideas of another work or occasion. Because they are capable of saying so much in so little, they are extremely useful to the poet.

"OUT, OUT—"

> The buzz-saw snarled and rattled in the yard
> And made dust and dropped stove-length sticks of wood,
> Sweet-scented stuff when the breeze drew across it.
> And from there those that lifted eyes could count
> Five mountain ranges one behind the other 5
> Under the sunset far into Vermont.
> And the saw snarled and rattled, snarled and rattled,
> As it ran light, or had to bear a load.
> And nothing happened: day was all but done.
> Call it a day, I wish they might have said 10
> To please the boy by giving him the half hour
> That a boy counts so much when saved from work.
> His sister stood beside them in her apron
> To tell them "Supper." At the word, the saw,
> As if to prove saws knew what supper meant, 15
> Leaped out at the boy's hand, or seemed to leap—
> He must have given the hand. However it was,
> Neither refused the meeting. But the hand!

*Jacques Barzun, *Teacher in America* (Boston: Little, Brown, 1945), p. 160.

The boy's first outcry was a rueful laugh,
As he swung toward them holding up the hand   20
Half in appeal, but half as if to keep
The life from spilling. Then the boy saw all –
Since he was old enough to know, big boy
Doing a man's work, though a child at heart –
He saw all spoiled. "Don't let him cut my hand off –   25
The doctor, when he comes. Don't let him, sister!"
So. But the hand was gone already.
The doctor put him in the dark of ether.
He lay and puffed his lips out with his breath.
And then – the watcher at his pulse took fright.   30
No one believed. They listened at his heart.
Little – less – nothing! – and that ended it.
No more to build on there. And they, since they
Were not the one dead, turned to their affairs.

Robert Frost (1874–1963)

QUESTIONS

1. How does this poem differ from a newspaper account that might have dealt with the same incident?
2. To whom does "they" (33) refer? The boy's family? The doctor and hospital attendants? Casual onlookers? Need we assume that all these people – whoever they are – turned immediately "to their affairs"? Does the ending of this poem seem to you callous or merely realistic? Would a more tearful and sentimental ending have made the poem better or worse? ·
3. What figure of speech is used in lines 21–22?

Allusions vary widely in the burden put on them by the poet to convey his meaning. Lord Chesterfield risked his whole meaning on his hearers' recognizing his allusion. Robert Frost in "Out, Out – " makes his meaning entirely clear even for the reader who does not recognize the allusion contained in his title. His theme is the uncertainty and unpredictability of life, which may be accidentally ended at any moment, and the tragic waste of human potentiality which takes place when such premature deaths occur. A boy who is already "doing a man's work" and gives every promise of having a useful life ahead of him is suddenly wiped out. There seems no rational explanation for either the accident or the death. The only comment to be made is, "No more to build on there."

Frost's title, however, is an allusion to one of the most famous passages in all English literature, and it offers a good illustration of how a poet may use allusion not only to reinforce emotion but also to help define his theme. The passage is that in *Macbeth* in which Macbeth has just been informed of his wife's death. A good many readers will recall the key phrase, "Out, out, brief candle!" with its underscoring of the tragic brevity and uncertainty of life that can be snuffed out at any moment. For some readers, however, the allusion will summon up the whole passage in act V, scene 5, in which this phrase occurs. Macbeth's words are:

> She should have died hereafter;
> There would have been a time for such a word.
> To-morrow, and to-morrow, and to-morrow
> Creeps in this petty pace from day to day
> To the last syllable of recorded time;   5
> And all our yesterdays have lighted fools
> The way to dusty death. <u>Out, out, brief candle!</u>
> Life's but a walking shadow, a poor player,
> That struts and frets his hour upon the stage
> And then is heard no more. It is a tale   10
> Told by an idiot, full of sound and fury,
> Signifying nothing.

Macbeth's first words underscore the theme of premature death. The boy also "should have died hereafter." The rest of the passage, with its marvelous evocation of the vanity and meaninglessness of life, expresses neither Shakespeare's philosophy nor, ultimately, Frost's, but it is MacBeth's philosophy at the time of his bereavement, and it is likely to express the feelings of us all when such tragic accidents occur. Life does indeed seem cruel and meaningless, a tale told by an idiot, signifying nothing, when human life and potentiality are thus without explanation so suddenly ended.

Allusions vary widely in the number of readers to whom they will be familiar. The poet, in using an allusion as in using a figure of speech, is always in danger of not being understood. In appealing powerfully to one reader, he may lose another reader altogether. But the poet must assume a certain fund of common experience with his readers. He could not even write about the ocean unless he could assume that his reader had seen the ocean or pictures of it. In the same way he will assume a certain common fund of literary experience. He is often justified in expecting a rather wide range of literary experience in his readers, for the people who read poetry for pleasure are generally people of good minds and good education who have read widely. But, obviously, beginning readers will not have this range, just as they will not know the meanings of as many words as will maturer readers. The student ought therefore to be prepared to look up certain allusions, just as he should be eager to look up in his dictionary the meanings of unfamiliar words. He will find that <u>every increase in</u> <u>knowledge will broaden his base for understanding both literature and life.</u>

*   *   *   *   *

IN JUST-

in Just-
spring   when the world is mud-
luscious the little
lame balloonman

whistles   far   and wee   5

and eddieandbill come
running from marbles and
piracies and it's
spring

when the world is puddle-wonderful   10

the queer
old balloonman whistles
far   and   wee
and bettyandisbel come dancing

from hop-scotch and jump-rope and   15

it's
spring
and
    the

      goat-footed   20

balloonMan   whistles
far
and
wee

e. e. cummings (1894–1962)

1. Why is the balloonman called "goat-footed"? How does the identification made by this mythological allusion enrich the meaning of the poem?

ON HIS BLINDNESS

When I consider how my light is spent
 Ere half my days in this dark world and wide,
 And that one talent which is death to hide
 Lodged with me useless, though my soul more bent
To serve therewith my Maker, and present   5
 My true account, lest he returning chide,
 "Doth God exact day-labor, light denied?"
 I fondly ask. But Patience, to prevent
That murmur, soon replies, "God doth not need
 Either man's work or his own gifts. Who best   10
 Bear his mild yoke, they serve him best. His state
Is kingly: thousands at his bidding speed,
 And post o'er land and ocean without rest;
 They also serve who only stand and wait."

John Milton (1608–1674)

QUESTIONS

1. Vocabulary: *spent* (1), *fondly* (8), *prevent* (8), *post* (13).
2. What two meanings has "talent" (3)? What is Milton's "one talent"?
3. The poem is unified and expanded in its dimensions by a Biblical allusion that Milton's original readers would have recognized immediately. What is it? If you do not know, look up Matthew 25:14–30. In what ways is the situation in the poem similar to that in the parable? In what ways is it different?
4. What is the point of the poem?

GOD IS A DISTANT, STATELY LOVER

God is a distant, stately lover –
Woos, as he states us, by his son:
Verily, a vicarious courtship –
Miles and Priscilla were such an one.

But lest the soul, like fair Priscilla,
Choose the envoy and spurn the groom,
Vouches, with hyperbolic archness,
Miles and John Alden were synonym.

Emily Dickinson (1830–1886)

QUESTIONS

1. Vocabulary: *vicarious* (3), *hyperbolic* (7), *archness* (7).
2. In Longfellow's long narrative poem *The Courtship of Miles Standish* – once familiar to every American school child – the widower Miles Standish, Captain of the Plymouth Colony, determines to marry the virtuous Puritan maiden Priscilla. A blunt old soldier with no gift for words, he requests his literate young friend John Alden to make the proposal for him, not knowing John loves her too. Faithful to friendship, but torn by his own love, John makes the proposal and is answered by Priscilla, "Why don't you speak for yourself, John?" Eventually the two young persons marry. – How, in Dickinson's poem, is God like Miles Standish? Who is His "John Alden"? Who is the "Priscilla" whom He woos? How does He insure himself against the kind of defeat Miles Standish suffered?
3. What is Dickinson satirizing in this poem?

1887

From Clee to heaven the beacon burns,
    The shires have seen it plain,
From north and south the sign returns
    And beacons burn again.

Look left, look right, the hills are bright,   5
    The dales are light between,
Because 'tis fifty years tonight
    That God has saved the Queen.

Now, when the flame they watch not towers
    About the soil they trod,   10
Lads, we'll remember friends of ours
    Who shared the work with God.

To skies that knit their heartstrings right,
    To fields that bred them brave,
The saviors come not home tonight: 15
    Themselves they could not save.

It dawns in Asia, tombstones show
    And Shropshire names are read;
And the Nile spills his overflow
    Beside the Severn's dead.   20

We pledge in peace by farm and town
    The Queen they served in war,
And fire the beacons up and down
    The land they perished for.

"God save the Queen" we living sing,   25
    From height to height 'tis heard;
And with the rest your voices ring,
    Lads of the Fifty-third.

Oh, god will save her, fear you not:
    Be you the men you've been,   30
Get you the sons your fathers got,
    And God will save the Queen.

A. E. Housman (1859–1936)

QUESTIONS

1. Vocabulary: *get* and *got* (31).
2. In 1887 England celebrated the fiftieth year of Queen Victoria's reign with beacon fires built on hilltops across the land. This poem, written in 1887, was published in a volume entitled *The Shropshire Lad*. Clee (1), in the Clee Hills, is a village, the Severn (20), a river; both are in Shropshire. Whom is the poet addressing? What is "the Fifty-third" (28)?
3. To what are lines 15–16 an allusion? If you do not know, check Mark 15:29–31. What is the poet's attitude toward the dead soldiers?
4. What is alluded to in lines 8, 25, 29, and 32? Who, in the poet's view, will really "save the Queen"? What kind of irony is this?

LEDA AND THE SWAN

A sudden blow: the great wings beating still
Above the staggering girl, her thighs caressed
By the dark webs, her nape caught in his bill,
He holds her helpless breast upon his breast.

How can those terrified vague fingers push   5
The feathered glory from her loosening thighs?

And how can body, laid in that white rush,
But feel the strange heart beating where it lies?

A shudder in the loins engenders there
The broken wall, the burning roof and tower   10
And Agamemnon dead.

                Being so caught up,
So mastered by the brute blood of the air,
Did she put on his knowledge with his power
Before the indifferent beak could let her drop?

William Butler Yeats (1865–1939)

QUESTIONS

1. What is the connection between Leda and "the broken wall, the burning roof
   and tower / And Agamemnon dead"? If you do not know, look up the myth
   of Leda, and, if necessary, the story of Agamemnon.
2. What is the significance of the question asked in the last two lines?

THE SHIELD OF ACHILLES

    She looked over his shoulder
        For vines and olive trees,
    Marble well-governed cities,
        And ships upon untamed seas,
    But there on the shining metal   5
        His hands had put instead
    An artificial wilderness
        And a sky like lead.

A plain without a feature, bare and brown,
    No blade of grass, no sign of neighborhood,   10
Nothing to eat and nowhere to sit down,
    Yet, congregated on its blankness, stood
    An unintelligible multitude.
A million eyes, a million boots in line,
Without expression, waiting for a sign.   15

Out of the air a voice without a face
   Proved by statistics that some cause was just
In tones as dry and level as the place:
   No one was cheered and nothing was discussed;
   Column by column in a cloud of dust   20
They marched away enduring a belief
Whose logic brought them, somewhere else, to grief.

     She looked over his shoulder
       For ritual pieties,
     White flower-garlanded heifers,   25
       Libation and sacrifice,
     But there on the shining metal
       Where the altar should have been,
     She saw by his flickering forge-light
       Quite another scene.   30

Barbed wire enclosed an arbitrary spot
   Where bored officials lounged (one cracked a joke)
And sentries sweated, for the day was hot:
   A crowd of ordinary decent folk
   Watched from without and neither moved nor spoke   35
As three pale figures were led forth and bound
To three posts driven upright in the ground.

The mass and majesty of this world, all
   That carries weight and always weighs the same,
Lay in the hands of others; they were small   40
   And could not hope for help and no help came:
   What their foes like to do was done, their shame
Was all the worst could wish; they lost their pride
And died as men before their bodies died.

     She looked over his shoulder   45
       For athletes at their games,
     Men and women in a dance
       Moving their sweet limbs
     Quick, quick, to music,
       But there on the shining shield   50
     His hands had set no dancing-floor
       But a weed-choked field.

A ragged urchin, aimless and alone,
    Loitered about that vacancy; a bird
Flew up to safety from his well-aimed stone: 55
    That girls are raped, that two boys knife a third,
    Were axioms to him, who'd never heard
Of any world where promises were kept
Or one could weep because another wept.

    The thin-lipped armorer,   60
        Hephaestos, hobbled away;
    Thetis of the shining breasts
        Cried out in dismay
    At what the god had wrought
        To please her son, the strong   65
    Iron-hearted man-slaying Achilles
        Who would not live long.

W. H. Auden (1907–1973)

QUESTIONS

1. Vocabulary: *libation* (26).
2. The description of Achilles' shield, made for him at the request of his mother Thetis by Hephaestos, god of the forge, is one of the most famous passages in the *Iliad* (Book XVIII). On the shield Hephaestos depicted scenes from the Hellenic world. From what world do the three scenes in the poem come? Comment specifically on each and on the contrast between each and the expectation of Thetis preceding it.
3. What possible allusion is made in lines 36–37, and what is its purpose?
4. What figure of speech occurs in line 14? What meanings has "arbitrary" (31)?

- what is expected and what actually happens

PROGRESS

    Man is mind
    cried old Descartes
    and Wordsworth answered
    Man is heart.

    Down a new road
    at last we come;
    our cry: *Libido*
    ergo sum.

Peter Meinke (b. 1932)

1. René Descartes (1596–1650) is widely regarded as the founder of modern philosophy. Line 1 refers generally to the tenor of his whole philosophy but should call up (in the context of the poem) the famous brief Latin phrase in which he stated the starting point of his philosophical system. What was it?
2. Line 4 attempts to sum up the tenor of thought in the poetry of Wordsworth (1770–1850). Do the poems reprinted on pages 111 and 351–53 support this summation?
3. To what body of thought do the last four lines refer? In the writings of what famous modern thinker and investigator (1856–1939) does it have its origin? How would you translate the Latin?
4. How should the title be taken?

THE GOODNIGHT

He stood still by her bed
Watching his daughter breathe,
The dark and silver head,
The fingers curled beneath,
And thought: Though she may have   5
Intelligence and charm
And luck, they will not save
Her life from every harm.

The lives of children are
Dangerous to their parents   10
With fire, water, air,
And other accidents;
And some, for a child's sake,
Anticipating doom,
Empty the world to make   15
The world safe as a room.

Who could endure the pain
That was Laocoön's?
Twisting, he saw again
In the same coil his sons.   20
Plumed in his father's skill,
Young Icarus flew higher
Toward the sun, until
He fell in rings of fire.

A man who cannot stand   25
Children's perilous play,
With lifted voice and hand
Drives the children away.
Out of sight, out of reach,
The tumbling children pass;   30
He sits on an empty beach,
Holding an empty glass.

Who said that tenderness
Will turn the heart to stone?
May I endure her weakness   35
As I endure my own.
Better to say goodnight
To breathing flesh and blood
Each night as though the night
Were always only good.   40

Louis Simpson (b. 1923)

QUESTIONS

1. Explain the apparent paradox in lines 9–10, the metaphorical overstatement in lines 15–16.
2. Explain the allusion to Laocoön in lines 17–20. If unfamiliar with it, look it up in a reference work, preferably an illustrated one. Is the word "coil" (20) metaphorical, literal, or both?
3. Explain the allusion to Icarus (lines 21–24). Is there a double meaning in "plumed" (21)? For what is "skill" (21) a metonymy? Is there any irony in this line?
4. Explain the meaning of lines 27–28, the symbolism in lines 31–32? What earlier lines do lines 31–32 echo?
5. Who is "her" (35)? How do the symbolical overtones of "night" (39) intensify the meaning of the last two lines?
6. What is the speaker's dilemma? How does he resolve it? Is he a wise father?

NARCISSUS, PHOTOGRAPHER

Mirror-mad,
he photographed reflections:
sunstorms in puddles,
cities in canals,

double portraits framed   5
in sunglasses,

the fat phantoms who dance
on the flanks of cars.

Nothing caught his eye
unless it bent   10
or glistered
over something else.

He trapped clouds in bottles
the way kids
trap grasshoppers.   15
Then one misty day

he was stopped
by the windshield.
Behind him,
an avenue of trees,   20

before him,
the mirror of that scene.
He seemed to enter
what, in fact, he left.

Erica Jong (b. 1942)

QUESTIONS

1. Why does the poet give the modern art-photographer in this poem a name
   taken from Greek mythology? What are the parallels?
2. What happens to the photographer? In what way is his conclusion ironic?
3. What meanings have the last two lines?

IN THE GARDEN

In the garden there strayed
A beautiful maid
As fair as the flowers of the morn;
The first hour of her life
She was made a man's wife,
And was buried before she was born.

Anonymous

QUESTION

1. Resolve the paradox by identifying the allusion.

9 Meaning and Idea

Little Jack Horner
Sat in a corner
Eating a Christmas pie.
He stuck in his thumb
And pulled out a plum
And said, "What a good boy am I!"

Anonymous

The meaning of a poem is the experience it expresses – nothing less. But the reader who, baffled by a particular poem, asks perplexedly, "What does it *mean?*" is usually after something more specific than this. He wants something that he can grasp entirely with his mind. We may therefore find it useful to make a distinction between the TOTAL MEANING of a poem – that which it communicates (and which can be communicated in no other way) – and its PROSE MEANING – the ingredient that can be separated out in the form of a prose paraphrase. If we make this distinction, however, we must be careful not to confuse the two kinds of meaning. The prose meaning is no more the poem than a plum is a pie or than a prune is a plum.

The prose meaning will not necessarily or perhaps even usually be an idea. It may be a story, it may be a description, it may be a statement of emotion, it may be a presentation of human character, or it may be some combination of these. "Sir Patrick Spens" (page 12) tells a story; "The Eagle" (page 5) is primarily descriptive; "A Red, Red Rose" (page 103) is an expression of emotion; "My Last Duchess" (page 119) is an account of human character. None of these poems is directly concerned with ideas. The message-hunter will be baffled and disappointed by poetry of this kind, for he will not find what he is looking for, and he may attempt to read some idea into the poem that is really not there. Yet ideas are also part of human experience, and therefore many poems are concerned, at least partially, with presenting ideas. But with these poems message-hunting is an even more dangerous activity. For the message-hunter is likely to think that the whole object of reading the poem is to find the message – that the idea is really the only important thing in it. Like Little Jack Horner, he will reach in and pluck it out and say, "What a good boy am I!" as if the pie existed for the plum.

The idea in a poem is only part of the total experience it communicates. The value and worth of the poem are determined by the value of the total experience, not by the truth or the nobility of the idea itself. This is not to say that the truth of the idea is unimportant, or that its validity should not be examined and appraised. But a good idea will not make a good poem, nor need an idea with which the reader does not agree ruin one. The good reader of poetry will be a reader receptive to all kinds of experience. He will be able to make that "willing suspension of disbelief" that Coleridge characterized as constituting poetic faith. When one attends a performance of *Hamlet* he is willing to forget for the time being that such a person as Hamlet never existed and that the events on the stage are fictions. The reader of poetry should also be willing to enter imaginatively, for the time being, into ideas he objectively regards as untrue. It is one way of understanding these ideas better and of enlarging his own experience. The Christian should be able to enjoy a good poem expressing atheistic ideas, and the atheist a good poem in praise of God. The optimist by temperament should be able to find pleasure in pessimistic poetry, and the pessimist in optimistic poetry. The teetotaler should be able to enjoy "The Rubáiyát of Omar Khayyám," and the winebibber a good poem in praise of austerity. The primary value of a poem depends not so much on the truth of the idea presented as on the power with which it is communicated and on its being made a convincing part of a meaningful total experience. We must feel that the idea has been truly and deeply *felt* by the poet and that he is doing somthing more than merely moralizing. The plum must be made part of a pie. If the plum is properly combined with other ingredients and if the pie is well cooked, it should be enjoyable even for persons who do not care for the brand of plums it is made of. Let us consider, for instance, the following two poems.

BARTER

Life has loveliness to sell,
    All beautiful and splendid things,
Blue waves whitened on a cliff,
    Soaring fire that sways and sings,
And children's faces looking up,   5
Holding wonder like a cup.

Life has loveliness to sell,
    Music like a curve of gold,
Scent of pine trees in the rain,
    Eyes that love you, arms that hold,   10
And for your spirit's still delight,
Holy thoughts that star the night.

Spend all you have for loveliness,
    Buy it and never count the cost;
For one white singing hour of peace   15
    Count many a year of strife well lost,
And for a breath of ecstasy
Give all you have been, or could be.

                                              Sara Teasdale (1884–1933)

STOPPING BY WOODS ON A SNOWY EVENING

Whose woods these are I think I know.
His house is in the village though;
He will not see me stopping here
To watch his woods fill up with snow.

My little horse must think it queer   5
To stop without a farmhouse near
Between the woods and frozen lake
The darkest evening of the year.

He gives his harness bells a shake
To ask if there is some mistake.   10
The only other sound's the sweep
Of easy wind and downy flake.

The woods are lovely, dark and deep,
But I have promises to keep,
And miles to go before I sleep,   15
And miles to go before I sleep.

Robert Frost (1874–1963)

QUESTIONS

1. How do these two poems differ in idea?
2. What contrasts are suggested between the speaker in the second poem and
   (a) his horse and (b) the owner of the woods?

Both of these poems present ideas, the first more or less explicitly, the second symbolically. Perhaps the best way to get at the idea of the second poem is to ask two questions. First, why does the speaker stop? Second, why does he go on? He stops, we answer, to watch the woods fill up with snow – to observe a scene of natural beauty. He goes on, we answer, because he has "promises" to keep, that is, he has obligations to fulfill. He is momentarily torn between his love of beauty and these other various and complex claims that life has upon him. The small conflict in the poem is symbolical of a larger conflict in life. One part of the sensitive thinking man would like to give up his life to the enjoyment of beauty and art. But another part is aware of larger duties and responsibilities – responsibilities owed, at least in part, to other human beings. The speaker in the poem would like to satisfy both impulses. But when the two come into conflict, he seems to suggest, the "promises" must be given precedence.

The first poem also presents a philosophy but an opposed one. For this poet, beauty is of such supreme value that any conflicting demand should be sacrificed to it. "Spend all you have for loveliness, / Buy it and never count the cost . . . And for a breath of ecstasy / Give all you have been, or could be." The reader, if he is a thinking person, will have to choose between these two philosophies – to commit himself to one or the other. But if he is a good reader of poetry, this commitment should not destroy for him his enjoyment of either poem. If it does, he is reading for plums and not for pies.

Nothing so far said in this chapter should be construed as meaning that the truth or falsity of the idea in a poem is a matter of no importance. *Other things being equal,* the good reader naturally will, and properly should, value more highly the poem whose idea he feels to be maturer and nearer to the heart of human experience. There may be some ideas, moreover, that he feels to be so vicious or so foolish or so beyond the pale of normal human decency as to discredit *by themselves* the poems in which he finds them. A rotten plum may spoil a pie. But a good reader will always be a person of considerable intellectual flexibility and tolerance, able to entertain sympathetically ideas other than his own. He will often like a poem whose idea he disagrees with better than one with an idea he accepts. And, above all, he will not confuse the prose meaning of any poem with its total meaning. He will not mistake plums for pies.

*   *   *   *   *

MY SWEETEST LESBIA

My sweetest Lesbia, let us live and love,
And though the sager sort our deeds reprove,
Let us not weigh them. Heaven's great lamps do dive
Into their west, and straight again revive,
But soon as once set is our little light,   5
Then must we sleep one ever-during night.

If all would lead their lives in love like me,
Then bloody swords and armor should not be;
No drum nor trumpet peaceful sleeps should move,
Unless alarm came from the camp of love.   10
But fools do live, and waste their little light,
And seek with pain their ever-during night.

When timely death my life and fortune ends,
Let not my hearse be vexed with mourning friends,
But let all lovers, rich in triumph, come   15
And with sweet pastimes grace my happy tomb;
And Lesbia, close up thou my little light,
And crown with love my ever-during night.

Thomas Campion (1567–1620)

QUESTIONS

1. This poem is partly imitation, partly translation, of one of a series of poems written by the famous Roman poet Catullus (c. 84–c. 54 B.C.) to his mistress, the wife of a Roman consul. As such, it constitutes a literary allusion which would have been widely familiar to its Renaissance readers. What proposal does the speaker make in stanza 1? On what philosophical grounds does he justify it? How is the phrase "the sager sort" (2) to be taken?

2. How does the speaker justify his proposal in stanza 2? Who are the "fools" spoken of in line 11?
3. With what is "timely death" (13) to be contrasted? With what does "rich in triumph" (15) compare or contrast? How does the speaker want his death to be commemorated? Why?
4. Contrast the philosophy advanced in this poem with that in Lovelace's "To Lucasta, On Going to the Wars" (page 102).

NATURE THE GENTLEST MOTHER IS

Nature the gentlest mother is,
Impatient of no child,
The feeblest or the waywardest.
Her admonition mild

In forest and the hill   5
By traveller be heard,
Restraining rampant squirrel
Or too impetuous bird.

How fair her conversation
A summer afternoon,   10
Her household her assembly;
And when the sun go down,

Her voice among the aisles
Incite the timid prayer
Of the minutest cricket,   15
The most unworthy flower.

When all the children sleep,
She turns as long away
As will suffice to light her lamps,
Then bending from the sky   20

With infinite affection
And infiniter care,
Her golden finger on her lip,
Wills silence everywhere.

Emily Dickinson (1830–1886)

1. The metaphorical concept of Nature as a mother (preserved in the phrase "Mother Nature") is an old one. How does Dickinson freshen it and renew it?
2. Comment on the meaning and appropriateness of the words "assembly" (11), "aisles" (13), "prayer" (14), "unworthy" (16). Do they have any associations in common? Are these associations present elsewhere in the poem? Comment on the meaning of "lamps" (19) and "golden finger" (23).
3. An idiosyncrasy of Dickinson's poetic style is her frequent preference for the subjunctive mood over the indicative. How would a standard grammarian render lines 6, 12, 14?

WHAT MYSTERY PERVADES A WELL!

What mystery pervades a well!
The water lives so far –
A neighbor from another world
Residing in a jar

Whose limit none have ever seen,   5
But just his lid of glass –
Like looking every time you please
In an abyss's face!

The grass does not appear afraid,
I often wonder he   10
Can stand so close and look so bold
At what is awe to me.

Related somehow they may be,
The sedge stands next the sea –
Where he is floorless, and of fear   15
No evidence gives he.

But nature is a stranger yet;
The ones that cite her most
Have never passed her haunted house,
Nor simplified her ghost.   20
To pity those that know her not
Is helped by the regret
That those who know her, know her less
The nearer her they get.

Emily Dickenson (1830–1886)

1. What difference in meaning or connotation exists between "mystery" (1) and "awe" (12)? What intervening words, images, and metaphors contribute to the transition?
2. Are the grass and the water in the well "related" (13)? Explain the analogy between the images in stanzas 3 and 4.
3. Comment on the figures of speech contained in the word "floorless" (15) and the meanings suggested by it. Why does Dickinson use the word "ghost" (20) rather than "spirit" (one of its synonyms)? Is nature dead?
4. Explain the paradoxes in the last stanza.
5. Compare this poem in content with the one before it. Do you find similar ambivalences in other nature poems by Dickinson in this book?

TO A WATERFOWL

Whither, midst falling dew,
While glow the heavens with the last steps of day,
Far, through their rosy depths, dost thou pursue
    Thy solitary way?

Vainly the fowler's eye   5
Might mark thy distant flight to do thee wrong,
As, darkly seen against the crimson sky,
    Thy figure floats along.

Seek'st thou the plashy brink
Of weedy lake, or marge of river wide,   10
Or where the rocking billows rise and sink
    On the chafed ocean side?

There is a Power whose care
Teaches thy way along that pathless coast –
The desert and illimitable air –   15
    Lone wandering, but not lost.

All day thy wings have fanned,
At that far height, the cold, thin atmosphere,
Yet stoop not, weary, to the welcome land,
    Though the dark night is near.   20

And soon that toil shall end;
Soon shalt thou find a summer home, and rest,
And scream among thy fellows; reeds shall bend,
    Soon, o'er thy sheltered nest.

Thou'rt gone, the abyss of heaven   25
Hath swallowed up thy form; yet, on my heart
Deeply has sunk the lesson thou hast given,
    And shall not soon depart.

He who, from zone to zone,
Guides through the boundless sky thy certain flight,   30
In the long way that I must tread alone,
    Will lead my steps aright.

William Cullen Bryant (1794–1878)

DESIGN

I found a dimpled spider, fat and white,
On a white heal-all, holding up a moth
Like a white piece of rigid satin cloth –
Assorted characters of death and blight
Mixed ready to begin the morning right,   5
Like the ingredients of a witches' broth –
A snow-drop spider, a flower like a froth,
And dead wings carried like a paper kite.

What had that flower to do with being white,
The wayside blue and innocent heal-all?   10
What brought the kindred spider to that height,
Then steered the white moth thither in the night?
What but design of darkness to appall? –
If design govern in a thing so small.

Robert Frost (1874–1963)

QUESTIONS

1. Vocabulary: *characters* (4).
2. The heal-all is a wildflower, usually blue or violet but occasionally white, found blooming along roadsides in the summer. It was once supposed to have healing qualities, hence its name. Of what significance, scientific and poetic, is the fact that the spider, the heal-all, and the moth are all white? Of what poetic significance is the fact that the spider is "dimpled" and "fat" and like a "snow-drop," and that the flower is "innocent" and named "heal-all"?
3. The "argument from design," as it was called, was a favorite eighteenth-century argument for the existence of God. What twist does Frost give the argument? What questions does the poem pose?

4. Contrast Frost's poem in content with "To a Waterfowl." Is it possible to admire both?

WHAT IF A MUCH OF A WHICH OF A WIND

what if a much of a which of a wind
gives the truth to summer's lie;
bloodies with dizzying leaves the sun
and yanks immortal stars awry?
Blow king to beggar and queen to seem   5
(blow friend to fiend: blow space to time)
— when skies are hanged and oceans drowned,
the single secret will still be man

what if a keen of a lean wind flays
screaming hills with sleet and snow: 10
strangles valleys by ropes of thing
and stifles forests in white ago?
Blow hope to terror; blow seeing to blind
(blow pity to envy and soul to mind)
— whose hearts are mountains, roots are trees,   15
it's they shall cry hello to the spring

what if a dawn of a doom of a dream
bites this universe in two,
peels forever out of his grave
and sprinkles nowhere with me and you?   20
Blow soon to never and never to twice
(blow life to isn't:blow death to was)
— all nothing's only our hugest home;
the most who die, the more we live

e. e. cummings (1894–1962)

QUESTIONS

1. What unconventional uses does cummings make of grammar and diction?
   Can you justify them?
2. What kind of storm is described? What does it signify?
3. What assertions does the poet make about man in each of the three stanzas?

WHEN SERPENTS BARGAIN FOR THE RIGHT TO SQUIRM

> when serpents bargain for the right to squirm
> and the sun strikes to gain a living wage –
> when thorns regard their roses with alarm
> and rainbows are insured against old age
>
> when every thrush may sing no new moon in   5
> if all screech-owls have not okayed his voice
> – and any wave signs on the dotted line
> or else an ocean is compelled to close
>
> when the oak begs permission of the birch
> to make an acorn – valleys accuse their   10
> mountains of having altitude – and march
> denounces april as a saboteur
>
> then we'll believe in that incredible
> unanimal mankind (and not until)

e. e. cummings (1894–1962)

QUESTIONS

1. What characteristics do the various activities not engaged in by nature have in common? What qualities of thought and feeling or kinds of behavior ought to replace these activities, in the poet's view?
2. What does the poet imply by calling man an "unanimal" (14)? What is the precise force here of "incredible" (13)?
3. How does the view of man implied in this poem differ from that implied in the preceding poem? Which of the two poems is *satirical* (see page 104)?

THE CAGED SKYLARK

> As a dare-gale skylark scanted in a dull cage
>   Man's mounting spirit in his bone-house, mean house, dwells –
>   That bird beyond the remembering his free fells;
> This in drudgery, day-laboring-out life's age.
>
> Though aloft on turf or perch or poor low stage,   5
>   Both sing sometimes the sweetest, sweetest spells,
>   Yet both droop deadly sometimes in their cells
> Or wring their barriers in bursts of fear or rage.

Not that the sweet-fowl, song-fowl, needs no rest –
Why, hear him, hear him babble and drop down to his nest,   10
   But his own nest, wild nest, no prison.

Man's spirit will be flesh-bound when found at best,
But uncumbered: meadow-down is not distressed
   For a rainbow footing it nor he for his bones risen.

whose spirit has risen

                    Gerard Manley Hopkins (1844–1889)

QUESTIONS

1. Vocabulary: *scanted* (1), *fells* (3). What meanings of "mean" (2) are appropriate here? "Turf" (5) is a piece of sod placed in a cage.
2. This poem, written by a poet-priest, expresses his belief in the orthodox Roman Catholic doctrine of the resurrection of the body. According to this belief man's immortal soul, after death, will be ultimately reunited with his body; this body, however, will be a weightless, perfected, glorified body, not the gross imperfect body of mortal life. Express the analogy in the poem as a pair of mathematical statements of proportion (in the form $a:b = c:d,$ and $e:f = g:h = i:j,$ using the following terms: caged skylark, mortal body, meadow-down, cage, rainbow, spirit-in-life, nest, immortal spirit, wild skylark, resurrected body.
3. Discuss the image of the last two lines as a figure for weightlessness. Why would not a shadow have been equally apt as a rainbow for this comparison?

THE IMMORTAL PART

       When I meet the morning beam
       Or lay me down at night to dream,
       I hear my bones within me say,
       "Another night, another day.
       "When shall this slough of sense be cast,   5
       This dust of thoughts be laid at last,
       The man of flesh and soul be slain
       And the man of bone remain?

       "This tongue that talks, these lungs that shout,
       These thews that hustle us about,   10
       This brain that fills the skull with schemes,
       And its humming hive of dreams, –

something to we shed

Meaning and Idea   147

"These today are proud in power
And lord it in their little hour:
The immortal bones obey control   15
Of dying flesh and dying soul.

" 'Tis long till eve and morn are gone:
Slow the endless night comes on,
And late to fullness grows the birth
That shall last as long as earth.   20

"Wanderers eastward, wanderers west.
Know you why you cannot rest?
'Tis that every mother's son
Travails with a skeleton.

"Lie down in the bed of dust;   25
Bear the fruit that bear you must;
Bring the eternal seed to light,
And morn is all the same as night.

"Rest you so from trouble sore,
Fear the heat o' the sun no more,   30
Nor the snowing winter wild,
Now you labor not with child.

"Empty vessel, garment cast,
We that wore you long shall last.
– Another night, another day."   35
So my bones within me say.

Therefore they shall do my will
Today while I am master still,
And flesh and soul, now both are strong,
Shall hale the sullen slaves along,   40

Before this fire of sense decay,
This smoke of thought blow clean away,
And leave with ancient night alone
The steadfast and enduring bone.

A. E. Housman (1859–1936)

1. Vocabulary: *slough* (5), *thews* (10), *travails* (24), *hale* (40).
2. Discuss the figures of speech in lines 3–16, 12, 19–27, 41–42, 43.
3. Do you recognize the allusion in stanza 8? If not, refer to page 338. How is the allusion appropriate here?
4. Contrast the meaning of the word "soul" in this poem with its meaning in "The Caged Skylark." How do the two poems differ in idea? Is there any pronounced difference between them in poetic merit?

ARS POETICA

A poem should be palpable and mute
As a globed fruit,

Dumb
As old medallions to the thumb,

Silent as the sleeve-worn stone   5
Of casement ledges where the moss has grown –

A poem should be wordless
As the flight of birds.

                              *

A poem should be motionless in time
As the moon climbs,   10

Leaving, as the moon releases
Twig by twig the night-entangled trees,

Leaving, as the moon behind the winter leaves,
Memory by memory the mind –

A poem should be motionless in time   15
As the moon climbs.

                              *

A poem should be equal to:
Not true.

For all the history of grief
An empty doorway and a maple leaf.   20

For love
The leaning grasses and two lights above the sea —

A poem should not mean
But be.

Archibald MacLeish (b. 1892)

QUESTIONS

1. How can a poem be "wordless" (7)? How can it be "motionless in time" (15)?
2. The Latin title, literally translatable as "The Art of Poetry," is a traditional title for works on the philosophy of poetry. What is *this* poet's philosophy of poetry? What does he mean by saying that a poem should not "mean" and should not be "true"?

10 Tone

Tone, in literature, may be defined as the writer's or speaker's attitude toward his subject, his audience, or himself. It is the emotional coloring, or the emotional meaning, of the work and is an extremely important part of the full meaning. In spoken language it is indicated by the inflections of the speaker's voice. If, for instance, a friend tells you, "I'm going to get married today," the facts of the statement are entirely clear. But the emotional meaning of the statement may vary widely according to the tone of voice with which it is uttered. The tone may be ecstatic ("Hooray! I'm going to get married today!"); it may be incredulous ("I can't believe it! I'm going to get married today"); it may be despairing ("Horrors! I'm going to get married today"); it may be resigned ("Might as well face it. I'm going to get married today"). Obviously, a correct interpretation of the tone will be an important part of understanding the full meaning. It may even have rather important consequences. If someone calls you a fool, your interpretation of the tone may determine whether you roll up your sleeves for a fight or walk off with your arm around his shoulder. If a girl says "No" to a proposal of marriage, your interpretation of her tone may determine whether you ask her again and win her or start going with someone else.

In poetry tone is likewise important. We have not really understood a poem unless we have accurately sensed whether the attitude it manifests is playful or solemn, mocking or reverent, calm or excited. But the correct determination of tone in literature is a much more delicate matter than it is with spoken language, for we do not have the speaker's voice to guide us. We must learn to recognize tone by other means. Almost all the elements of poetry go into indicating its tone: connotation, imagery, and metaphor; irony and understatement; rhythm, sentence construction, and formal pattern. There is therefore no simple formula for recognizing tone. It is an end product of all the elements in a poem. The best we can do is illustrate.

Robert Frost's "Stopping by Woods on a Snowy Evening" (page 138) seems a simple poem, but it has always afforded trouble to beginning readers. A very good student, asked to interpret it, once wrote this: "The poem means that we are forever passing up pleasures to go onward to what we wrongly consider our obligations. We would like to watch the snow fall on the peaceful countryside, but we always have to rush home to supper and other engagements. Mr. Frost feels that the average man considers life too short to stop and take time to appreciate true pleasures." This student did a good job in recognizing the central conflict of the poem. He went astray in recognizing its tone. Let's examine why.

In the first place, the fact that the speaker in the poem *does* stop to watch the snow fall in the woods immediately establishes him as a human being with more sensitivity and feeling for beauty than most. He is not one of the people of Wordsworth's sonnet (page 353) who, "getting and spending," have laid waste their powers and lost the capacity to be stirred by nature. Frost's speaker is contrasted with his horse, who, as a creature of habit and an animal without esthetic perception, cannot understand the speaker's reason for stopping. There is also a suggestion of contrast with the "owner" of the woods, who, if he saw the speaker stopping, might be as puzzled as the horse. (Who most truly "profits" from the woods – its absentee owner or the person who can enjoy its beauty?) The speaker goes on because he has "promises to keep." But the word "promises," though it may here have a wry ironic undertone of regret, has a favorable connotation: people almost universally agree that promises ought to be kept. If the poet had used a different term, say, "things to do," or "business to attend to," or "financial affairs to take care of," or "money to make," the connotations would have been quite different. As it is, the tone of the poem tells us that the poet is sympathetic to the speaker, is endorsing rather than censuring his action. Perhaps we may go even further. In the concluding two lines, because of their climactic position, because they are repeated, and because "sleep" in poetry is often used figuratively to refer to death, there is a suggestion of symbolic interpretation: "and many years to live before I die." If we accept this interpretation, it poses a parallel between giving oneself up to contemplation of the woods and dying. The poet's total implication would seem to be that beauty is a distinctively human value that deserves its place in a full life but that to devote one's life to its pursuit, at the expense of other obligations and duties, is tantamount to one's death as a responsible being. The poet therefore accepts the choice the speaker makes, though not without a touch of regret.

Differences in tone, and their importance, can perhaps be studied best in poems with similar content. Consider, for instance, the following pair.

THE VILLAIN

> While joy gave clouds the light of stars,
>   That beamed where'er they looked;
> And calves and lambs had tottering knees,
>   Excited, while they sucked;
> While every bird enjoyed his song,   5
> Without one thought of harm or wrong –
> I turned my head and saw the wind,
>   Not far from where I stood,
> Dragging the corn by her golden hair,
>   Into a dark and lonely wood.   10

> *W. H. Davies (1871–1940)*

QUESTIONS

1. Vocabulary: *corn* (9).
2. From what realm of experience is the image in the title and the last two lines taken? What implications does your answer have for the way this image should be taken – that is, for its relation to reality?

APPARENTLY WITH NO SURPRISE

> Apparently with no surprise
> To any happy flower,
> The frost beheads it at its play
> In accidental power.

> The blond assassin passes on,
> The sun proceeds unmoved
> To measure off another day
> For an approving God.

> *Emily Dickinson (1830–1886)*

1. What is the "blond assassin"?
2. What ironies are involved in this poem?

Both of these poems are concerned with nature; both use contrast as their basic organizing principle – a contrast between innocence and evil, joy and tragedy. But in tone the two poems are sharply different. The first is light and fanciful; its tone is one of delight or delighted surprise. The second, though superficially fanciful, is basically grim, almost savage; its tone is one of horror. Let's examine the difference.

In "The Villain" the images of the first six lines all suggest joy and innocence. The last four introduce the sinister. The poet, on turning his head, sees a villain dragging a beautiful maiden toward a dark wood to commit there some unmentionable deed, or so his metaphor tells us. But our response is one not of horror but of delight, for we realize that the poet does not mean us to take his metaphor seriously. He has actually seen only the wind blowing through the wheat and bending its golden tops gracefully toward a shady wood. The beauty of the scene has delighted him, and he has been further delighted by the fanciful metaphor which he has found to express it. The reader shares his delight both in the scene and in the metaphor.

The second poem makes the same contrast of joyful innocence (the "happy flower . . . at its play") with the sinister ("the blond assassin"). The chief difference would seem to be that the villain is this time the frost rather than the wind. But this time the poet, though her metaphor is no less fanciful, is earnest in what she is saying. For the frost actually *does* kill the flower. What makes the horror of the killing even worse is that nothing else in nature is disturbed over it or seems even to notice it. The sun "proceeds unmoved / To measure off another day." Nothing in nature stops or pauses. The flower itself is not surprised. And even God – the God who we have all been told is benevolent and concerned over the least sparrow's fall – seems to approve of what has happened, for he shows no displeasure, and it was he who created the frost as well as the flower. Further irony lies in the fact that the "assassin" (the word's connotations are of terror and violence) is not dark but "blond," or white (the connotations here are of innocence and beauty). The destructive agent, in other words, is among the most exquisite creations of God's handiwork. The poet, then, is shocked at what has happened, and is even more shocked that nothing else in nature is shocked. What has happened seems inconsistent with a rule of benevolence in the universe. In her ironic reference to an "approving God," therefore, the poet is raising a dreadful question: are the forces that created and govern the universe actually benevolent? And if we think that the poet is unduly disturbed over the death of a flower, we may consider that what is true for the flower is true throughout nature. Death – even early or accidental death, in terrible juxtaposition with beauty – is its constant condition; the fate that befalls the flower befalls us all.

These two poems, then, though superficially similar, are basically as different as night and day. And the difference is primarily one of tone.

Accurate determination of tone, therefore, is extremely important, whether in the reading of poetry or the interpretation of a woman's "No." For the good reader it will be instinctive and automatic. For the beginning reader it will require study. But beyond the general suggestions for reading that have already been made, no specific instructions can be given. Recognition of tone requires an increasing familiarity with the meanings and connotations of words, alertness to the presence of irony and other figures, and, above all, careful reading. Poetry cannot be read as one would skim a newspaper or a mystery novel, looking merely for facts.

EXERCISE

1. Marvell's "To His Coy Mistress" (page 75), Housman's "Loveliest of trees" (page 77), and Herrick's "To the Virgins, to Make Much of Time" (page 88) all treat a traditional poetic theme known as the *carpe diem* ("seize the day") theme. They differ, however, in tone. Characterize the tone of each, and point out the differences in poetic management that account for the difference in tone.

2. Describe and account for the differences in tone between the poems in each of the following pairs: (a) "Spring" by Shakespeare (page 11) and "When the hounds of spring" by Swinburne (page 170); (b) "Break of Day" (page 32) and "The Good-Morrow" (page 305), both by Donne; (c) "God is a distant, stately lover" by Dickinson (page 127) and "Batter my heart, three-personed God" by Donne (page 111); (d) "When green buds hang in the elm" by Housman (page 43) and "Nothing Gold Can Stay" by Frost (page 179); (e) "Elegy for Alfred Hubbard" by Connor (page 159) and "The Mill" by Wilbur (page 350).

* * * * *

THE COMING OF WISDOM WITH TIME

Though leaves are many, the root is one;
Through all the lying days of my youth
I swayed my leaves and flowers in the sun;
Now I may wither into the truth.

William Butler Yeats (1865–1939)

QUESTION

1. Is the poet exulting over a gain or lamenting over a loss?

SINCE THERE'S NO HELP

Since there's no help, come let us kiss and part;
Nay, I have done, you get no more of me,
And I am glad, yea, glad with all my heart
That thus so cleanly I myself can free;
Shake hands forever, cancel all our vows,   5
And when we meet at any time again,
Be it not seen in either of our brows
That we one jot of former love retain.
Now at the last gasp of Love's latest breath,
When, his pulse failing, Passion speechless lies,   10
When Faith is kneeling by his bed of death,
And Innocence is closing up his eyes,
Now, if thou wouldst, when all have given him over,
From death to life thou mightst him yet recover.

Michael Drayton (1563–1631)

QUESTIONS

1. What difference in tone do you find between the first eight lines and the last six? What differences in rhythm and the kind of language used help to establish this difference in tone?
2. How many figures are there in the allegorical scene in lines 9–12? Why is "Love" dying?
3. Define the dramatic situation as precisely as possible, taking into consideration both the man's attitude and the woman's.

TOADS REVISITED

Walking around in the park
Should feel better than work:
The lake, the sunshine,
The grass to lie on,

Blurred playground noises   5
Beyond black-stockinged nurses –
Not a bad place to be.
Yet it doesn't suit me,

Being one of the men
You meet of an afternoon: 10
Palsied old step-takers,
Hare-eyed clerks with the jitters,

Wax-fleshed out-patients
Still vague from accidents,
And characters in long coats   15
Deep in the litter-baskets –

All dodging the toad work
By being stupid or weak.
Think of being them!
Hearing the hours chime,   20

Watching the bread delivered,
The sun by clouds covered,
The children going home;
Think of being them,

Turning over their failures   25
By some bed of lobelias,
Nowhere to go but indoors,
No friends but empty chairs –

No, give me my in-tray,
My loaf-haired secretary,   30
My shall-I-keep-the-call-in-Sir:
What else can I answer,

When the lights come on at four
At the end of another year?
Give me your arm, old toad;   35
Help me down Cemetery Road.

Philip Larkin (b. 1922)

QUESTIONS

1. As the title suggests, the poet is returning in this poem (published in 1964) to
   a subject treated in an earlier poem (published in 1955) (see page 72). How
   has the poet's attitude changed toward his subject? In which poem is the tone
   more ambivalent? How are the changes indicated?
2. What symbolism is suggested in lines 33–34? What meanings has "Cemetery
   Road" (36)?
3. How do you account for the poet's change in attitude?

TO A FRIEND WHOSE WORK HAS COME TO TRIUMPH

Consider Icarus, pasting those sticky wings on,
testing that strange little tug at his shoulder blade,
and think of that first flawless moment over the lawn
of the labyrinth. Think of the difference it made!
There below are the trees, as awkward as camels;   5
and here are the shocked starlings pumping past
and think of innocent Icarus who is doing quite well:
larger than a sail, over the fog and the blast
of the plushy ocean, he goes. Admire his wings!
Feel the fire at his neck and see how casually   10
he glances up and is caught, wondrously tunneling
into that hot eye. Who cares that he fell back to the sea?
See him acclaiming the sun and come plunging down
while his sensible daddy goes straight into town.

Anne Sexton (1928–1974)

QUESTIONS

1. The poem is based on two allusions. The first is to the Greek myth of
   Daedalus and Icarus (look it up if you are unfamiliar with it). What is the
   second? (If you fail to recognize it, check above the poem's title in the index
   of this book.)

2. Is this a poem of warning or of tribute to the friend mentioned in the title? In answering this question, consider carefully (a) the difference in language and tone between lines 1–13 and 14, (b) the function of the allusion contained in the title.
3. This poem is roughly an English sonnet (see pages 221–23). It has the same rime scheme (though many of the rimes are approximate); and most of its lines (though none are iambic) have five beats. Exceptional are lines 12 and 14. Discuss the difference in rhythm of these two lines, and relate the rhythm of each to its content.

ELEGY FOR ALFRED HUBBARD

Hubbard is dead, the old plumber;
who will mend our burst pipes now,
the tap that has dripped all the summer,
testing the sink's overflow?

No other like him. Young men with knowledge   5
of new techniques, theories from books,
may better his work straight from college,
but who will challenge his squint-eyed looks

in kitchen, bathroom, under floorboards,
rules of thumb which were often wrong;   10
seek as erringly stopcocks in cupboards,
or make a job last half as long?

He was a man who knew the ginnels,
alleyways, streets – the whole district,
family secrets, minor annals,   15
time-honored fictions fused to fact.

Seventy years of gossip muttered
under his cap, his tufty thatch,
so that his talk was slow and clotted,
hard to follow, and too much.   20

As though nothing fell, none vanished,
and time were the maze of Cheetham Hill,
in which the dead – with jobs unfinished –
waited to hear him ring the bell.

For much he never got round to doing,   25
but meant to, when weather bucked up,
or worsened, or when his pipe was drawing,
or when he'd finished this cup.

I thought time, he forgot so often,
had forgotten him but here's Death's pomp   30
over his house, and by the coffin
the son who will inherit his blowlamp,

tools, workshop, cart, and cornet
(pride of Cheetham Prize Brass Band),
and there's his mourning widow, Janet,   35
stood at the gate he'd promised to mend.

Soon he will make his final journey;
shaved and silent, strangely trim,
with never a pause to talk to any-
body: how arrow-like, for him!   40

In St. Mark's church, whose dismal tower
he pointed and painted when a lad,
they will sing his praises amidst flowers
while, somewhere, a cellar starts to flood,

and the housewife banging his front-door knocker   45
is not surprised to find him gone,
and runs for Thwaite, who's a better worker,
and sticks at a job until it's done.

Tony Connor (b. 1930)

QUESTIONS

1. Vocabulary: *annals* (15), *pomp* (30). "Ginnels" (13) are tunnels that punctuate rows of houses, giving access to the "backs." "Pointed" (42) means mortared.
2. Characterize Hubbard. How does this "elegy" differ from the *eulogy* that will be said for him in St. Mark's Church (41–43)? Compose his eulogy.
3. What is the poet's attitude toward his subject?

ONE DIGNITY DELAYS FOR ALL

One dignity delays for all,
One mitred afternoon.
None can avoid this purple,
None avoid this crown.

Coach it insures, and footmen,   5
Chamber and state and throng;
Bells, also, in the village,
As we ride grand along.

What dignified attendants,
What service when we pause!   10
How loyally at parting
Their hundred hats they raise!

How pomp surpassing ermine
When simple you and I
Present our meek escutcheon   15
And claim the rank to die!

Emily Dickinson (1830–1886)

QUESTIONS

1. Vocabulary: *mitred* (2), *state* (6), *escutcheon* (15).
2. What is the "dignity" that delays for all? What is its nature? What is being
   described in stanzas 2 and 3?
3. What figures of speech are combined in "our meek escutcheon" (15)? What
   metaphorically does it represent?

'TWAS WARM AT FIRST LIKE US

'Twas warm at first like us,
Until there crept upon
A chill, like frost upon a glass,
Till all the scene be gone.

The forehead copied stone,   5
The fingers grew too cold
To ache, and like a skater's brook
The busy eyes congealed.

It straightened – that was all,
It crowded cold to cold,   10
It multiplied indifference
As Pride were all it could.

And even when with cords
'Twas lowered like a weight,
It made no signal, nor demurred,   15
But dropped like adamant.

Emily Dickinson (1830–1886)

QUESTIONS

1. Vocabulary: *adamant* (16).
2. What is "It" in the opening line? What is being described in the poem, and between what points in time?
3. How would you describe the tone of this poem? How does it contrast with that of the preceding?

CROSSING THE BAR

Sunset and evening star,
    And one clear call for me!
And may there be no moaning of the bar
    When I put out to sea,

But such a tide as moving seems asleep,   5
    Too full for sound and foam,
When that which drew from out the boundless deep
    Turns again home.

Twilight and evening bell,
    And after that the dark!   10
And may there be no sadness of farewell
    When I embark;

For though from out our bourne of Time and Place
    The flood may bear me far,
I hope to see my Pilot face to face   15
    When I have crossed the bar.

Alfred, Lord Tennyson (1809–1892)

QUESTIONS

1. Vocabulary: *bourne* (13).
2. What two sets of figures does Tennyson use for approaching death? What is the precise moment of death in each set?
3. In troubled weather the wind and waves above the sandbar across a harbor's mouth make a moaning sound. What metaphorical meaning has the "moaning of the bar" here (3)? For what kind of death is the poet wishing? Why does he want "no sadness of farewell" (11)?
4. What is "that which drew from out the boundless deep" (7)? What is "the boundless deep"? To what is it opposed in the poem? Why is "Pilot" (15) capitalized?

THE OXEN

Christmas Eve, and twelve of the clock.
    "Now they are all on their knees,"
An elder said as we sat in a flock
    By the embers in hearthside ease.

We pictured the meek mild creatures where   5
    They dwelt in their strawy pen,
Nor did it occur to one of us there
    To doubt they were kneeling then.

So fair a fancy few would weave
    In these years! Yet, I feel,   10
If someone said on Christmas Eve,
    "Come; see the oxen kneel

"In the lonely barton° by yonder comb°   farm; valley
    Our childhood used to know,"
I should go with him in the gloom,   15
    Hoping it might be so.

                    Thomas Hardy (1840–1928)

QUESTIONS

1. Is the simple superstition referred to in the poem here opposed to, or identified with, religious faith? With what implications for the meaning of the poem?
2. What are "these years" (10) and how do they contrast with the years of the

poet's boyhood? What event in intellectual history between 1840 and 1915 (the date of composition of this poem) was most responsible for the change?

3. Both "Crossing the Bar" and "The Oxen" in their last lines use a form of the verb *hope*. By full discussion of tone, establish the precise meaning of hope in each poem. What degree of expectation does it imply? How should the word be handled in reading Tennyson's poem aloud?

A MAD ANSWER OF A MADMAN

> One asked a madman if a wife he had.
> "A wife?" quoth he. "I never was so mad."

Robert Hayman (b. 1628?)

QUESTION

1. Considering its title, in how many ways might this epigram be interpreted? Considering its tone, which interpretation is uppermost?

LOVE

> There's the wonderful love of a beautiful maid,
>   And the love of a staunch true man,
> And the love of a baby that's unafraid –
>   All have existed since time began.
> But the most wonderful love, the Love of all loves,
>   Even greater than the love for Mother,
> Is the infinite, tenderest, passionate love
>   Of one dead drunk for another.

Anonymous

QUESTION

1. The radical shift in tone makes "Love" come off. If such a shift were unintentional in a poem, what would our view be?

11 Musical Devices

I t is obvious to the most uninitiated reader that poetry makes a greater use of the "music" of language than does language that is not poetry. The poet, unlike the person who uses language to convey only information, chooses words for sound as well as for meaning, and uses the sound as a means of reinforcing meaning. So prominent is this musical quality of poetry that some writers have made it the distinguishing term in their definitions of poetry. Edgar Allan Poe, for instance, describes poetry as "music . . . combined with a pleasurable idea." Whether or not it deserves this much importance, verbal music, like connotation, imagery, and figurative language, is one of the important resources that enable the poet to do something more than communicate mere information. The poet may indeed sometimes pursue verbal music for its own sake; more often, at least in first-rate poetry, it is an adjunct to the total meaning or communication of the poem.

There are two broad ways by which the poet achieves musical quality: by the choice and arrangement of sounds and by the arrangement of accents. In this chapter we will consider one aspect of the first of these.

An essential element in all music is repetition. In fact, we might say that all art consists of giving structure to two elements: repetition and variation. All things we enjoy greatly and lastingly have these two elements. We enjoy the sea endlessly because it is always the same yet always different. We enjoy a baseball game because it contains the same complex combination of pattern and variation. Our love of art, then, is rooted in human psychology. We like the familiar, we like variety, but we like them combined. If we get too much sameness, the result is monotony and tedium; if we get too much variety, the result is bewilderment and confusion. The composer of music, therefore, repeats certain musical tones; repeats them in certain combinations, or chords; and repeats them in certain patterns, or melodies. The poet likewise repeats certain sounds in certain combinations and arrangements, and thus gives organization and structure to his verse. Consider the following short example.

THE TURTLE

> The turtle lives 'twixt plated decks
> Which practically conceal its sex.
> I think it clever of the turtle
> In such a fix to be so fertile.

Ogden Nash (1902–1971)

Here is a little joke, a paradox of animal life to which the author has cleverly drawn our attention. An experiment will show us, however, that much of its appeal lies not so much in what it says as in the manner in which it says it. If, for instance, we recast the verse as prose: "The turtle lives in a shell which almost conceals its sex. It is ingenious of the turtle, in such a situation, to be so prolific," the joke falls flat. Some of its appeal must lie in its metrical form. So now we cast it in unrimed verse:

> Because he lives between two decks,
> It's hard to tell a turtle's gender.
> The turtle is a clever beast
> In such a plight to be so fertile.

Here, perhaps, is *some* improvement, but still the piquancy of the original is missing. Much of that appeal must have consisted in the use of rime – the repetition of sound in "decks" and "sex," "turtle" and "fertile." So we try once more:

> The turtle lives 'twixt plated decks
> Which practically conceal its sex.
> I think it clever of the turtle
> In such a plight to be so fertile.

But for the perceptive reader there is still something missing – he does not at first see what – but some little touch that makes the difference between a good piece of verse and a little masterpiece in its kind. And then he sees it: "plight" has been substituted for "fix."

But why should "fix" make such a difference? Its meaning is little different from that of "plight"; its only important difference is in sound. But there we are. The final x in "fix" catches up the concluding consonant sound in "sex," and its initial f is repeated in the initial consonant sound of "fertile." Not only do these sound recurrences provide a subtle gratification to the ear, but they also give the verse structure; they emphasize and draw together the key words of the piece: "sex," "fix," and "fertile."

The poet may repeat any unit of sound from the smallest to the largest. He may repeat individual vowel and consonant sounds, whole syllables, words, phrases, lines, or groups of lines. In each instance, in a good poem, the repetition will serve several purposes: it will please the ear, it will emphasize the words in which the repetition occurs, and it will give structure to the poem. The popularity and initial impressiveness of such repetitions is evidenced by their becoming in many instances embedded in the language as clichés like "wild and woolly," "first and foremost," "footloose and fancy-free," "penny-wise, pound-foolish," "dead as a doornail," "might and main," "sink or swim," "do or die," "pell-mell," "helter-skelter," "harum-scarum," "hocus-pocus." Some of these kinds of repetition have names, as we will see.

A syllable consists of a vowel sound that may be preceded or followed by consonant sounds. Any of these sounds may be repeated. The repetition of initial consonant sounds, as in "tried and true," "safe and sound," "fish or fowl," "rime or reason," is ALLITERATION. The repetition of vowel sounds, as in "mad as a hatter," "time out of mind," "free and easy," "slapdash," is ASSONANCE. The repetition of final consonant sounds, as in "First and last," "odds and ends," "short and sweet," "a stroke of luck," or Shakespeare's "struts and frets" (page 125) is CONSONANCE.*

Repetitions may be used alone or in combination. Alliteration and assonance are combined in such phrases as "time and tide," "thick and

---

*There is no established terminology for these various repetitions. *Alliteration* is used by some writers to mean any repetition of consonant sounds. *Assonance* has been used to mean the similarity as well as the identity of vowel sounds, or even the similarity of any sounds whatever. *Consonance* has often been reserved for words in which both the initial *and* final consonant sounds correspond, as in *green* and *groan, moon* and *mine*. *Rime* (or rhyme) has been used to mean any sound repetition, including alliteration, assonance, and consonance. In the absence of clear agreement on the meanings of these terms, the terminology chosen here has appeared most useful, with support in usage. Labels are useful in analysis. The student should, however, learn to recognize the devices and, more important, to see their function, without worrying too much over nomenclature.

thin," "kith and kin," "alas and alack," "fit as a fiddle," and Edgar Allan Poe's famous line, "The viol, the violet, and the vine." Alliteration and consonance are combined in such phrases as "crisscross," "last but not least," "lone and lorn," "good as gold," Housman's "Malt does more than Milton can" (page 17), "strangling in a string" (page 55) and "fleet foot" (page 318), and e. e. cummings's "blow friend to fiend" and "a doom of a dream" (page 145). The combination of assonance and consonance is rime.

RIME is the repetition of the accented vowel sound and all succeeding sounds. It is called MASCULINE when the rime sounds involve only one syllable, as in *decks* and *sex* or *support* and *retort*. It is FEMININE when the rime sounds involve two or more syllables, as in *turtle* and *fertile* or *spitefully* and *delightfully*. It is referred to as INTERNAL RIME when one or both riming words are within the line and as END RIME when both riming words are at the *ends* of lines. End rime is probably the most frequently used and most consciously sought-after sound repetition in English poetry. Because it comes at the end of the line, it receives emphasis as a musical effect and perhaps contributes more than any other musical resource except rhythm and meter to give poetry its musical effect as well as its structure. There exists, however, a large body of poetry that does not employ rime and for which rime would not be appropriate. Also, there has always been a tendency, especially noticeable in modern poetry, to substitute approximate rimes for perfect rimes at the ends of lines. APPROXIMATE RIMES include words with any kind of sound similarity, from close to fairly remote. Under approximate rime we include alliteration, assonance, and consonance or their combinations when used at the end of the line; half-rime (feminine rimes in which only half of the word rimes – the accented half, as in *lightly* and *frightful*, or the unaccented half, as in *yellow* and *willow*); and other similarities too elusive to name. "A narrow fellow in the grass" (page 55), "Dr. Sigmund Freud Discovers the Sea Shell" (page 65), "Toads" (page 72) and "Toads Revisited" (page 157), "Mr. Z" (page 117), "Poem in October" (page 225), and "Wind" (page 320), among others, employ various kinds of approximate rime.

THAT NIGHT WHEN JOY BEGAN

> That night when joy began
> Our narrowest veins to flush,
> We waited for the flash
> Of morning's levelled gun.

But morning let us pass, 5
And day by day relief
Outgrew his nervous laugh,
Grows credulous of peace.

As mile by mile is seen
No trespasser's reproach, 10
And love's best glasses reach
No fields but are his own.

W. H. Auden (1907–1973)

QUESTIONS

1. What has been the past experience with love of the two people in the poem? What is their present experience? What precisely is the tone of the poem?
2. What basic metaphor underlies the poem? Work it out stanza by stanza. What is "the flash of morning's levelled gun"? Does line 10 mean that no trespasser reproaches the lovers or that no one reproaches the lovers for being trespassers? Does "glasses" (11) refer to spectacles, tumblers, or field glasses? Point out three personifications.
3. The rime pattern in this poem is intricate and exact. Work it out, considering alliteration, assonance, and consonance.

In addition to the repetition of individual sounds and syllables, the poet may repeat whole words, phrases, lines, or groups of lines. When such repetition is done according to some fixed pattern, it is called a REFRAIN. The refrain is especially common in songlike poetry. Examples are to be found in Shakespeare's "Winter" (page 6) and "Spring" (page 11).

It is not to be thought that we have exhausted the possibilities of sound repetition by giving names to a few of the more prominent kinds. The complete study of possible kinds of sound repetition in poetry would be so complex that it would break down under its own machinery. Some of the subtlest and loveliest effects escape our net of names. In as short a phrase as this from the prose of John Ruskin – "ivy as light and lovely as the vine" – we notice alliteration in *light* and *lovely,* assonance in *ivy, light,* and *vine,* and consonance in *ivy* and *lovely,* but we have no name to connect the *v* in *vine* with the *v*'s in *ivy* and *lovely,* or the second *l* in *lovely* with the first *l,* or the final syllables of *ivy* and *lovely* with each other; but these are all an effective part of the music of the line. Also contributing to the music of poetry is the use of related rather than identical sounds, such as *m* and *n* or *p* and *b* or the vowel sounds in *boat, boot,* and *book.*

These various musical repetitions, for a trained reader, will ordinarily make an almost subconscious contribution to his reading of the poem: the reader will feel their effect without necessarily being aware of what has caused it. There is value, however, in occasionally analyzing a poem for these devices in order to increase awareness of them. A few words of caution are necessary. First, the repetitions are entirely a matter of sound; spelling is irrelevant. *Bear* and *pair* are rimes, but *through* and *rough* are not. *Cell* and *sin, folly* and *philosophy* alliterate, but *sin* and *sugar, gun* and *gem* do not. Second, alliteration, assonance, consonance, and masculine rime are matters that ordinarily involve only stressed or accented syllables; for only such syllables ordinarily make enough impression on the ear to be significant in the sound pattern of the poem. We should hardly consider *which* and *its* in the second line of "The Turtle," for instance, as an example of assonance, for neither word is stressed enough in the reading to make it significant as a sound. Third, the words involved in these repetitions must be close enough together that the ear retains the sound, consciously or subconsciously, from its first occurrence to its second. This distance varies according to circumstances, but for alliteration, assonance, and consonance the words ordinarily have to be in the same line or adjacent lines. End rime bridges a longer gap.

WHEN THE HOUNDS OF SPRING

> When the hounds of spring are on winter's traces,
>   The mother of months in meadow or plain
> Fills the shadows and windy places
>   With lisp of leaves and ripple of rain;
> And the brown bright nightingale amorous   5
> Is half assuaged for Itylus,
> For the Thracian ships and the foreign faces,
>   The tongueless vigil, and all the pain.
>
> Come with bows bent and with emptying of quivers,
>   Maiden most perfect, lady of light,   10
> With a noise of winds and many rivers,
>   With a clamor of waters, and with might;
> Bind on thy sandals, O thou most fleet,
> Over the splendor and speed of thy feet;
> For the faint east quickens, the wan west shivers, 15
>   Round the feet of the day and the feet of the night.

Where shall we find her, how shall we sing to her,
    Fold our hands round her knees, and cling?
O that man's heart were as fire and could spring to her,
    Fire, or the strength of the streams that spring!   20
For the stars and the winds are unto her
As raiment, as songs of the harp-player;
For the risen stars and the fallen cling to her,
    And the southwest-wind and the west-wind sing.

For winter's rains and ruins are over,   25
    And all the season of snows and sins;
The days dividing lover and lover,
    The light that loses, the night that wins;
And time remembered is grief forgotten,
And frosts are slain and flowers begotten,   30
And in green underwood and cover
    Blossom by blossom the spring begins.

The full streams feed on flower of rushes,
    Ripe grasses trammel a traveling foot,
The faint fresh flame of the young year flushes   35
    From leaf to flower and flower to fruit;
And fruit and leaf are as gold and fire,
And the oat is heard above the lyre,
And the hoofèd heel of a satyr crushes
    The chestnut-husk at the chestnut-root,   40

And Pan by noon and Bacchus by night,
    Fleeter of foot than the fleet-foot kid,
Follows with dancing and fills with delight
    The Maenad and the Bassarid;
And soft as lips that laugh and hide   45
The laughing leaves of the trees divide,
And screen from seeing and leave in sight
    The god pursuing, the maiden hid.

The ivy falls with the Bacchanal's hair
    Over her eyebrows hiding her eyes;   50
The wild vine slipping down leaves bare
    Her bright breast shortening into sighs;

The wild vine slips with the weight of its leaves,
But the berried ivy catches and cleaves
To the limbs that glitter, the feet that scare   55
   The wolf that follows, the fawn that flies.

Algernon Charles Swinburne (1837–1909)

QUESTIONS

1. Vocabulary: *assuaged* (6), *trammel* (34), *satyr* (39), *kid* (42).
2. What is the subject of the poem? What is its tone?
3. The poet views the coming of spring in terms of Greek mythology. Can you suggest reasons why? The "mother of months" (2) is Artemis, goddess of the moon and of wild nature, usually pictured as a virgin huntress with bow, arrows, and hounds. Lines 5–8 refer to the legend of Philomela, whose brother-in-law, the king of Thrace, violated her and cut out her tongue. In revenge, she and her sister served the king's son Itylus to him as food, and fled. Later she was changed into a nightingale. Bacchus (41) is the god of wine, and the Maenad and Bassarid (44) and Bacchanal (49) are female worshippers of Bacchus. What characteristics of spring does Swinburne describe? What activities of the gods does he recount? What is meant by "The light that loses, the night that wins" (28)?
4. Copy stanzas 1 and 5 (double space if you typewrite), and, using different-colored pencils, encircle and tie together all examples of alliteration, assonance, consonance, and rime. Do these exhaust the kinds of musical repetition which Swinburne uses in the poem?
5. Swinburne has been criticized because the "music" of many of his poems distracts from, rather than contributes to, their meaning. Do you think this criticism applicable to this poem?

We should not leave the impression that the use of these musical devices is necessarily or always valuable. Like the other resources of poetry, they can be judged only in the light of the poem's total intention. Many of the greatest works of English poetry – for instance, *Hamlet* and *King Lear* and *Paradise Lost* – do not employ end rime. Both alliteration and rime, especially feminine rime, if used excessively or unskillfully, become humorous or silly. If the intention is humorous, the result is delightful; if not, fatal. Shakespeare, who knew how to use all these devices to the utmost advantage, parodied their unskillful use in lines like "The preyful princess pierced and pricked a pretty pleasing prickett" in *Love's Labor's Lost* and

> Wherat with blade, with bloody, blameful blade,
> He bravely broached his boiling bloody breast

in *Midsummer Night's Dream.* Swinburne parodied his own highly alliterative style in "Nephelidia" with lines like "Life is the lust of a lamp for the light that is dark till the dawn of the day when we die." Used skillfully and judiciously, however, musical devices provide a palpable and delicate pleasure to the ear and, even more important, add dimension to meaning.

EXERCISE

1. Discuss the various ways in which the following poems make use of refrain:
   a. "Winter," page 6.
   b. "Spring," page 11.
   c. "The Pasture," page 15.
   d. "Southern Cop," page 113.
   e. "in Just-," page 126.
   f. "The Shield of Achilles," page 130.
   g. "My sweetest Lesbia," page 140.
   h. "what if a much of a which of a wind," page 145.
   i. "Song: To Cynthia," page 189.
   j. "John Gorham," page 195.
   k. "Edward," page 230.
   l. "Cha Till Maccruimein," page 250.
   m. "The Lamb," page 284.
   n. "Fear no more the heat o' the sun," page 338.
   o. "Do not go gentle into that good night," page 345.

*   *   *   *   *

GOD'S GRANDEUR

> The world is charged with the grandeur of God.
>   It will flame out, like shining from shook foil;
>   It gathers to a greatness, like the ooze of oil
> Crushed. Why do men then now not reck his rod?
> Generations have trod, have trod, have trod;   5
>   And all is seared with trade; bleared, smeared with toil;
>   And wears man's smudge and shares man's smell: the soil

Is bare now, nor can foot feel, being shod.
And for all this, nature is never spent;
   There lives the dearest freshness deep down things;   10
And though the last lights off the black West went
   Oh, morning, at the brown brink eastward, springs –
Because the Holy Ghost over the bent
   World broods with warm breast and with ah! bright wings.

Gerald Manley Hopkins (1844–1889)

QUESTIONS

1. What is the theme of this sonnet?
2. The image in lines 3 – 4 possibly refers to olive oil being collected in great vats from crushed olives, but the image is much disputed. Explain the simile in line 2 and the symbols in lines 7–8 and 11–12.
3. Explain "reck his rod" (4), "spent" (9), "bent" (13).
4. Using different-colored pencils, encircle and connect examples of alliteration, assonance, consonance, and internal rime. Do these help to carry the meaning?

WE REAL COOL

The Pool Players.
Seven at the Golden Shovel.

    We real cool. We
    Left school. We

    Lurk late. We   5
    Strike straight. We

    Sing sin. We
    Thin gin. We

    Jazz June. We
    Die soon.   10

Gwendolyn Brooks (b. 1917)

QUESTIONS

1. In addition to end rime, what other musical devices does this poem employ?
2. Try reading this poem with the pronouns at the beginning of the lines instead of at the end. What is lost?

3. English teachers in a certain urban school were criticized recently for having their students read this poem: it was said to be immoral. Was the criticism justified? Why or why not?

I HEAR AN ARMY

I hear an army charging upon the land,
    And the thunder of horses plunging, foam about their knees:
Arrogant, in black armor, behind them stand,
    Disdaining the reins, with fluttering whips, the charioteers.

They cry unto the night their battle-name: 5
    I moan in sleep when I hear afar their whirling laughter.
They cleave the gloom of dreams, a blinding flame,
    Clanging, clanging upon the heart as upon an anvil.

They come shaking in triumph their long, green hair:
    They come out of the sea and run shouting by the shore.   10
My heart, have you no wisdom thus to despair?
    My love, my love, my love, why have you left me alone?

James Joyce (1882–1941)

QUESTIONS

1. What is the rime scheme of the poem? What kinds of rime does it employ?
2. Find examples of assonance, consonance, and alliteration in the poem: circle similar sounds and connect them. Do any of these sound correspondences seem to you to contribute to the meaning? Are there any other types of sound repetition in the poem?
3. What is the situation in the poem? (Who is the speaker? Where is he? Why is he in despair? What are the army and the charioteers?)
4. What different kinds of imagery are used in the poem? What figures of speech? How do they contribute to the meaning of the poem?

PARTING, WITHOUT A SEQUEL

She has finished and sealed the letter
At last, which he so richly has deserved,
With characters venomous and hatefully curved,
And nothing could be better.

But even as she gave it   5
Saying to the blue-capped functioner of doom,
"Into his hands," she hoped the leering groom
Might somewhere lose and leave it.

Then all the blood
Forsook the face. She was too pale for tears,   10
Observing the ruin of her younger years.
She went and stood

Under her father's vaunting oak
Who kept his peace in wind and sun and glistened
Stoical in the rain; to whom she listened   15
If he spoke.

And now the agitation of the rain
Rasped his sere leaves, and he talked low and gentle
Reproaching the wan daughter by the lintel;
Ceasing and beginning again.   20

Away went the messenger's bicycle,
Her serpent's track went up the hill forever,
And all the time she stood there hot as fever
And cold as any icicle.

John Crowe Ransom (1888–1974)

QUESTIONS

1. Identify the figures of speech in lines 3 and 22 and discuss their effectiveness. Are there traces of dramatic irony in the poem? Where?

2. Is the oak literal or figurative? Neither? Both? Discuss the meanings of "vaunting" (13), "stoical" (15), "sere" (18), and "lintel" (19).

3. Do you find any trite language in the poem? Where? What does it tell us about the girl's action?

4. W. H. Auden has defined poetry as "the clear expression of mixed feelings." Discuss the applicability of the definition to this poem. Try it out on other poems.

5. A feminine rime that involves two syllables is known also as a DOUBLE RIME. Find examples in the poem of both perfect and approximate double rimes. A feminine rime that involves three syllables is a TRIPLE RIME. Find one example of a triple rime. Which lines employ masculine or SINGLE RIMES, either perfect or approximate?

WINTER OCEAN

Many-maned scud-thumper, tub
of male whales, maker of worn wood, shrub-
ruster, sky-mocker, rave!
portly pusher of waves, wind-slave.

John Updike (b. 1932)

QUESTIONS

1. The fun of this poem lies chiefly in two features: in its invention of elaborate epithets (descriptive names) for something familiar (in Old English poetry, partially imitated here, these descriptive names were called *kennings*), and in its equally elaborate sound correspondences. How apt are the names? List or chart the sound correspondences. Are they also appropriate?
2. What figure of speech is most central to the poem?

Apostrophe - address to the ocean

A PROMPT, EXECUTIVE BIRD

A prompt, executive bird is the Jay,
Bold as a Bailiff's hymn,
Brittle and brief in quality –
Warrant in every line;

Sitting a bough like a Brigadier,
Confident and straight,
Much is the mien of him in March
As a Magistrate.

Emily Dickinson (1830–1886)

QUESTIONS

Sheriff's deputy

1. Vocabulary: *Bailiff* (2), *warrant* (4).   Authorization, warrant, pledge
2. What aspect of the Jay is considered in stanza 1? What aspect in stanza 2? What characterization of the Jay do these aspects combine to produce? What do Bailiffs, Brigadiers, and Magistrates have in common?
3. How do alliteration, consonance, rime, and other sound qualities enhance the characterization?

ON WENLOCK EDGE

On Wenlock Edge the wood's in trouble;
  His forest fleece the Wrekin heaves;
The gale, it plies the saplings double,
  And thick on Severn snow the leaves.

'Twould blow like this through holt and hangar   5
  When Uricon the city stood:
'Tis the old wind in the old anger,
  But then it threshed another wood.

Then, 'twas before my time, the Roman
  At yonder heaving hill would stare: 10
The blood that warms an English yeoman,
  The thoughts that hurt him, they were there.

There, like the wind through woods in riot,
  Through him the gale of life blew high;
The tree of man was never quiet: 15
  Then 'twas the Roman, now 'tis I.

The gale, it plies the saplings double,
  It blows so hard, 'twill soon be gone:
Today the Roman and his trouble
  Are ashes under Uricon.   20

A. E. Housman (1859–1936)

QUESTIONS

1. Vocabulary: *yeoman* (11). "Holt"(5) is a wooded hill: "hanger" (5) is a wood on the side of a steep hill or bank; both words derive from Old English or Anglo-Saxon.
2. Wenlock Edge (1) is a long ridge of hills in county Shropshire, England; the Wrekin (2) (pronounced *reek′ in*) is a solitary round-topped hill not far distant, an opposing feature of the landscape; the river Severn (4) flows through Shropshire; the ruins of the ancient Roman city Uricon (6) have been partially excavated near modern Wroxeter. Who is the speaker? Why does he mention "the Roman" (9)? Compare Housman's strategy in this respect with that in "On Moonlit heath and lonesome bank" (page 54).
3. For what do the trees of the first two stanzas become symbols? For what does the wind? How is "wind" related to *breath* and *spirit* (see dictionary), and what is implied by Housman's choice of it and of "gale" over these more

traditional figures? What is implied by the juxtaposition of the "blood that warms" and the "thoughts that hurt" in lines 11–12?

4. What consolation does the speaker offer himself in the final stanza?
5. Discuss the use and effect of alliteration, assonance, consonance, masculine and feminine rime, and other repetitions in the poem.

NOTHING GOLD CAN STAY

Nature's first green is gold,
Her hardest hue to hold.
Her early leaf's a flower;
But only so an hour.
Then leaf subsides to leaf.
So Eden sank to grief,
So dawn goes down to day.
Nothing gold can stay.

Robert Frost (1874–1963)

QUESTIONS

1. Explain the paradoxes in lines 1 and 3.
2. Discuss the poem as a series of symbols. What are the symbolical meanings of "gold" in the final line of the poem?
3. Discuss the contributions of alliteration, assonance, consonance, rime, and other repetitions to the effectiveness of the poem.

THREE GREY GEESE

Three grey geese in a green field grazing,
Grey were the geese and green was the grazing.

Nursery Rhyme

12 Rhythm and Meter

Our love of rhythm and meter is rooted even deeper in us than our love for musical repetition. It is related to the beat of our hearts, the pulse of our blood, the intake and outflow of air from our lungs. Everything that we do naturally and gracefully we do rhythmically. There is rhythm in the way we walk, the way we swim, the way we ride a horse, the way we swing a golf club or a baseball bat. So native is rhythm to us that we read it, when we can, into the mechanical world around us. Our clocks go tick-tick-tick-tick, but we hear them go tick-tock, tick-tock in an endless trochaic. The click of the railway wheels beneath us patterns itself into a tune in our heads. There is a strong appeal for us in language that is rhythmical.

The term RHYTHM refers to any wavelike recurrence of motion or sound. In speech it is the natural rise and fall of language. All language is to some degree rhythmical, for all language involves some kind of alternation between accented and unaccented syllables. Language varies considerably, however, in the degree to which it exhibits rhythm. In some forms of speech the rhythm is so unobtrusive or so unpatterned that we are scarcely, if at all, aware of it. In other forms of speech the rhythm is so pronounced that we may be tempted to tap our foot to it.

METER is the kind of rhythm we can tap our foot to. In language that is metrical the accents are so arranged as to occur at apparently equal intervals of time, and it is this interval we mark off with the tap of our foot. Metrical language is called VERSE. Nonmetrical language is PROSE. Not all poetry is metrical, nor is all metrical language poetry. *Verse* and *poetry* are not synonymous terms, nor is a *versifier* necessarily a *poet.*

The study of meter is a fascinating but highly complex subject. It is by no means an absolute prerequisite to an enjoyment, even a rich enjoyment, of poetry. But a knowledge of its fundamentals does have certain values. It can make the beginning reader more aware of the rhythmical effects of poetry and of how poetry should be read. It can enable the more advanced reader to analyze how certain effects are achieved, to see how rhythm is adapted to thought, and to explain what makes one poem (in this respect) better than another. The beginning student ought to have at least an elementary knowledge of the subject. It is not so difficult as its terminology might suggest.

In every word of more than one syllable, one syllable is *accented* or *stressed,* that is, given more prominence in pronunciation than the rest.* We say to*day,* tomo*r*row, *yes*terday, *dai*ly, inter*vene.* If words of even one syllable are arranged into a sentence, we give certain words, or syllables, more prominence in pronunciation than the rest. We say: "He *went* to the *store,*" or *"Jack* is *driv*ing his *car."* There is nothing mysterious about this; it is the normal process of language. The only difference between prose and verse is that in prose these accents occur more-or-less haphazardly; in verse the poet has arranged them to occur at regular intervals.

The word *meter* comes from a word meaning "measure." To measure something we must have a unit of measurement. For measuring length we use the inch, the foot, and the yard; for measuring time we use the second, the minute, and the hour. For measuring verse we use the foot, the line, and (sometimes) the stanza.

The basic metrical unit, the FOOT, consists normally of one accented syllable plus one or two unaccented syllables, though occasionally there may be no unaccented syllables, and very rarely there may be three. For diagramming verse, various systems of visual symbols have been invented. In this book we shall use a short curved line to indicate an unaccented syllable, a short horizonal line to indicate an accented syllable, and a

---

*Though the words *accent* and *stress* are generally used interchangeably, as here, a distinction is sometimes made between them in technical discussions. *Accent,* the relative prominence given a syllable in relation to its neighbors, is then said to result from one or more of four causes: *stress,* or force of utterance, producing loudness; *duration; pitch;* and *juncture,* the manner of transition between successive sounds. Of these, *stress,* in English verse, is most important.

vertical bar to indicate the division between feet. The basic kinds of feet are thus as follows:

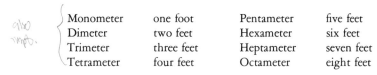

Example	Name of foot	Name of meter*
‿ — to-*day*	Iamb	Iambic ⎱ ⎰ Duple meters
— ‿ *dai*-ly	Trochee	Trochaic
‿ ‿ — in-ter-*vene*	Anapest	Anapestic ⎱ ⎰ Triple meters
— ‿ ‿ *yes*-ter-day	Dactyl	Dactylic
— — *day*-*break*	Spondee	(Spondaic)
— *day*	Monosyllabic foot	

(handwritten margin notes: "Vory impt.")

The secondary unit of measurement, the LINE, is measured by naming the number of feet in it. The following names are used:

Monometer	one foot	Pentameter	five feet
Dimeter	two feet	Hexameter	six feet
Trimeter	three feet	Heptameter	seven feet
Tetrameter	four feet	Octameter	eight feet

(handwritten margin note: "also impt.")

The third unit, the STANZA, consists of a group of lines whose metrical pattern is repeated throughout the poem. Since not all verse is written in stanzas, we shall save our discussion of this unit till a later chapter.

The process of measuring verse is referred to as SCANSION. To *scan* any specimen of verse, we do three things: (1) we identify the prevailing foot, (2) we name the number of feet in a line – if this length follows any regular pattern, and (3) we describe the stanza pattern – if there is one. Suppose we try out our skill on the poem "To Lucasta, Going to the Wars" (page 102).

The first step in scanning a poem is to read it normally, listening to

---

*In the spondee the accent is thought of as being distributed equally or almost equally over the two syllables and is sometimes referred to as a hovering accent. No whole poems are written in spondees or monosyllabic feet; hence there are only four basic meters: iambic, trochaic, anapestic, and dactylic. Iambic and trochaic are DUPLE METERS because they employ two-syllable feet; anapestic and dactylic are TRIPLE METERS because they employ three-syllable feet.

where the accents fall, and perhaps keeping time with your hand. In "To Lucasta" we immediately run into difficulty, for the first line is highly irregular and may leave us uncertain as to just where the accents fall. Let us pass over it, then, and look for easier lines. Though the second stanza, we discover, is more regular than the first, the third stanza is the most regular of the three. So let us begin with it. Lines 9, 11, and 12 go regularly, and we mark them as follows:

$$\cup \ \_ \ | \ \cup \ \_ \ | \ \cup \ \_ | \cup \ \_ \ |$$
Yet this in-con-stan-cy is such

As you too shall a-dore;   10

$$\cup \ \_ \ | \ \cup \ \_ \ | \ \cup \ \_ \ | \ \cup \ \_ \ |$$
I could not love thee, Dear, so much,

$$\cup \ \_| \ \cup \ \_ | \cup \ \_ \ |$$
Loved I not hon-or more.

Line 10 might also be marked regularly, but if we listen carefully we shall probably detect a slightly stronger stress on *too,* though it comes in an unstressed position, than on either of the adjacent syllables. So we'll mark it thus:

$$\cup \ \_ \ | \ \_ \ \ \_ \ | \cup \_ \ |$$
As you too shall a-dore.

We now see that this stanza is written in lines of alternating iambic tetrameter and iambic trimeter. Knowing this, we return to the first and second stanzas, expecting them, since they look similar, to conform to a similar pattern.

In the second stanza, lines 7 and 8 are perfectly regular, so we mark them confidently, but lines 5 and 6 offer some variation. Here is what we hear:

$$\_ \ \ \cup \ \_ \ \ \_ \ \ \cup \ \ \_ \ \cup \ \_$$
True, a new mis-tress now I chase,   5

$$\cup \ \ \_ \ \ \_ \ \cup \ \cup \ \ \_$$
The first foe in the field;

$$\cup \ \ \_ \ | \cup \ \ \_ \ | \cup \ \ \_ \ | \ \cup \ \ \_ \ |$$
And with a strong-er faith em-brace

$$\cup \ \ \_ \ | \ \cup \ \_ \ | \ \cup \ \ \_ \ |$$
A sword, a horse, a shield.

Since we are expecting lines 5 and 6 to conform to the established pattern, we shall assume that they are respectively a tetrameter and a trimeter line, and we shall mark the divisions between the feet in such a way as to yield the maximum number of iambs. The result is as follows:

$$\_ \ \ \cup| \ \_ \ \ \ \_ \ | \cup \ \ \_ \ |\cup \ \_ \ |$$
True, a new mis-tress now I chase,   5

$$\cup \ \ \_ \ | \ \_ \ \cup | \cup \ \ \_ \ |$$
The first foe in the field.

We are now ready for the difficult first stanza. Following the same process of first marking the accents where we hear them and then dividing the feet so as to yield tetrameter and trimeter lines with the maximum possible number of iambic feet, we get something like the following:

$$\_ \ \cup \ | \ \_ \quad \_ \ | \ \_ \ \cup \ | \ \cup \quad \_ \ |$$
Tell me not, Sweet, I am un-kind,

$$\cup \quad \_ \ | \ \cup \quad \_ \ | \ \cup \ \_ |$$
That from the nun-ner-y

$$\cup \quad \_ | \ \_ \quad \_ \ | \ \cup \quad \_ \ | \cup \quad \_ \ |$$
Of thy chaste breast and qui-et mind

$$\cup \quad \_ \ | \ \cup \quad \_ \ | \cup \ \_ |$$
To war and arms I fly.

We are now ready to make a few generalizations about scansion.

1. A good reader will not ordinarily stop to scan a poem he is reading, and he certainly will not read a poem with the exaggerated emphasis on accented syllables that we sometimes give them in order to make the scansion more apparent. However, occasional scansion of a poem does have value. We hope to make this more apparent in the next chapter.

2. Scansion is at best a gross way of describing the rhythmical quality of a poem. It depends on classifying all syllables into either accented or unaccented categories and on ignoring the sometimes considerable difference between degrees of accent. Actually "accented" and "unaccented" are relative terms, and seldom will two syllables have exactly the same degree of accent. Whether we call a syllable accented or unaccented depends, moreover, on its degree of accent relative to the syllables on either side of it. In line 7 of "To Lucasta," for instance, the accent on "with" is not nearly so great as the accent on "strong," and in line 2 the accent on the final *y* in "nunnery" is *lighter* than that on the *un*accented "thee" in line 11. Scansion therefore is incapable of dealing with the subtlest rhythmical effects in poetry. It is nevertheless a useful device, and probably any device more sensitive would be so complicated as to be no longer useful.

3. Scansion is not an altogether exact science. Within certain limits we may say that a certain scansion is right or wrong, but beyond these limits there is legitimate room for personal interpretation and disagreement between qualified readers. Lines 11 and 12 of "To Lucasta," for instance, have been scanned above as perfectly regular. But a different reader might read line 11 thus:

$$\_ \quad \cup \quad | \ \cup \ \_ | \ \_ \quad \_ \ | \ \cup \quad \_ \ |$$
I could not love thee, Dear, so much,

or line 12 thus:

$$\_ \quad \_ | \ \_ \quad \_ \ | \cup \quad \_ \ |$$
Loved I not hon-or more.

The divisions between feet, moreover, are highly arbitrary and have little meaning except to help us name the meter of the poem. They correspond to no real divisions in the reading of the line, coming often, as they do, in the middle of a word. They are placed where they are usually only for the purpose of yielding the most possible of a single kind of foot. Accordingly, line 6 has been marked:

$$\breve{} \; \underline{} \, | \; \underline{} \; \breve{} \, | \; \breve{} \; \underline{} \, |$$
The first foe in the field,

though it might more plausibly have been marked:

$$\breve{} \; \underline{} \, | \; \underline{} \; \breve{} \, | \; \breve{} \; \underline{} \, |$$
The first foe in the field.

4. Finally—and this is the most important generalization of all—perfect regularity of meter is no criterion of merit. Beginning students sometimes get the notion that it is. If the meter is smooth and perfectly regular, they feel that the poet has handled his meter successfully and deserves all credit for it. Actually there is nothing easier than for any moderately talented versifier to make language go ta-*dum* ta-*dum* ta-*dum*. But there are two reasons why this is not generally desirable. The first is that, as we have said, all art consists essentially of repetition and variation. If a meter alternates too regularly between light and heavy beats, the result is to banish variation; the meter becomes mechanical and, for any sensitive reader, monotonous. The second is that, once a basic meter has been established, any deviations from it become highly significant and are the means by which the poet can use meter to reinforce meaning. If a meter is too perfectly regular, the probability is that the poet, instead of adapting rhythm to meaning, has simply forced his meaning into a metrical straitjacket.

Actually what gives the skillful use of meter its greatest effectiveness is that it consists, not of one rhythm, but of two. One of these is the *expected* rhythm. The other is the *heard* rhythm. Once we have determined the basic meter of a poem, say, iambic tetrameter, we have an expectation that this rhythm will continue. Thus a silent drumbeat is set up in our minds, and this drumbeat constitutes the expected rhythm. But the actual rhythm of the words—the heard rhythm—will sometimes confirm this expected rhythm and sometimes not. Thus the two rhythms are counterpointed against each other, and the appeal of the verse is magnified just as when two melodies are counterpointed against each other in music or as when we see two swallows flying together and around each other, following the same general course but with individual variations and making a much more eye-catching pattern than one swallow flying alone. If the heard rhythm conforms too closely to the expected rhythm, the meter becomes dull and uninteresting. If it departs too far from the expected rhythm, there ceases to be an expected rhythm. If the irregularity is too great, meter disappears, and the result is prose rhythm or free verse.

There are several ways by which variation can be introduced into the poet's use of meter. The most obvious way is by the substitution of different kinds of feet for regular feet. In our scansion of "To Lucasta," for instance, we noted one spondaic and two trochaic substitutions in the very first line. A less obvious but equally important means of variation is through simple phrasing and variation of degrees of accent. Lines 2, 4, 8, and 12 of "To Lucasta" have all been marked as regular, but actually there is considerable difference between them. Line 4 is quite regular, for the phrasing corresponds with the metrical pattern, and the line can be read ta-*dum* ta-*dum* ta-*dum*. Line 8 is even more regular, for the unaccented syllables are all *very* light, the accented syllables are all *very* strong, and the divisions between the feet are marked off by grammatical pauses indicated in the punctuation. This line goes ta-*dumm!* ta-*dumm!* ta-*dumm!* Line 12, on the other hand, is less regular, because the word "honor" cuts across the division between two feet. We should read it ta-*dum* ta-*dum*pty *dum*. And line 2 is even less regular because not only does "nunnery" cut across the division between two feet, but its final syllable is so lightly stressed as hardly to be accented at all. We should read this line something like ta-*dum* ta-*dum*pteree. Finally, variation can be introduced by grammatical and rhetorical pauses. Line 11 of "To Lucasta," though scanned as regular, actually introduces variation because of the pause indicated by the commas around *Dear.*

The uses of rhythm and meter are several. Like the musical repetitions of sound, the musical repetitions of accent can be pleasing for their own sake. In addition, rhythm works as an emotional stimulus and serves, when used skillfully, to heighten our attention and awareness to what is going on in a poem. Finally, by his choice of meter, and by his skillful use of variation within the metrical framework, the poet can adapt the sound of his verse to its content and thus make meter a powerful reinforcement of meaning. We should avoid, however, the notion that there is any mystical correspondence between certain meters and certain emotions. There are no "happy" meters and no "melancholy" ones. The poet's choice of meter is probably less important than how he handles it after he has chosen it. However, some meters are swifter than others, some slower; some are more lilting than others, some more dignified. The poet can choose a meter that is appropriate or one that is inappropriate to his content, and by his handling of it can increase the appropriateness or inappropriateness. If he chooses a swift, lilting meter for a serious and grave subject, the meter will probably act to keep the reader from feeling any really deep emotion. But if he chooses a more dignified meter, it will intensify the emotion. In all great poetry, meter works intimately with the other elements of the poem to produce the appropriate total effect.

We must not forget, of course, that poetry need not be metrical at all. Like alliteration and rime, like metaphor and irony, like even imagery, meter is simply one resource the poet may or may not use. His job is to employ his resources to the best advantage for the object he has in mind—the kind of experience he wishes to express. And on no other basis can we judge him.

EXERCISES

1. Two additional terms that every student should be familiar with and should be careful to discriminate between are *blank verse* and *free verse*. BLANK VERSE is a very specific meter: *iambic pentameter, unrimed.* It has a special name because it is the principal English meter, that is, the meter that has been used for a large proportion of the greatest English poetry, including the tragedies of Shakespeare and the epics of Milton. Iambic pentameter in English seems especially suitable for the serious treatment of serious themes. The natural movement of the English language tends to be iambic. Lines shorter than pentameter tend to be songlike, not suited to sustained treatment of serious material. Lines longer than pentameter tend to break up into shorter units, the hexameter line being read as two three-foot units, the heptameter line as a four-foot and a three-foot unit, and so on. Rime, while highly appropriate to most short poems, often proves a handicap for a long and lofty work. (The word *blank* implies that the end of the line is "blank," that is, bare of rime.) The above generalizations of course represent tendencies, not laws.

   FREE VERSE, by our definition, is not verse at all; that is, it is not metrical. It may be rimed or unrimed. The word *free* means that it is free of metrical restrictions. The only difference between free verse and rhythmical prose is that free verse introduces one additional rhythmical unit, the line. The arrangement into lines divides the material into rhythmical units or cadences. Beyond its line arrangement there are no necessary differences between it and rhythmical prose.

   Of the following poems, some are in free verse (F), some in blank verse (B), and some in other (O) meters. Determine into which category each belongs and indicate by putting an F, B, or O after it.

   a. "Dulce et Decorum Est," page 8. ○
   b. "Elegy for Yards, Pounds, and Gallons," page 47. F

d. "Ulysses," page 92.

e. "Fire and Ice," page 92.

f. "Out, Out —," page 123.

g. "in Just —," page 126.

h. "Paranoia," page 286.

i. "When I Heard the Learn'd Astronomer," page 349.

j. "There was a Boy," page 352.

2. Another useful distinction is that between end-stopped lines and run-on lines. An END-STOPPED LINE is one in which the end of the line corresponds with a natural speech pause; a RUN-ON LINE is one in which the sense of the line hurries on into the next line. (There are, of course, all degrees of end-stop and run-on. A line ending with a period or semicolon is heavily end-stopped. A line without punctuation at the end but representing a slight pause between phrases or sense units would be lightly end-stopped.) The use of run-on lines is one way the poet can make use of grammatical or rhetorical pauses to vary his basic meter. Examine, for instance, Swift's "A Description of the Morning" (page 345) and Browning's "My Last Duchess" (page 119). Both of these poems are written in the same meter: iambic pentameter, rimed in couplets. Is their general rhythmical effect quite similar or markedly different? What accounts for the difference? Does this contrast support our statement that the poet's choice of meter is probably less important than the way he handles it?

*   *   *   *   *

VIRTUE

Sweet day, so cool, so calm, so bright,
    The bridal of the earth and sky;
The dew shall weep thy fall to night,
    For thou must die.

Sweet rose, whose hue, angry and brave,   5
    Bids the rash gazer wipe his eye;
Thy root is ever in its grave,
    And thou must die.

Sweet spring, full of sweet days and roses,
    A box where sweets compacted lie;   10
My music shows ye have your closes,
    And all must die.

Only a sweet and virtuous soul,
   Like seasoned timber, never gives;
But though the whole world turn to coal,   15
   Then chiefly lives.

George Herbert (1593–1633)

QUESTIONS

1. Vocabulary: *brave* (5), *closes* (11).
2. How are the four stanzas interconnected? How do they build to a climax? How does the fourth contrast with the first three?
3. Scan the poem, identify its meter, and point out the principal variations from the expected rhythm.

SONG: TO CYNTHIA

Queen and huntress, chaste and fair,
Now the sun is laid to sleep,
Seated in thy silver chair,
State in wonted manner keep:
   Hesperus entreats thy light,   5
   Goddess excellently bright.

Earth, let not thy envious shade
Dare itself to interpose;
Cynthia's shining orb was made
Heaven to clear, when day did close: 10
   Bless us then with wishèd sight,
   Goddess excellently bright.

Lay thy bow of pearl apart,
And thy crystal shining quiver;
Give unto the flying hart   15
Space to breathe, how short soever,
   Thou that mak'st a day of night,
   Goddess excellently bright.

Ben Jonson (1573?–1637)

QUESTIONS

1. Vocabulary: *Cynthia* (title); *wonted* (4), *Hesperus* (5), *hart* (15).
2. This poem combines mythology and astronomy. What mythological

attributes of Cynthia are referred to? In astronomical terms, what request is made in each stanza? What figure of speech is present throughout the poem?

3. The advice for scanning a poem given on page 182–to read it normally, listening to where the accents fall–must be modified in one respect. The poem often sets up a pattern so strong that it overrides the rhetorical accentuation of normal reading. This poem, for instance, quickly establishes a tetrameter pattern in which the first syllable of the line invariably receives an accent. Therefore, though we should *normally* read line 14 like this:

$$\smile \ \smile \ \_ \ \smile \ \_ \ \smile \ \_ \ \smile$$
And thy crys-tal shin-ing quiv-er,

the overall pattern of the poem compels us to give the first syllable at least a light accent:

$$\_ \ \smile \ \_ \ \smile \ \_ \ \smile \ \_ \ \smile$$
And thy crys-tal shin-ing quiv-er.

What syllables in lines 3 and 5 does the pattern similarly require us to promote to lightly accented status?

4. Keeping the above in mind, scan stanza 1 without putting in the bar divisions. Should the poem on the basis of this stanza be regarded as iambic or trochaic? Could it be either? Some metrists have discarded the distinction between iambic and trochaic and between anapestic and dactylic as being artificial. The only real distinction, they feel, is between duple and triple meters. Does this stanza support their claim?

5. If you were forced to classify this poem as iambic or trochaic, what two lines later in the poem would determine the decision?

THE "JE NE SAIS QUOI"

Yes, I'm in love, I feel it now,
    And Celia has undone me;
And yet I'll swear I can't tell how
    The pleasing plague stole on me.

'Tis not her face that love creates,   5
    For there no Graces revel;
'Tis not her shape, for there the Fates
    Have rather been uncivil.

'Tis not her air, for sure in that,
    There's nothing more than common;   10
And all her sense is only chat,
    Like any other woman.

Her voice, her touch, might give the alarm—
　'Tis both perhaps, or neither;
In short, 'tis that <u>provoking charm</u>　　　　15
　Of Celia altogether.

William Whitehead (1715–1785)

QUESTIONS

1. *Je ne sais quoi* is a French expression meaning "I do not know what"—an indefinable something. Does the use of approximate rimes rather than perfect rimes in the even lines of this poem help to establish the quality of uncertainty which is the subject of the poem?
2. Find examples of OXYMORON (a compact paradox in which two successive words seemingly contradict each other) in the first and last stanzas. What broad paradox underlies the whole poem?
3. What is the reason for the capitalization and pluralization of "grace" and "fate" in the second stanza? What is the image here conveyed? Is "love" (5) the subject or object of the verb?
4. Because of the feminine rimes of the even-numbered lines, you will find, on scanning the poem, that there is an extra unaccented syllable left over in these lines. For instance, the first two lines may be scanned as follows:

$$\breve{\,}\ \_\ |\ \breve{\,}\ \_\ |\ \breve{\,}\ \_\ |\ \breve{\,}\ \_\ |$$
Yes, I'm in love, I feel it now,
$$\breve{\,}\ \_\ |\ \breve{\,}\ \_\ |\ \breve{\,}\ \_\ |\ \breve{\,}$$
And Cel-ia has un-done me.

It will often happen that one or two unaccented syllables are left over—at the end of the line with iambic and anapestic meter, at the beginning of the line with trochaic and dactylic meter. Although we ignore these unaccented extras in naming the meter (the above poem is written in alternating iambic tetrameter and iambic trimeter), they make considerable difference in the rhythmical effect. They are another way the poet can vary his basic meter.

IF EVERYTHING HAPPENS THAT CAN'T BE DONE

if everything happens that can't be done
(and anything's righter
than books
could plan)
the stupidest teacher will almost guess　　　　5
(with a run

Rhythm and Meter　**191**

skip
around we go yes)
there's nothing as something as one

one hasn't a why or because or although   10
(and buds know better
than books
don't grow)
one's anything old being everything new
(with a what   15
which
around we come who)
one's everyanything so

so world is a leaf so tree is a bough
(and birds sing sweeter   20
than books
tell how)
so here is away and so your is a my
(with a down
up   25
around again fly)
forever was never till now

now i love you and you love me
(and books are shuter
than books   30
can be)
and deep in the high that does nothing but fall
(with a shout
each
around we go all)   35
there's somebody calling who's we

we're anything brighter than even the sun
(we're everything greater
than books
might mean)   40

we're everyanything more than believe
(with a spin
leap
alive we're alive)
we're wonderful one times one   45

e. e. cummings (1894–1962)

QUESTIONS

1. Explain the last line. Of what very familiar idea is this poem a fresh treatment?
2. The poem is based on a contrast between heart and mind, or love and learning. Which does the poet prefer? What symbols does he use for each?
3. What is the tone of the poem?
4. Which lines of each stanza regularly rime with each other (either perfect or approximate rime)? How does the poet link the stanzas together?
5. What is the basic metrical scheme of the poem? What does the meter contribute to the tone? What line (in the fourth stanza) most clearly states the subject and occasion of the poem? How does meter underline its significance?
6. Can you suggest any reason why the poet wrote lines 2–4 and 6–8 of each stanza as three lines rather than one? What metrical variations does the poet use in lines 6–8 of each stanza and with what effect?

OH WHO IS THAT YOUNG SINNER

Oh who is that young sinner with the handcuffs on his wrists?
And what has he been after that they groan and shake their fists?
And wherefore is he wearing such a conscience-stricken air?
Oh they're taking him to prison for the color of his hair.

'Tis a shame to human nature, such a head of hair as his;   5
In the good old time 'twas hanging for the color that it is;
Though hanging isn't bad enough and flaying would be fair
For the nameless and abominable color of his hair.

Oh a deal of pains he's taken and a pretty price he's paid
To hide his poll or dye it of a mentionable shade;   10
But they've pulled the beggar's hat off for the world to see and stare,
And they're taking him to justice for the color of his hair.

all repetitive

Now 'tis ~~oakum~~ for his fingers and the treadmill for his feet,
And the quarry-gang on Portland in the cold and in the heat,
And between his spells of labor in the time he has to spare   15
He can curse the God that made him for the color of his hair.

A. E. Housman (1859–1936)

QUESTIONS

1. Vocabulary: *poll* (10), *oakum* (13). Portland (14), an English peninsula, is the site of a famous criminal prison.
2. What kind of irony does the poem exhibit? Explain.
3. What symbolical meanings are suggested by "the color of his hair"?
4. This poem represents a kind of meter that we have not yet discussed. It *may* be scanned as iambic heptameter:

```
 ∪   _ | ∪   _ |  ∪    _ | ∪   _ |  ∪   _ | ∪    _ |  ∪    _ |
Oh  who  is  that young sin-ner with the hand-cuffs on  his  wrists?
```

But you will probably find yourself reading it as a four-beat line:

```
 ∪   _ | ∪  ∪    ∪    _ | ∪   ∪   ∪    _ | ∪   ∪  ∪    _ |
Oh  who  is  that young sin-ner with the hand-cuffs on  his  wrists?
```

Although the meter is duple insofar as there is an alternation between un-accented and accented syllables, there is also an alternation in the degree of stress on the accented syllables: the first, third, fifth, and seventh stresses being heavier than the second, fourth, and sixth; the result is that the two-syllable feet tend to group themselves into larger units. We may scan it as follows, using a short line for a light accent, a longer one for a heavy accent:

```
 ∪   _ | ∪   _    ∪    _  ∪   _   ∪   _ | ∪   _  ∪    _ |
Oh  who  is  that young sin-ner with the hand-cuffs on  his  wrists?

 ∪   _ | ∪   _   ∪   _ | ∪   _   ∪    _ | ∪   _   ∪    _ |
And what has  he  been af-ter that they groan. and shake their fists?

 ∪   _ | ∪   _  ∪   _ | ∪   _   ∪   _ | ∪   _   ∪  _ |
And where-fore is  he  wear-ing such a  con-science strick-en air?

 _   ∪   _ | ∪   _   ∪   _ | ∪   _   ∪  _ | ∪   _   ∪   _ |
Oh they're tak-ing him to pris-on for the col-or of his hair.
```

This kind of meter, in which there is an alternation between heavy and light stresses, is known as DIPODIC (two-footed) VERSE. The alternation may not be perfect throughout, but it will be frequent enough to establish a pattern in the reader's mind. Now scan the last three stanzas.

JOHN GORHAM

"Tell me what you're doing over here, John Gorham,
Sighing hard and seeming to be sorry when you're not;
Make me laugh or let me go now, for long faces in the moonlight
Are a sign for me to say again a word that you forgot." –

"I'm over here to tell you what the moon already   5
May have said or maybe shouted ever since a year ago;
I'm over here to tell you what you are, Jane Wayland,
And to make you rather sorry, I should say, for being so." –

"Tell me what you're saying to me now, John Gorham,
Or you'll never see as much of me as ribbons any more;   10
I'll vanish in as many ways as I have toes and fingers,
And you'll not follow far for one where flocks have been before." –

"I'm sorry now you never saw the flocks, Jane Wayland,
But you're the one to make of them as many as you need.
And then about the vanishing. It's I who mean to vanish;   15
And when I'm here no longer you'll be done with me indeed." –

"That's a way to tell me what I am, John Gorham!
How am I to know myself until I make you smile?
Try to look as if the moon were making faces at you,
And a little more as if you meant to stay a little while." –   20

"You are what it is that over rose-blown gardens
Makes a pretty flutter for a season in the sun;
You are what it is that with a mouse, Jane Wayland,
Catches him and lets him go and eats him up for fun." –

"Sure I never took you for a mouse, John Gorham;   25
All you say is easy, but so far from being true
That I wish you wouldn't ever be again the one to think so;
For it isn't cats and butterflies that I would be to you." –

"All your little animals are in one picture –
One I've had before me since a year ago to-night;   30
And the picture where they live will be of you, Jane Wayland,
Till you find a way to kill them or to keep them out of sight." –

"Won't you ever see me as I am, John Gorham,
Leaving out the foolishness and all I never meant?
Somewhere in me there's a woman, if you know the way to find her.   35
Will you like me any better if I prove it and repent?" –

"I doubt if I shall ever have the time, Jane Wayland;
And I dare say all this moonlight lying round us might as well
Fall for nothing on the shards of broken urns that are forgotten,
As on two that have no longer much of anything to tell."   40

Edwin Arlington Robinson (1869–1935)

QUESTIONS

1. Vocabulary: *shards* (39).
2. Define as precisely as possible the occasion in the poem.
3. What kind of person is John Gorham? Jane Wayland? Do you think the poet is more sympathetic with one than with the other?
4. We are never told exactly what was said (4) or what happened (6) "a year ago." Does the withholding of this information weaken the poem, or is the author's purpose complete without it?
5. Like the preceding poem, this is written in dipodic verse, but with greater variation. The first stanza may perhaps be scanned thus:

"Tell | me what you're do-ing o-ver here, | John Gor-ham,

Sigh-ing hard and seem-ing to be sor-ry when you're not;

Make me laugh | or let me go | now, for long fac-es in the

moon-light

Are a sign | for me to say a-gain a word | that you for-got."

As this scansion makes clear, dipodic meter is a complex meter, with large possibilities for substitute feet. Yet it should be apparent to anyone with a sense of rhythm that the lines of this poem have four primary beats, and that the basic foot is composed of syllables that are respectively unaccented, lightly accented, unaccented, and heavily accented. But almost any of these syllables except the heavily accented one may be left out, as they regularly are in the initial feet of both this poem and the preceding one. In addition this poem regularly has an unaccented syllable left over at the end of the first and third lines of each stanza. Point out other variations. Now try scanning another stanza.

Down by the <u>salley</u> gardens my love and I did meet;
She passed the salley gardens with little snow-white feet.
She bid me take love easy, as the leaves grow on the tree;
But I, being young and foolish, with her would not agree.
In a field by the river my love and I did stand,
And on my leaning shoulder she laid her snow-white hand.
She bid me take life easy, as the grass grows on the <u>weirs;</u> *an embankment along*
But I was young and foolish, and now am full of tears. *a river fence*

William Butler Yeats (1865–1939)

QUESTION

1. This poem introduces an additional kind of metrical variation – the metrical pause or rest. Unlike grammatical and rhetorical pauses, the metrical pause affects scansion. If you beat out the rhythm of this poem with your hand, you will find that the fourth beat of each line (possibly excepting lines 3 and 7) regularly falls *between* syllables. A METRICAL PAUSE, then, is a pause that re-places an accented syllable. It is usually found in verse that has a pronounced lilt or swing. The first line of Yeats's poem may be scanned as follows (the metrical pause is represented with an *x*):

— ∪ | ∪ — | ∪ — | ∪ | ∪ — | ∪ — | ∪   — |
Down by the sal- ley gar- dens,*x* my love and I did meet.

The third line might be scanned in several ways, as the following alternatives suggest:

∪ — | ∪ — | ∪ — | ∪ — | ∪ — | ∪ — | ∪   — |
She bid me take life eas- y, as the leaves grow on the trees,
∪ — | ∪ — | — — | ∪ | ∪ ∪ — | — ∪ | ∪   — |
She bid me take life eas- y, *x* as the leaves grow on the trees.

Scan the rest of the poem.

HAD I THE CHOICE   *catalogue*   *poets*

Had I the choice to <u>tally</u> greatest bards,
   (paint in words)
To <u>limn</u> their portraits, stately, beautiful, and emulate at will,
Homer with all his wars and warriors – Hector, Achilles, Ajax,
Or Shakespeare's woe-entangled Hamlet, Lear, Othello – Tennyson's fair
   ladies,   *an elaborate metaphor*
Meter or wit the best, or choice <u>conceit</u> to <u>wield</u> in perfect rhyme,
   delight of singers;   *exercise, use,*
                                        govern

These, these, O sea, all these I'd gladly barter,
Would you the undulation of one wave, its trick to me transfer,
Or breathe one breath of yours upon my verse,
And leave its odor there.

Walt Whitman (1819–1892)

QUESTIONS

1. Vocabulary: *tally* (1), *limn* (2), *conceit* (5).
2. What poetic qualities does Whitman propose to barter in exchange for what? What qualities do the sea and its waves symbolize?
3. What kind of "verse" is this? Why does Whitman prefer it to "meter" and "perfect rhyme"?

THE AIM WAS SONG

Before man came to blow it right
    The wind once blew itself untaught,
And did its loudest day and night
    In any rough place where it caught.

Man came to tell it what was wrong: 5
    It hadn't found the place to blow;
It blew too hard – the aim was song.
    And listen – how it ought to go!

He took a little in his mouth,
    And held it long enough for north   10
To be converted into south,
    And then by measure blew it forth.

By measure. It was word and note,
    The wind the wind had meant to be –
A little through the lips and throat.   15
    The aim was song – the wind could see.

Robert Frost (1874–1963)

QUESTIONS

1. Frost invents a myth about the origin of poetry. What implications does it suggest about the relation of man to nature and of poetry to nature?
2. Contrast the thought and form of this poem with Whitman's.
3. Scan the poem and identify its meter. How does the poet give variety to a regular metrical pattern?

13 Sound and Meaning

Rhythm and sound cooperate to produce what we call the music of poetry. This music, as we have pointed out, may serve two general functions: it may be enjoyable in itself; it may be used to reinforce meaning and intensify the communication.

Pure pleasure in sound and rhythm exists from a very early age in the human being – probably from the age the baby first starts cooing in its cradle, certainly from the age that children begin chanting nursery rimes and skipping rope. The appeal of the following verse, for instance, depends almost entirely on its "music":

$$\overline{\text{Pease}} \mid \overline{\text{por}}\text{-}\overset{\smile}{\text{ridge}} \mid \overline{\text{hot,}} \mid$$
$$\overline{\text{Pease}} \mid \overline{\text{por}}\text{-}\overset{\smile}{\text{ridge}} \mid \overline{\text{cold,}} \mid$$
$$\overline{\text{Pease}} \mid \overline{\text{por}}\text{-}\overset{\smile}{\text{ridge}} \mid \overline{\text{in}} \overset{\smile}{\text{the}} \mid \overline{\text{pot}} \mid$$
$$\overline{\text{Nine}} \mid \overline{\text{days}} \mid \overline{\text{old.}} \mid$$

There is very little sense here; the attraction comes from the emphatic rhythm, the emphatic rimes (with a strong contrast between the short vowel and short final consonant of *hot-pot* and the long vowel and long final consonant combination of *cold-old*), and the heavy alliteration (exactly half the words begin with *p*). From nonsense rimes such as this, many of us graduate into a love of more meaningful poems whose appeal resides largely in the sound they make. Much of the pleasure that we find in Swinburne's "When the hounds of spring" (page 170) lies in its musical quality. Other famous examples are Vachel Lindsay's "The Congo" and Edgar Allan Poe's "The Bells."

The peculiar function of poetry as distinguished from music, however, is to convey not sounds but meaning or experience *through* sounds. In third and fourth-rate poetry sound and rhythm sometimes distract attention from sense. In first-rate poetry the sound exists, not for its own sake, not for mere decoration, but as a medium of meaning. Its function is to support the leading player, not to steal the scene.

There are numerous ways in which the poet may reinforce meaning through sound. Without claiming to exhaust them, perhaps we can include most of the chief means under four general headings.

First, the poet can choose words whose sound in some degree suggests their meaning. In its narrowest sense this is called onomatopoeia. ONOMATOPOEIA, strictly defined, means the use of words which, at least supposedly, sound like what they mean, such as *hiss, snap,* and *bang.*

SONG: HARK, HARK!

> Hark, hark!
> Bow-wow.
> The watch-dogs bark!
> Bow-wow.
> Hark, hark! I hear
> The strain of strutting chanticleer
> Cry, "Cock-a-doodle-doo!"

William Shakespeare (1564–1616)

In this lyric, "bark," "bow-wow," and "cock-a-doodle-doo" are onomatopoetic words. In addition Shakespeare has reinforced the onomatopoetic effect with the repeated use of "hark," which sounds like "bark." The usefulness of onomatopoeia, of course, is strictly limited, because it can be used only where the poet is describing sound, and most poems do not describe sound. And the use of pure onomatopoeia, as in the above example, is likely to be fairly trivial except as it forms an incidental part of a more complex poem. But by combining onomatopoeia with other devices that help convey meaning, the poet can achieve subtle and beautiful effects whose recognition is one of the keenest pleasures in reading poetry.

In addition to onomatopoetic words there is another group of words, sometimes called PHONETIC INTENSIVES, whose sound, by a process as yet obscure, to some degree suggests their meaning. An initial *fl-* sound, for instance, is often associated with the idea of moving light, as in *flame, flare, flash, flicker, flimmer.* An initial *gl-* also frequently accompanies the idea of light, usually unmoving, as in *glare, gleam, glint, glow, glisten.* An initial *sl-* often introduces words meaning "smoothly wet," as in *slippery, slick, slide, slime, slop, slosh, slobber, slushy.* Short *-i-* often goes with the idea of smallness, as in *inch, imp, thin, slim, little, bit, chip, sliver, chink, slit, sip, whit, tittle, snip, wink, glint, glimmer, flicker, pigmy, midge, chick, kid, kitten, minikin, miniature.* Long *-o-* or *-oo-* may suggest melancholy or sorrow, as in *moan, groan, woe, mourn, forlorn, toll, doom, gloom, moody.* Medial and final *-are* sometimes goes with the idea of a big light or noise, as *flare, glare, stare, blare.* Medial *-att-* suggests some kind of particled movement, as in *spatter, scatter, shatter, chatter, rattle, prattle, clatter, batter.* Final *-er* and *-le* indicate repetition, as in *glitter, flutter, shimmer, whisper, jabber, chatter, clatter, sputter, flicker, twitter, mutter,* and *ripple, bubble, twinkle, sparkle, rattle, rumble, jingle.* None of these various sounds is invariably associated with the idea that it seems to suggest, and, in fact, a short *-i-* is found in *thick* as well as *thin,* in *big* as well as *little.* Language is a complex phenomenon. But there is enough association between these sounds and ideas to suggest some sort of intrinsic if obscure relationship, and a word like *flicker,* though not onomatopoetic, for it does not refer to sound, would seem somehow to suggest its sense, the *fl-* suggesting moving light, the *-i-* suggesting smallness, the *-ck* suggesting sudden cessation of movement (as in *crack, peck, pick, hack,* and *flick*), and the *-er* suggesting repetition. The above list of sound-idea correspondences is only a very partial one. A complete list, though it would involve only a small proportion of words in the language, would probably be a longer list than that of the more strictly onomatopoetic words, to which they are related.

SPLINTER

The voice of the last cricket
across the first frost
is one kind of good-by.
It is so thin a splinter of singing.

Carl Sandburg (1878–1967)

QUESTIONS

1. Why is "so thin a splinter" a better choice of metaphor than *so small an atom* or *so meager a morsel*?
2. How does the poet intensify the effect of the two phonetic intensives in line 4?

Second, the poet can choose sounds and group them so that the effect is smooth and pleasant sounding (*euphonious*) or rough and harsh sounding (*cacophonous*). The vowels are in general more pleasing than the consonants, for the vowels are musical tones, whereas the consonants are merely noises. A line with a high percentage of vowel sounds in proportion to consonant sounds will therefore tend to be more melodious than one in which the proportion is low. The vowels and consonants themselves differ considerably in quality. The "long" vowels, such as those in *fate, reed, rime, coat, food,* and *dune* are fuller and more resonant than the "short" vowels, as in *fat, red, rim, cot, foot,* and *dun.* Of the consonants, some are fairly mellifluous, such as the "liquids," *l, m, n,* and *r*; the soft *v* and *f* sounds; the semi-vowels *w* and *y*; and such combinations as *th* and *wh.* Others, such as the "explosives," *b, d, g, k, p,* and *t,* are harsher and sharper in their effect. These differences in sound are the poet's materials. However, he will not necessarily seek out the sounds that are pleasing and attempt to combine them in melodious combinations. Rather, he will use euphonious and cacophonous combinations as they are appropriate to his content. Consider, for instance, the following poem.

UPON JULIA'S VOICE

> So smooth, so sweet, so silv'ry is thy voice,
> As, could they hear, the Damned would make no noise,
> But listen to thee (walking in thy chamber)
> Melting melodious words to Lutes of Amber.

Robert Herrick (1591–1674)

QUESTION

1. Literally, an amber lute is as nonsensical as a silver voice. What connotations do "Amber" and "silv'ry" have that contribute to the meaning of this poem?

There are no strictly onomatopoetic words in this poem, and yet the sound seems marvelously adapted to the sense. Especially remarkable are the first and last lines, those most directly concerned with Julia's voice. In the first line the sounds that most strike the ear are the unvoiced *s*'s and the soft *v*'s, supported by *th*: "So *smooth, so sweet, so silv'ry is thy voice*." In the fourth line the predominating sounds are the liquid consonants *m, l,* and *r,* supported by a *w*: "*Melting melodious words to Lutes of Amber.*" The least euphonious line in the poem, on the other hand, is the second, where the subject is the tormented in hell, not Julia's voice. Here the prominent sounds are the *d*'s, supported by a voiced *s* (a voiced *s* buzzes, unlike the unvoiced *s*'s in line 1), and two *k* sounds: "A*s*, coul*d* they hear, the *d*amne*d* would ma*k*e no noi*s*e." Throughout the poem there is a remarkable correspondence between the pleasant-sounding and the pleasant in idea, the unpleasant-sounding and the unpleasant in idea.

A third way in which a poet can reinforce meaning through sound is by controlling the speed and movement of his lines by his choice and use of meter, by his choice and arrangement of vowel and consonant sounds, and by his disposition of pauses. In meter the unaccented syllables go faster than the accented syllables; hence the triple meters are swifter than the duple. But the poet can vary the tempo of any meter by the use of substitute feet. Whenever two or more unaccented syllables come together, the effect will be to speed up the pace of the line; when two or more accented syllables come together, the effect will be to slow it down. This pace will also be affected by the vowel lengths and by whether the sounds are easily run together. The long vowels take longer to pronounce than the short ones. Some words are easily run together, while others demand that the position of the mouth be re-formed before the next word is uttered. It takes much longer, for instance, to say, "Watch dogs catch much meat" than to say, "My aunt is away," though the number of syllables is the same. And finally the poet can slow down the speed of a line through the introduction of grammatical and rhetorical pauses. Consider lines 54–56 from Tennyson's "Ulysses" (page 92):

> ∪ — | ∪ — | ∪ — | ∪ — | ∪ — |
> The lights be-gin to twin-kle from the rocks;
> ∪ — | — — | ∪ — | — — | ∪ — |
> The long day wanes; the slow moon climbs; the deep
> — — | ∪ — | ∪ — | ∪
> Moans round with man-y voi-ces . . .

In these lines Tennyson wished the movement to be slow, in accordance with the slow waning of the long day and the slow climbing of the moon. His meter is iambic pentameter. This is not a swift meter, but in lines 55–56 he slows it down, (1) by introducing three spondaic feet, thus bringing three accented syllables together in three separate places; (2) by choosing for his accented syllables words that have long vowel sounds or dipthongs that the voice hangs on to: "long," "day," "wanes," "slow," "moon," "climbs," "deep," "moans," "round"; (3) by choosing words that are not easily run together (except for "day" and "slow," each of these words begins and ends with consonant sounds that demand varying degrees of readjustment of the mouth before pronunciation is continued); (4) by introducing two grammatical pauses, after "wanes" and "climbs," and a rhetorical pause after "deep." The result is an extremely effective use of the movement of the verse to accord with the movement suggested by the words.*

A fourth way for a poet to fit sound to sense is to control both sound and meter in such a way as to put emphasis on words that are important in meaning. He can do this by marking out such words by alliteration, assonance, consonance, or rime; by placing them before a pause; or by skillfully placing or displacing them in the metrical pattern. Look again at Shakespeare's "Spring" (page 11):

When dai-sies pied and vio-lets blue

And la-dy-smocks all sil-ver-white

And cuck-oo-buds of yel-low hue

Do paint the mea-dows with de-light,

The cuck-oo then, on ev-ery tree,

Mocks mar-ried men; for thus sings he,

"Cuckoo!

Cuckoo, cuckoo!" O, word of fear,

Unpleasing to a married ear!

The scansion is regular until the beginning of the sixth line: there we find a spondaic substitution in the first foot. In addition, the first three words in this line are heavily alliterated, all beginning with *m*. And further, each of these words ends in a consonant, thus preventing their being run together. The result is to throw heavy emphasis on these three words: to give them, one might almost say, a tone of solemnity, or mock-solemnity. Whether or not the solemnity is in the sound, the emphasis on these three words is appropriate, for it serves to signal the shift in tone that takes place at this point. The first five lines have contained nothing but delightful images; the concluding four introduce the note of irony.

Just as Shakespeare uses metrical irregularity, plus alliteration, to give emphasis to important words, Tennyson, in the concluding line of

---

*In addition, Tennyson uses one onomatopoetic word ("moans") and one phonetic intensive ("twinkle").

"Ulysses," uses marked regularity, plus skillful use of grammatical pause, to achieve the same effect:

<pre>
       ∪   — | ∪ —| ∪   — | ∪ — | ∪   — |
Though much is ta-ken, much a-bides; and though
   ∪ — | ∪   — | ∪   — | ∪   ∪ — | — |
We are not now that strength which in old days
   —   — | ∪   — | ∪ — | ∪   ∪ — | ∪ — |
Moved earth and heav-en, that which we are, we are:
   — —| ∪   — | ∪ —| ∪—|∪   — |
One e-qual tem-per of he-ro-ic hearts,
   —   — | ∪   — | ∪ — | ∪   — | ∪ — |
Made weak by time and fate, but strong in will
  ∪   — | ∪   —| ∪   —| ∪   — | ∪ — |
To strive, to seek, to find, and not to yield.
</pre>

The blank verse rhythm throughout "Ulysses" is remarkably subtle and varied, but the last line is not only regular in its scansion but heavily regular, for a number of reasons. First, all the words are monosyllables: no words cross over the divisions between feet. Second, the unaccented syllables are all very small and unimportant words—four "to's" and one "and," whereas the accented syllables consist of four important verbs and a very important "not." Third, each of the verbs is followed by a grammatical pause pointed off by a mark of punctuation. The result is to cause a pronounced alternation between light and heavy syllables that brings the accent down on the four verbs and the "not" with sledgehammer blows. The line rings out like a challenge, which it is.

THE SPAN OF LIFE

The old dog barks backward without getting up.
I can remember when he was a pup.

Robert Frost (1874–1963)

QUESTIONS

1. Is the dog a dog only or also a symbol?
2. The first line presents a visual and auditory image; the second line makes a comment. But does the second line *call up images?* Does it suggest more than it says? Would the poem have been more or less effective if the second line had been, "He was frisky and lively when he was a pup"?

We may well conclude our discussion of the adaptation of sound to sense by analyzing this very brief poem. It consists of one riming anapestic tetrameter couplet. Its content is a contrast between the decrepitude of an old dog and his friskiness as a pup. The scansion is as follows:

$$\breve{\text{The}} \mid \overline{\text{old}} \mid \overline{\text{dog}} \quad \overline{\text{barks}} \quad \overline{\text{back}}\text{-ward} \mid \breve{\text{with}}\text{-out} \quad \breve{\text{get}}\text{-ting} \quad \overline{\text{up.}}$$

$$\overline{\text{I}} \mid \breve{\text{can}} \quad \breve{\text{re}}\text{-mem-}\overline{\text{ber}} \mid \breve{\text{when}} \quad \breve{\text{he}} \mid \breve{\text{was}} \quad \breve{\text{a}} \quad \overline{\text{pup.}}$$

How is sound fitted to sense? In the first place, the triple meter chosen by the poet is a swift meter, but in the first line he has jammed it up in a remarkable way by substituting a kind of foot so rare that we do not even have a name for it. It might be called a triple spondee: at any rate it is a foot in which the accent is distributed over three syllables. This foot, following the accented syllable in the first foot, creates a situation where four accented syllables are pushed up together. In addition, each of these accented syllables begins and ends with a strong consonant sound or cluster of consonant sounds, so that they cannot be run together in pronunciation: the mouth must be re-formed between each syllable: "The *old dog barks backward.*" The result is to slow down the line drastically to almost destroy its rhythmical quality, and to make it difficult to utter. Indeed, the line is as decrepit as the old dog who turns his head to greet his master but does not get up. When we get to the second line, however, the contrast is startling. The rhythm is swift and regular, the syllables end in vowels or liquid consonants and are easily run together, the whole line ripples fluently off the tongue. In addition, where the first line has a high proportion of explosive and cacophonous consonants – "The *old dog barks backward without getting up*" – the second line contains predominantly consonants which are smoother and more graceful – "I *can remember when he was a pup.*" Thus the motion and the sound of the lines are remarkably in accord with the visual images they suggest. In addition, in the first line the poet has supported the onomatopoetic word *barks* with a near echo *back,* so that the sound reinforces the auditory image. If the poem does a great deal in just two lines, this skillful adaptation of sound to sense is one very important reason.

In analyzing verse for correspondence between sound and sense, we need to be very cautious not to make exaggerated claims. A great deal of nonsense has been written about the moods of certain meters and the effects of certain sounds, and it is easy to suggest correspondences that exist really only in our imaginations. Nevertheless, the first-rate poet has nearly always an instinctive tact about handling his sound so that it in some degree supports his meaning; the inferior poet is usually obtuse to these correspondences. One of the few absolute rules that can be applied to the judgment of poetry is that the form should be adequate to the content. This rule does not mean that there must always be a close and easily demonstrable correspondence. It does mean that there will be no glaring discrepancies. Poor poets, and even good poets in their third-rate work, sometimes go horribly wrong.

The two selections that introduce this chapter illustrate, first, the use of sound in verse almost purely for its own sake ("Pease porridge hot"), and second, the use of sound in verse almost purely to *imitate* meaning ("Hark, hark! Bow-wow"), and they are, as significant poetry, perhaps the most trivial pieces in the whole book. But in between these extremes there is an abundant range of poetic possibilities where sound is pleasurable for itself without violating meaning and where sound to varying degrees corresponds with and corroborates meaning; and in this rich middle range, for the reader who can learn to perceive them, lie many of the greatest pleasures of reading poetry.

EXERCISE

1. In which of the following pairs of quotations is sound more successfully adapted to sense? As precisely as possible, explain why. (The poet whose name is given is in each case the author of the superior version.)

   a. (1) Go forth – and Virtue, ever in your sight,
         Shall be your guide by day, your guard by night.
      (2) Go forth – and Virtue, ever in your sight,
         Shall point your way by day, and keep you safe at night.
         Charles Churchill

   b. (1) How charming is divine philosophy!
         Not harsh and rough as foolish men suppose
         But musical as is the lute of Phoebus.
      (2) How charming is divine philosophy!
         Not harsh and crabbed as dull fools suppose
         But musical as is Apollo's lute.
         Milton

   c. (1) All day the fleeing crows croak hoarsely over the snow.
      (2) All day the out-cast crows croak hoarsely across the whiteness.
         Elizabeth Coatsworth

   d. (1) Your talk attests how bells of singing gold
         Would sound at evening over silent water.
      (2) Your low voice tells how bells of singing gold
         Would sound at twilight over silent water.
         Edwin Arlington Robinson

e. (1) A thousand streamlets flowing through the lawn,
  The moan of doves in gnarled ancient oaks,
  And quiet murmuring of countless bees.
 (2) Myriads of rivulets hurrying through the lawn,
  The moan of doves in immemorial elms,
  And murmuring of innumerable bees.

Tennyson

f. (1) It is the lark that sings so out of tune,
  Straining harsh discords and unpleasing sharps.
 (2) It is the lark that warbles out of tune
  With harsh discordant voice and hateful flats.

Shakespeare

g. (1) "Artillery" and "armaments" and "implements of war"
  Are phrases too severe to please the gentle Muse.
 (2) Bombs, drums, guns, bastions, batteries, bayonets, bullets, –
  Hard words, which stick in the soft Muses' gullets.

Byron

h. (1) The hands of the sisters Death and Night incessantly softly wash
   again, and ever again, this soiled world.
 (2) The hands of the soft twins Death and Night repeatedly wash
   again, and ever again, this dirty world.

Whitman

i. (1) The curfew sounds the knell of parting day,
  The lowing cattle slowly cross the lea,
  The plowman goes wearily plodding his homeward way,
  Leaving the world to the darkening night and me.
 (2) The curfew tolls the knell of parting day,
  The lowing herd wind slowly o'er the lea,
  The plowman homeward plods his weary way,
  And leaves the world to darkness and to me.

Thomas Gray

j. (1) Let me chastise this odious, gilded bug,
  This painted son of dirt, that smells and bites.
 (2) Yet let me flap this bug with gilded wings,
  This painted child of dirt, that stinks and stings.

Pope

*   *   *   *   *

SOUND AND SENSE

True ease in writing comes from art, not chance,
As those move easiest who have learned to dance.
'Tis not enough no harshness gives offense,
The sound must seem an echo to the sense:
Soft is the strain when Zephyr gently blows,   5
And the smooth stream in smoother numbers flows;
But when loud surges lash the sounding shore,
The hoarse, rough verse should like the torrent roar;
When Ajax strives some rock's vast weight to throw,
The line too labors, and the words move slow;   10
Not so, when swift Camilla scours the plain,
Flies o'er the unbending corn, and skims along the main.
Hear how Timotheus' varied lays surprise,
And bid alternate passions fall and rise!

Alexander Pope (1688–1744)

QUESTIONS

1. Vocabulary: *numbers* (6), *lays* (13).
2. This excerpt is from a long poem (called *An Essay on Criticism*) on the arts of writing and judging poetry. Which line is the topic sentence of the passage?
3. There are four classical allusions: Zephyr (5) was god of the west wind; Ajax (9), a Greek warrior noted for his strength; Camilla (11), a legendary queen reputedly so fleet of foot that she could run over a field of grain without bending the blades or over the sea without wetting her feet; Timotheus (13), a famous Greek rhapsodic poet. Does the use of these allusions enable Pope to achieve greater economy?
4. Copy the passage and scan it. Then, considering both meter and sounds, show how Pope practices what he preaches. (Incidentally, on which syllable should "alternate" in line 14 be accented?)

I LIKE TO SEE IT LAP THE MILES

I like to see it lap the miles,
And lick the valleys up,
And stop to feed itself at tanks;
And then, prodigious, step

Around a pile of mountains,   5
And, supercilious, peer

In shanties by the sides of roads;
And then a quarry pare

To fit its ribs,
And crawl between,   10
Complaining all the while
In horrid, hooting stanza;
Then chase itself down hill

And neigh like Boanerges;   _the sons of thunder_
Then, punctual as a star,   _Vicaş name for_
                             ranting creatures   15
Stop – docile and omnipotent –   _an-powerful_
At its own stable door.

Emily Dickinson (1830–1886)

QUESTIONS

1. Vocabulary: *prodigious* (4), *supercilious* (6), *Boanerges* (14).
2. What basic metaphor underlies the poem? Identify the literal and the metaphorical terms and explain how you were able to make both identifications.
3. What additional figures of speech do you find in lines 8, 12, 15, 16, and 17? Explain their appropriateness.
4. Point out examples of alliteration, assonance, and consonance. Does this poem have a rime scheme?
5. Considering such things as sounds and sound repetitions, grammatical pauses, run-on lines, monosyllabic and polysyllabic words, onomatopoeia, and meter, explain in detail how sound is fitted to sense in this poem.

BRAINSTORM

The house was shaken by a rising wind
That rattled window and door. He sat alone
In an upstairs room and heard these things: a blind
Ran up with a bang, a door slammed, a groan
Came from some hidden joist, a leaky tap,   _beam_   5
At any silence of the wind walked like
A blind man through the house. Timber and sap
Revolt, he thought, from washer, baulk and spike.   _heavy nail_
Bent to his book, continued unafraid
Until the crows came down from their loud flight   10
To walk along the rooftree overhead.

Their horny feet, so near but out of sight,
Scratched on the slate; when they were blown away
He heard their wings beat till they came again,
While the wind rose, and the house seemed to sway,   15
And window panes began to blind with rain.
The house was talking, not to him, he thought,
But to the crows; the crows were talking back
In their black voices. The secret might be out:
Houses are only trees stretched on the rack.   20
And once the crows knew, all nature would know.
Fur, leaf and feather would invade the form,
Nail rust with rain and shingle warp with snow,
Vine tear the wall, till any straw-borne storm
Could rip both roof and rooftree off and show   25
Naked to nature what they had kept warm.
He came to feel the crows walk on his head
As if he were the house, their crooked feet
Scratched, through the hair, his scalp. He might be dead,
It seemed, and all the noises underneath   30
Be but the cooling of the sinews, veins,
Juices, and sodden sacks suddenly let go;
While in his ruins of wiring, his burst mains,
The rainy wind had been set free to blow
Until the green uprising and mob rule   35
That ran the world had taken over him,
Split him like seed, and set him in the school
Where any crutch can learn to be a limb.

Inside his head he heard the stormy crows.

Howard Nemerov (b. 1920)

QUESTIONS

1. Vocabulary: *Brainstorm* (title), *baulk* (8), *rooftree* (11), *mains* (35).
2. With what conflict is the poem concerned? Trace the progress of the protagonist's thoughts and imaginings about this conflict.
3. Discuss the figurative language used in the poem, especially in lines 5–7, 16–19, 20, 22, 32–33, and 35–38. What is the "school" of line 37? What kind or kinds of "limb" are indicated in line 38?
4. Show how sound is adapted to sense in this poem.

HEAVEN-HAVEN

A Nun Takes the Veil

> I have desired to go
> Where springs not fail,
> To fields where flies no sharp and sided hail
> And a few lilies blow.
>
> And I have asked to be
> Where no storms come,
> Where the green swell is in the havens dumb,
> And out of the swing of the sea.

Gerard Manley Hopkins (1844–1889)

QUESTIONS

1. Who is the speaker and what is the situation? Explain the metaphors that form the substance of the poem. What things are being compared?
2. Comment on the meaning of "springs" (2) and on the effectiveness of the poet's choice of "lilies" (4).
3. How do the sound repetitions of the title reinforce the meaning? Are there other instances in the poem where sound reinforces meaning?
4. Scan the poem. (The meter is basically iambic, but there is a great deal of variation.) How does the meter reinforce meaning, especially in the last line? What purpose is served by the displacement of "not" (2) from its normal order?

ANTHEM FOR DOOMED YOUTH

> What passing-bells for these who die as cattle?
> Only the monstrous anger of the guns.
> Only the stuttering rifles' rapid rattle
> Can patter out their hasty orisons.
> No mockeries now for them; no prayers nor bells,   5
> Nor any voice of mourning save the choirs, —
> The shrill, demented choirs of wailing shells;
> And bugles calling for them from sad shires.
>
> What candles may be held to speed them all?
> Not in the hands of boys, but in their eyes   10
> Shall shine the holy glimmers of good-byes.

The pallor of girls' brows shall be their pall;
Their flowers the tenderness of patient minds,
And each slow dusk a drawing-down of blinds.

Wilfred Owen (1893–1918)

QUESTIONS

1. Vocabulary: *passing-bells* (1), *orisons* (4), *shires* (8), *pall* (12).
2. How do the octave and the sestet of this sonnet differ in (a) geographical setting, (b) subject matter, (c) kind of imagery used, and (d) tone? Who are the "boys" (10) and "girls" (12) referred to in the sestet? – It was the custom during World War I to draw down the blinds in homes where a son had been lost. (14).
3. What central metaphorical image runs throughout the poem? What secondary metaphors build up the central one?
4. Why are the "doomed youth" said to die "as cattle"? Why would prayers, bells, etc., be "mockeries" for them (5)?
5. Show how sound is adapted to sense throughout the poem.

THE DARK HILLS

Dark hills at evening in the west,
Where sunset hovers like a sound
Of golden horns that sang to rest
Old bones of warriors under ground,
Far now from all the bannered ways
Where flash the legions of the sun,
You fade – as if the last of days
Were fading, and all wars were done.

Edwin Arlington Robinson (1869–1935)

QUESTIONS

1. This poem consists of one sentence; analyze it grammatically. What is its skeleton? Is the poem primarily narrative, descriptive, or philosophical? What is the poem about?
2. Point out and explain the figures of speech in the poem. What are "the bannered ways" (5) and "the legions of the sun" (6)? What unity of idea does the figurative language have? What overtones of suggestion does the poem have?
3. Analyze the poem for musical devices. How is sound fitted to sense?

EIGHT O'CLOCK

He stood, and heard the steeple *— the notes at the quarters of the hour*
    Sprinkle the quarters on the morning town. *meely divinely*
One, two, three, four, to market-place and people
    It tossed them down.

Strapped, noosed, nighing his hour, *nearing*
    He stood and counted them and cursed his luck;
And then the clock collected in the tower
    Its strength, and struck.

A. E. Housman (1859–1936)

QUESTIONS

1. Vocabulary: *quarters* (2).
2. Eight A.M. is the traditional hour in England for putting condemned men to death. Discuss the force of "morning" (2) and "struck" (8). Discuss the appropriateness of the image of the clock collecting its strength. Can you suggest any reason for the use of "nighing" (5) rather than *nearing?*
3. Scan the poem and note its musical devices. Comment on the adaptation of sound to sense.

ALL DAY I HEAR

All day I hear the noise of waters
    Making moan,
Sad as the sea-bird is, when going
    Forth alone,
He hears the winds cry to the waters'   5
    Monotone.

The grey winds, the cold winds are blowing
    Where I go.
I hear the noise of many waters
    Far below.   10
All day, all night, I hear them flowing
    To and fro.

James Joyce (1882–1941)

1. What is the central purpose of the poem? Is it primarily descriptive?
2. What kinds of imagery does the poem contain?
3. Discuss the adaptation of sound to meaning, commenting on the use of onomatopoeia, phonetic intensives, alliteration, consonance, rime, vowel quality, stanzaic structure, the counterpointing of the rhythmically varied long lines with the rhythmically regular short lines.

LIGHTLY STEPPED A YELLOW STAR

> Lightly stepped a yellow star
> To its lofty place.
> Loosed the moon her silver hat
> From her lustral face.
> All of evening softly lit
> As an astral hall.
> "Father," I observed to Heaven,
> "You are punctual."

Emily Dickinson (1830–1886)

QUESTIONS

1. Vocabulary: *astral* (6). What meanings have "lightly" (1) and "Heaven" (7)?
2. Discuss adaptation of sound to meaning. What technical term is particularly applicable to this poem?
3. Explain the last two lines.

THE DANCE

> In Breughel's great picture, The Kermess,
> the dancers go round, they go round and
> around, the squeal and the blare and the
> tweedle of bagpipes, a bugle and fiddles
> tipping their bellies (round as the thick-   5
> sided glasses whose wash they impound)
> their hips and their bellies off balance
> to turn them. Kicking and rolling about
> the Fair Grounds, swinging their butts, those

shanks must be sound to bear up under such   10
rollicking measures, prance as they dance
in Breughel's great picture, The Kermess.

William Carlos Williams (1883–1963)

rolling

QUESTION

1. Peter Breughel, the Elder, was a sixteenth-century Flemish painter of peasant life. A *kermess* is an annual outdoor festival or fair. How do the form, the meter, and the sounds of this poem reinforce its content?

LITTLE DICKY DILVER

Little Dicky Dilver
Had a wife of silver;
He took a stick and broke her back
And sold her to the miller;
The miller wouldn't have her
So he threw her in the river.

Mother Goose Rhyme

QUESTION

1. Comment on sound and meaning in the title and in the one line that doesn't rime (at least approximately) with the others.

14 Pattern

A rt, ultimately, is organization. It is a searching after order, after form. The primal artistic act was God's creation of the universe out of chaos, shaping the formless into form; and every artist since, on a lesser scale, has sought to imitate Him – by selection and arrangement to reduce the chaotic in experience to a meaningful and pleasing order. For this reason we evaluate a poem partially by the same criteria that an English instructor uses to evaluate a theme – by its unity, its coherence, and its proper placing of emphasis. In a well-constructed poem there is neither too little nor too much; every part of the poem belongs where it is and could be placed nowhere else; any interchanging of two stanzas, two lines, two words, or even two accents, would to some extent damage the poem and make it less effective. We come to feel, with a truly first-rate poem, that the choice and placement of every word is inevitable, that it could not be otherwise.

In addition to the internal ordering of materials, images, ideas, and sounds, the poet may also impose some external pattern on his poem, may give it not only an inside logical order but an outside symmetry. In doing so, he appeals to the human instinct for design, the instinct that makes primitive men tattoo and paint their bodies, later men to decorate their swords and shields with beautiful and complex designs, and modern men to choose patterned ties, carpets, curtains, and wallpapers. The poet appeals to our love of the shapely.

In general, there are three broad kinds of form into which the poet may cast his work: continuous form, stanzaic form, and fixed form.

In CONTINUOUS FORM, as illustrated by "Had I the Choice" (page 197), "Dover Beach" (page 280), "Ulysses" (page 92), and "My Last Duchess" (page 119), the element of formal design is slight. The lines follow each other without formal grouping, the only breaks being dictated by units of meaning, as paragraph breaks are in prose. Even here there are degrees of formal pattern. The free verse "Had I the Choice" has neither regular meter nor rime. "Dover Beach," on the other hand, is metrical; it has no regularity in length of line, but the meter is prevailingly iambic. "Ulysses" is regular in both meter and length of line; it is unrimed iambic pentameter, or blank verse. And to these regularities "My Last Duchess" adds regularity of rime, for it is written in riming iambic pentameter couplets. Thus, in increasing degrees, the authors of "Dover Beach," "Ulysses," and "My Last Duchess" have chosen a predetermined pattern in which to cast their work.

In STANZAIC FORM the poet writes in a series of STANZAS, that is, repeated units having the same number of lines, the same metrical pattern, and often an identical rime scheme. The poet may choose some traditional stanza pattern (for poetry, like colleges, is rich in tradition) or invent his own. The traditional stanza patterns (for example, terza rima, ballad meter, rime royal, Spenserian stanza) are many, and the student specializing in literature will wish to familiarize himself with some of them; the general student should know that they exist. Often the use of one of these traditional stanza forms constitutes a kind of literary allusion. The reader who is conscious of its traditional use or of its use by a previous great poet will be aware of subtleties in the communication that a less well-read reader may miss.

As with continuous form, there are degrees of formal pattern in stanzaic form. In "Poem in October" (page 225), for instance, the stanzas are alike in length of line but are without a regular pattern of rime. In "To Lucasta" (page 102), a rime pattern is added to a metrical pattern. In Shakespeare's "Winter" (page 6) and "Spring" (page 11), a refrain is employed in addition to the patterns of meter and rime. The following poem illustrates additional elements of design:

THE GREEDY THE PEOPLE

> the greedy the people
> (as if as can yes)
> they sell and they buy
> and they die for because
> though the bell in the steeple   5
> says Why

the chary the wary
(as all as can each)
they don't and they do
and they turn to a which   *something*   10
though the moon in her glory
says Who   *going back?*

the busy the millions
(as you're as can i'm)
they flock and they flee   15
through a thunder of seem
though the stars in their silence
say Be

the cunning the craven
(as think as can feel)   20
they when and they how
and they live for until
though the sun in his heaven
says Now

the timid the tender   25
(as doubt as can trust)
they work and they pray
and they bow to a must   *decay*
though the earth in her splendor
says May   30

e. e. cummings (1894–1962)

QUESTIONS

1. This poem is a constellation of interlocking patterns. To appreciate them
   fully, read it first in the normal fashion, one line after another; then read all
   the first lines of the stanzas, followed by the second lines, the third lines, and
   so on. Having done this, describe (1) the rime scheme; (b) the metrical
   design; (c) the sound pattern (How are the two main words in each of the
   first lines related?); (d) the syntactical pattern. Prepare a model of the poem in
   which the recurring words are written out, blanks are left for varying words,
   and recurring parts of speech are indicated in parentheses. The model for the
   third lines would be: *they [verb] and they [verb]*. Describe the pattern of
   meaning. How do the first four lines of each stanza relate to the last two?
   What blanks in your model are to be filled in by words related in meaning?

2. A trademark of e. e. cummings as a poet is his imaginative freedom with parts

of speech. For instance, in line 21 he uses conjunctions as verbs. What different parts of speech does he use as nouns in the fourth line of each stanza? Can you see meanings for these unusual nouns? Explain the contrast between the last words in the fourth and sixth lines of each stanza. What two meanings has the final word of the poem.

3. Sum up briefly the meaning of the poem.

A stanza form may be described by designating four things: the rime scheme (if there is one), the position of the refrain (if there is one), the prevailing metrical foot, and the number of feet in each line. Rime scheme is traditionally designated by using letters of the alphabet to indicate the riming lines, and x for unrimed lines. Refrain lines may be indicated by a capital letter, and the number of feet in the line by a numerical exponent after the letter. Thus the stanza pattern of Browning's "Meeting at Night" (page 51) is iambic tetrameter $abccba$ (or iambic $abccba^4$); that of cummings's "if everything happens that can't be done" (page 191) is anapestic $a^4x^2x^1a^1b^4x^1x^1b^2a^3$; that of Shakespeare's "Spring" (page 11) is iambic $ababcc^4X^1DD^4$.

A FIXED FORM is a traditional pattern that applies to a whole poem. In French poetry many fixed forms have been widely used: rondeaus, roundels, villanelles, triolets, sestinas, ballades, double ballades, and others. In English poetry, though most of the fixed forms have been experimented with, perhaps only two – the limerick and the sonnet – have really taken hold.

The LIMERICK, though really a subliterary form, will serve to illustrate the fixed form in general. Its pattern is anapestic $aa^3bb^2a^3$:

> ∪   _ |∪   ∪   _|∪   ∪   _| ∪
> There was a young la-dy of Ni-ger
> ∪   _ | ∪ ∪   _ | ∪ ∪ _|∪
> Who smiled as she rode on a ti-ger;
>   ∪   ∪   _ | ∪   ∪   _ |
> They re-turned from the ride
>   ∪   ∪ _|∪ ∪   _ |
>   With the la-dy in–side,
> ∪   ∪   _ | ∪ ∪   _| ∪ ∪ _|∪
> And the smile on the face of the ti-ger.

Anonymous

The limerick form is used exclusively for humorous and nonsense verse, for which, with its swift catchy meter, short lines, and emphatic rimes, it is particularly suitable. By trying to recast these little jokes and bits of nonsense in a different meter and pattern or into prose, we may discover how much of their effect they owe particularly to the limerick form. There is, of course, no magical or mysterious identity between certain forms and certain types of content, but there may be more or less correspondence. A form may be appropriate or inappropriate. The limerick form is apparently inappropriate for the serious treatment of serious material.

The SONNET is less rigidly prescribed than the limerick. It must be fourteen lines in length, and it almost always is iambic pentameter, but in structure and rime scheme there may be considerable leeway. Most sonnets, however, conform more or less closely to one of two general models or types, the Italian and the English.

The ITALIAN or *Petrarchan* SONNET (so called because the Italian poet Petrarch practiced it so extensively) is divided usually between eight lines called the octave, using two rimes arranged *abbaabba,* and six lines called the sestet, using any arrangement of either two or three rimes: *cdcdcd* and *cdecde* are common patterns. Usually in the Italian sonnet, corresponding to the division between octave and sestet indicated by the rime scheme (and sometimes marked off in printing by a space), there is a division of thought. The octave presents a situation and the sestet a comment, or the octave an idea and the sestet an example, or the octave a question and the sestet an answer.

ON FIRST LOOKING INTO CHAPMAN'S HOMER

> Much have I travelled in the realms of gold,
>   And many goodly states and kingdoms seen;
>   Round many western islands have I been
> Which bards in fealty to Apollo hold.
> Oft of one wide expanse had I been told   5
>   That deep-browed Homer ruled as his demesne;
>   Yet did I never breathe its pure serene
> Till I heard Chapman speak out loud and bold:
> Then felt I like some watcher of the skies
>   When a new planet swims into his ken;   10
> Or like stout Cortez when with eagle eyes
>   He stared at the Pacific – and all his men
> Looked at each other with a wild surmise –
>   Silent, upon a peak in Darien.

John Keats (1795–1821)

QUESTIONS

1. Vocabulary: *fealty* (4), *Apollo* (4), *demesne* (6), *ken* (10), *Darien* (14).
2. John Keats, at twenty-one, could not read Greek, and was probably

acquainted with Homer's *Iliad* and *Odyssey* only through the translations of Alexander Pope, which to him would have seemed prosy and stilted. Then one day he and a friend found a vigorous poetic translation by the Elizabethan poet George Chapman. Keats and his friend, enthralled, sat up late at night excitedly reading aloud to each other from Chapman's book. Toward morning Keats walked home and, before going to bed, wrote the above sonnet and sent it to his friend. What common ideas underlie the three major figures of speech in the poem?

3. What is the rime scheme? What division of thought corresponds to the division between octave and sestet?

4. Balboa, not Cortez, discovered the Pacific. Does this mistake seriously detract from the value of the poem? Why or why not?

The ENGLISH or *Shakespearean* SONNET (invented by the English poet Surrey and made famous by Shakespeare) is composed of three quatrains and a concluding couplet, riming *abab cdcd efef gg*. Again, there is usually a correspondence between the units marked off by the rimes and the development of the thought. The three quatrains, for instance, may present three examples and the couplet a conclusion or (as in the following example) three metaphorical statements of one idea plus an application.

THAT TIME OF YEAR

That time of year thou mayst in me behold
When yellow leaves, or none, or few, do hang
Upon those boughs which shake against the cold,
Bare ruined choirs where late the sweet birds sang.
In me thou see'st the twilight of such day   5
As after sunset fadeth in the west,
Which by and by black night doth take away,
Death's second self, that seals up all in rest.
In me thou see'st the glowing of such fire,
That on the ashes of his youth doth lie   10
As the deathbed whereon it must expire,
Consumed with that which it was nourished by.
    This thou perceivest, which makes thy love more strong,
    To love that well which thou must leave ere long.

William Shakespeare (1564–1616)

More concerned w/ time
than love itself –
time's death

222   Pattern

1. What are the three major images introduced by the three quatrains? What do they have in common? Can you see any reason for presenting them in this particular order, or might they be rearranged without loss?
2. Each of the images is to some degree complicated rather than simple. For instance, what additional image is introduced by "bare ruined choirs" (4)? Explain its appropriateness.
3. What additional comparisons are introduced in the second and third quatrains?
4. Explain line 12.

At first glance it may seem absurd that a poet should choose to confine himself in an arbitrary fourteen-line mold with prescribed meter and rime scheme. He does so partly from the desire to carry on a tradition, as all of us carry out certain traditions for their own sake, else why should we bring a tree indoors at Christmas time? But, in addition, the tradition of the sonnet has proved a useful one for, like the limerick, it seems effective for certain types of subject matter and treatment. Though this area cannot be as narrowly limited or as rigidly described as for the limerick, the sonnet is usually most effective when used for the serious treatment of love but has also been used for the discussion of death, religion, political situations, and related subjects. Again, there is no magical affinity between form and subject, or treatment, and excellent sonnets have been written outside these traditional areas. The sonnet tradition has also proved useful because it has provided a challenge to the poet. The inferior poet, of course, is often defeated by that challenge: he will use unnecessary words to fill out his meter or inappropriate words for the sake of his rime. The good poet is inspired by the challenge: it will call forth ideas and images that might not otherwise have come. He will subdue his form rather than be subdued by it; he will make it do his will. There is no doubt that the presence of a net makes good tennis players more precise in their shots than they otherwise would be. And finally, there is in all form the pleasure of form itself.

EXERCISES

1. Review what you know about *ballad stanza* (see question 4 after "Sir Patrick Spens," page 12, and "Ballad of Birmingham," page 14). Then show how "On moonlit heath and lonesome bank" (page 54), "Oh see how thick the goldcup flowers" (page 233), "Edward" (page 230), and "Cha Till Maccruimein" (page 250) complicate the form.

2. "The Walking" (page 337) and "Do not go gentle into that good night" (page 345) are both examples of the French fixed form known as the *villanelle*. After reading the poems, define the *villanelle*.
3. "Acquainted with the Night" (page 309) is written in the stanzaic form known as *terza rima* (most famous for its use by Dante in *The Divine Comedy*). Read the poem and give a description of *terza rima*.
4. Reread the following sonnets; classify each (where possible) as primarily Italian or primarily English; then specify how closely each sticks to or how far it departs from (in pattern and structure) the polarities represented by "On First Looking into Chapman's Homer" and "That time of year": (a) "When my love swears that she is made of truth," page 37; (b) "The Silken Tent," page 71; (c) "Ozymandias," page 109; (d) "Batter my heart, three-personed God," page 111; (e) "On His Blindness," page 127; (f) "Leda and the Swan," page 129; (g) "Design," page 144; (h) "The Caged Skylark," page 146; (i) "Since there's not help," page 156; (j) "To a Friend Whose Work Has Come to Triumph," page 158; (k) "God's Grandeur," page 173; (l) "Anthem for Doomed Youth," page 212.

*　　*　　*　　*　　*

A HANDFUL OF LIMERICKS*

I sat next the Duchess at tea.
It was just as I feared it would be:
　　Her rumblings abdominal
　　Were simply abominable,
And everyone thought it was me.

There was a young lady of Lynn
Who was so uncommonly thin
　　That when she essayed
　　To drink lemonade
She slipped through the straw and fell in.

A tutor who tooted the flute
Tried to tutor two tooters to toot.
　　Said the two to the tutor,
　　"Is it harder to toot or
To tutor two tooters to toot?"

*Most limericks are anonymous. If not written anonymously, they soon become so, unfortunately for the glory of their authors, because of repeated oral transmission and reprinting without accreditation.

There was a young maid who said, "Why
Can't I look in my ear with my eye?
    If I put my mind to it,
    I'm sure I can do it.
You never can tell till you try."

There was an old man of Peru
Who dreamt he was eating his shoe.
    He awoke in the night
    In a terrible fright,
And found it was perfectly true!

A decrepit old gas man named Peter,
While hunting around for the meter,
    Touched a leak with his light.
    He arose out of sight,
And, as anyone can see by reading this, he
        also destroyed the meter.

Well, it's partly the shape of the thing
That gives the old limerick wing;
    These accordion pleats
    Full of airy conceits
Take it up like a kite on a string.

POEM IN OCTOBER

It was my thirtieth year to heaven
Woke to my hearing from harbor and neighbor wood
    And the mussel pooled and the heron
            Priested shore
        The morning beckon   5
With water praying and call of seagull and rook
And the knock of sailing boats on the net webbed wall
        Myself to set foot
            That second
    In the still sleeping town and set forth.   10

    My birthday began with the water-
Birds and the birds of the winged trees flying my name

Above the farms and the white horses
    And I rose
      In rainy autumn   15
And walked abroad in a shower of all my days.
High tide and the heron dived when I took the road
    Over the border
      And the gates
Of the town closed as the town awoke.   20.

A springful of larks in a rolling
Cloud and the roadside bushes brimming with whistling
    Blackbirds and the sun of October
      Summery
      On the hill's shoulder,   25
Here were fond climates and sweet singers suddenly
Come in the morning where I wandered and listened
    To the rain wringing
      Wind blow cold
In the woods faraway under me.   30

Pale rain over the dwindling harbor
And over the sea wet church the size of a snail
    With its horns through mist and the castle
      Brown as owls
      But all the gardens   35
Of spring and summer were blooming in the tall tales
Beyond the border and under the lark full cloud.
    There could I marvel
      My birthday
Away but the weather turned around.   40

It turned away from the blithe country
And down the other air and the blue altered sky
    Streamed again a wonder of summer
      With apples
      Pears and red currants   45
And I saw in the turning so clearly a child's
Forgotten mornings when he walked with his mother
    Through the parables
      Of sun light
And the legends of the green chapels   50

And the twice told fields of infancy
That his tears burned my cheeks and his heart moved in mine.
    These were the woods the river and sea
        Where a boy
        In the listening   55
Summertime of the dead whispered the truth of his joy
To the trees and the stones and the fish in the tide.
    And the mystery
        Sang alive
    Still in the water and singingbirds.   60

    And there could I marvel my birthday
Away but the weather turned around. And the true
    Joy of the long dead child sang burning
        In the sun.
        It was my thirtieth   65
Year to heaven stood there then in the summer noon
Though the town below lay leaved with October blood.
      O may my heart's truth
        Still be sung
    On this high hill in a year's turning.   70

Dylan Thomas (1914–1953)

QUESTIONS

1. The setting is a small fishing village on the coast of Wales. The poet's first name in Welsh means "water" (12). Trace the poet's walk in relation to the village, the weather, and the time of day.
2. "The weather turned around" is an expression indicating a change in the weather or the direction of the wind. In what psychological sense does the weather turn around during the poet's walk? Who is "the long dead child" (63), and what kind of child was he? With what wish does the poem close?
3. Explain "thirtieth year to heaven" (1), "horns" (33), "tall tales" (36), "green chapels" (50), "October blood" (67).
4. The elaborate stanza pattern in this poem is based not on the meter (which is very free) but on a syllable count. How many syllables are there in each line of the stanza? (In line 1 "thirtieth" is counted as only two syllables.) Notice that the stanzas 1 and 3 consist of exactly one sentence each.
5. The poem makes a considerable use of approximate rime, though not according to a regular pattern. Point out examples.

TWO JAPANESE HAIKU

The lightning flashes!
And slashing through the darkness,
A night-heron's screech.

A lightning gleam:
into darkness travels
a night heron's scream.

Matsuo Bashō (1644–1694)

The falling flower
I saw drift back to the branch
Was a butterfly.

Fallen flowers rise
back to the branch – I watch:
oh . . . butterflies!

Moritake (1452–1540)

QUESTION

The haiku, a Japanese form, consists of three lines with five, seven, and five syllables respectively. The translators of the left-hand versions above (Earl Miner and Babette Deutsch respectively) preserve this syllable count; the translator of the right-hand versions (Harold G. Henderson) seeks to preserve the sense of formal structure by making the first and last lines rime. Moritake's haiku, as Miss Deutsch points out, "refers to the Buddhist proverb that the fallen flower never returns to the branch; the broken mirror never again reflects." From these two examples, what would you say are the characteristics of effective haiku?

A WREATH

A wreathèd garland of deservèd praise,
Of praise deservèd, unto thee I give,
I give to thee, who knowest all my ways,
My crooked winding ways, wherein I live,
Wherein I die, not live: for life is straight,   5
Straight as a line, and ever tends to thee,
To thee, who art more far above deceit
Than deceit seems above simplicity.
Give me simplicity, that I may live,
So live and like, that I may know, thy ways,   10
Know them and practise them: then shall I give
For this poor wreath, give thee a crown of praise.

George Herbert (1593–1633)

QUESTIONS

1. To whom is the poem addressed? How do you know?
2. What are the meanings of "die," "live," and "life" (5)? Why does "deceit" seem "above simplicity" (8)? What is the meaning of the final line?
3. What metaphorical use does the poem make of circles, straight lines, and "crooked winding ways"?
4. What is the central metaphor of the poem? How does the form of the poem reflect its content?

GULL SKELETON

> In the first verse I find his skeleton
> nested in shore grass, late one autumn day.
> The loss of life and the life which is decay
> have been so gentle, so clasped one-to-one
>
> that what they left is perfect; and here in   5
> the second verse I kneel to pick it up:
> bones like the fine white china of a cup,
> chambered for lightness, dangerously thin,
>
> their one clear purpose forcing them toward flight
> even now, from the warm solace of my hand.   10
> In the third verse I bend to that demand
> and – quickly, against the deepening of night,
>
> because I *can* in poems – remake his wild eye,
> his claws, and the tense heat his muscles keep,
> his wings' knit feathers, then free him to his steep   15
> climb, in the last verse, up the streaming sky.

Jonathan Revere (b. 1939)

QUESTIONS

1. What two subjects are treated simultaneously in this poem? How are they related to each other? What statement does the poem make about poetry?
2. Point out and comment on the poem's use of assonance, consonance, and other sound repetitions. Discuss its use of simile, metaphor, paradox, and symbol.
3. Describe the stanza form of the poem. Discuss the movement and function of its unique feature of design.

FROM ROMEO AND JULIET

ROMEO   If I profane with my unworthiest hand
          This holy shrine, the gentle sin is this;
          My lips, two blushing pilgrims, ready stand
          To smooth that rough touch with a tender kiss.

JULIET   Good pilgrim, you do wrong your hand too much,   5
          Which mannerly devotion shows in this;
          For saints have hands that pilgrims' hands do touch,
          And palm to palm is holy palmers' kiss.

ROMEO   Have not saints lips, and holy palmers too?

JULIET   Ay, pilgrim, lips that they must use in prayer.   10

ROMEO   O! then, dear saint, let lips do what hands do;
          They pray, Grant thou, lest faith turn to despair.

JULIET   Saints do not move,° though grant for prayers' sake.   *propose,*

ROMEO   Then move not, while my prayers' effect I take.   *instigate*

William Shakespeare (1564–1616)

QUESTIONS

1. These fourteen lines have been lifted out of Act I, scene 5, of Shakespeare's play. They are the first words exchanged between Romeo and Juliet, who are meeting, for the first time, at a masquerade ball given by her father. Romeo is dressed as a pilgrim. Struck by Juliet's beauty, he has come up to greet her. What stage action accompanies this passage?
2. What is the basic metaphor employed? How does it affect the tone of the relationship between Romeo and Juliet?
3. What play on words do you find in lines 8 and 13–14? What two meanings has line 11?
4. By meter and rime scheme, these lines form a sonnet. Do you think this was coincidental or intentional on Shakespeare's part? Discuss.

EDWARD

        "Why dois° your brand° sae drap wi bluid,   *does; sword*
                Edward, Edward,
        Why dois your brand sae drap wi bluid,
            And why sae sad gang° yee O?"   *go*
        "O I hae killed my hauke sae guid,   5
                Mither, mither,
        O I hae killed my hauke sae guid,
            And I had nae mair bot hee O."

"Your haukis bluid was nevir sae reid,
             Edward, Edward,   10
Your haukis bluid was nevir sae reid,
   My deir son I tell thee O."
"O I hae killed my reid-roan steid,
             Mither, mither,
O I hae killed my reid-roan steid,   15
   That erst° was sae fair and frie° O."   formerly;
                                               spirited

"Your steid was auld, and ye hae got mair,
             Edward, Edward,
Your steid was auld, and ye hae got mair,
   Sum other dule° ye drie° O."   grief; suffer 20
"O I hae killed my fadir deir,
             Mither, mither,
O I hae killed my fadir deir,
   Alas, and wae is mee O!"

"And whatten penance wul ye drie for that,   25
             Edward, Edward,
And whatten penance wul ye drie for that?
   My deir son, now tell me O."
"Ile set my feit in yonder boat,
             Mither, mither,   30
Ile set my feit in yonder boat,
   And Ile fare ovir the sea O."

"And what wul ye doe wi your towirs and your ha,°   hall
             Edward, Edward,
And what wul ye doe wi your towirs and your ha,   35
   That were sae fair to see O?"
"Ile let thame stand tul they doun fa,°   fall
             Mither, mither,
Ile let thame stand tul they doun fa,
   For here nevir mair maun° I bee O."   must   40

"And what wul ye leive to your bairns° and your wife,   children
             Edward, Edward,
And what wul ye leive to your bairns and your wife,
   Whan ye gang ovir the sea O?"   44

"The warldis° room, late them beg thrae° life,   world's;
        Mither, mither,   through
The warldis room, late them beg thrae life,
    For thame nevir mair wul I see O."

"And what wul ye leive to your ain mither deir,
        Edward, Edward?   50
And what wul ye leive to your ain mither deir?
    My deir son, now tell me O."
"The curse of hell frae me sall ye beir,
        Mither, mither,
The curse of hell frae me sall ye beir,   55
    Sic° counseils ye gave to me O."   Such

Anonymous

QUESTIONS

1. What has Edward done and why? Where do the two climaxes of the poem come?

2. Tell as much as you can about Edward and his feelings toward what he has done. From what class of society is he? Why does he at first give false answers to his mother's questions? What reversal of feelings and loyalties has he undergone? Do his answers about his hawk and steed perhaps indicate his present feelings toward his father? How do you explain his behavior to his wife and children? What are his present feelings toward his mother?

3. Tell as much as you can about Edward's mother. Why does she ask what Edward has done—doesn't she already know? Is there any clue as to the motivation of her deed? How skillful is she in her questioning? What do we learn about her from her dismissal of Edward's steed as "auld" and only one of many (17)? From her asking Edward what penance *he* will do for his act (25)? From her reference to herself as Edward's "ain mither deir" (49)?

4. Structure and pattern are both important in this poem. Could any of the stanzas be interchanged without loss, or do they build up steadily to the two climaxes? What effect has the constant repetition of the two short refrains, "Edward, Edward" and "Mither, mither"? What is the effect of the final "O" at the end of each speech? Does the repetition of each question and answer simply waste words or does it add to the suspense and emotional intensity? (Try reading the poem omitting the third and seventh lines of each stanza. Is it improved or weakened?)

5. Much of what happened is implied, much is omitted. Does the poem gain anything in power from what is *not* told?

Show, not tell

OH SEE HOW THICK THE GOLDCUP FLOWERS

Oh see how thick the goldcup flowers
    Are lying in field and lane,
With dandelions to tell the hours
    That never are told again.
Oh may I squire you round the meads   5
    And pick you posies gay?
– 'Twill do no harm to take my arm.
    "You may, young man, you may."

Ah, spring was sent for lass and lad,
    'Tis now the blood runs gold,   10
And man and maid had best be glad
    Before the world is old.
What flowers today may flower tomorrow,
    But never as good as new.
– Suppose I wound my arm right round –   15
"'Tis true, young man, 'tis true."

Some lads there are, 'tis shame to say,
    That only court to thieve,
And once they bear the bloom away
    'Tis little enough they leave.   20
Then keep your heart for men like me
    And safe from trustless chaps.
My love is true and all for you.
    "Perhaps, young man, perhaps."

Oh, look in my eyes then, can you doubt?   25
    – Why, 'tis a mile from town.
How green the grass is all about!
    We might as well sit down.
– Ah, life, what is it but a flower?
    Why must true lovers sigh?   30
Be kind, have pity, my own, my pretty, –
    "Good-bye, young man, good-bye."

A. E. Housman (1859–1936)

QUESTIONS

1. Vocabulary: *tell* (3), *told* (4).
2. Much of the fascination of this poem lies in its steady progression of thought

and action through a fixed pattern of formal design. Describe fully the formal design – the elements that remain constant throughout the four stanzas.
3. Now describe the progression – or is it two progressions? Do the girl's replies run parallel or counter in direction to the young man's pleadings?
4. Flower imagery runs throughout the poem – some of it literal, some figurative. Describe the young man's use of it in each stanza. How original is his use of it?
5. In "Loveliest of trees" (page 77), Housman clearly endorses the *carpe diem* philosophy of the speaker. Does he support it here as well? That is, on whose side does "wisdom" lie – the young man's or the girl's? Support your answer fully, both from examination of internal evidence and by comparison or contrast with "Loveliest of trees."

400-METER FREESTYLE

THE GUN full swing the swimmer catapults and cracks

                           s

                           i

                           x

feet away onto that perfect glass he catches at   5

a

n

  d

throws behind him scoop after scoop cunningly moving

                           t   10

                           h

                           e

water back to move him forward. Thrift is his wonderful

s

e   15

c

ret; he has schooled out all extravagance. No muscle

                           r

                           i

                           p   20

ples without compensation wrist cock to heel snap to

h

i

s

mobile mouth that siphons in the air that nurtures   25

                                                    h

                                                    i

                                                    m

at   half   an   inch   above   sea   level   so   to   speak.

T   30

h

e

astonishing whites of the soles of his feet   rise

                                                a

                                                    n   35

                                                    d

salute us on the turns. He flips, converts, and is gone

a

l

l   40

in one. We watch him for signs. His arms are steady at

                                                    t

                                                        h

                                                        e

catch, his cadent feet tick in the stretch, they know   ·   45

t

h

e

lesson well. Lungs know, too; he does not list for

                                                a   50

                                                    i

                                                    r

he   drives   along   on   little   sips   carefully   expended

b

u   55

t

that plum red heart pumps hard cries hurt how soon

                                                i

                                                    t

                                                    s   60

near one more and makes its final surge   TIME: 4:25:9

                                          Maxine Kumin (b. 1925)

1. To what quality or qualities does this poem essentially pay tribute? What sentence in the poem most nearly expresses its theme?
2. Does the poem itself exhibit the qualities which it praises? Discuss.
3. How does the visual form of the poem reflect its content?

SLOWLY

Heavy is my heart,
    Dark are thine eyes.
Thou and I must part
    Ere the sun rise.

Ere the sun rise
    Thou and I must part.
Dark are thine eyes,
    Heavy is my heart.

Mary Coleridge (1861–1907)

QUESTION

1. How is the pattern of the poem related to its title and meaning?

A CHRISTMAS TREE

Star
If you are
A love compassionate,
You will walk with us this year.
We face a glacial distance, who are here
Huddld
At your feet.

William Burford (b. 1927)

QUESTION

1. Why do you think the author misspelled "huddled" in line 6?

15 Bad Poetry and Good

The attempt to evaluate a poem should never be made before the poem is understood; and, unless you have developed the capacity to feel some poetry deeply, any judgments you make will be worthless. A person who likes no wines can hardly be a judge of them. But the ability to make judgments, to discriminate between good and bad, great and good, good and half-good, is surely a primary object of all liberal education, and one's appreciation of poetry is incomplete unless it includes discrimination. Of the mass of verse that appears each year in print, as of all literature, most is "flat, stale, and unprofitable"; a very, very little is of any enduring value.

In judging a poem, as in judging any work of art, we need to ask three basic questions: (1) *What is its central purpose?* (2) *How fully has this purpose been accomplished?* (3) *How important is this purpose?* The first question we need to answer in order to understand the poem. The last two questions are those by which we evaluate it. The first of these measures the poem on a scale of perfection. The second measures it on a scale of significance. And, just as the area of a rectangle is determined by multiplying its measurements on two scales, breadth and height, so the greatness of a poem is determined by multiplying its measurements on two scales, perfection and significance. If the poem measures well on the first of these scales, we call it a good poem, at least of its kind. If it measures well on both scales, we call it a great poem.*

The measurement of a poem is a much more complex process, of course, than is the measurement of a rectangle. It cannot be done as exactly. Agreement on the measurements will never be complete. Yet over a period of time the judgments of qualified readers† tend to coalesce: there comes to be more agreement than disagreement. There is almost universal agreement, for instance, that Shakespeare is the greatest of English poets. Although there might be sharp disagreements among qualified readers as to whether Donne or Keats is the superior poet, or Wordsworth or Chaucer, or Shelley or Pope, there is almost universal agreement among them that each of these is superior to Kipling or Longfellow. And there is almost universal agreement that Kipling and Longfellow are superior to James Whitcomb Riley and Edgar Guest.

But your problem is to be able to discriminate, not between already established reputations, but between poems—poems you have not seen before and of which, perhaps, you do not even know the author. Here, of course, you will not always be right—even the most qualified readers occasionally go badly astray—but you should, we hope, be able to make broad distinctions with a higher average of success than you could when you began this book. And, unless you allow yourself to petrify, your ability to do this should improve throughout your college years and beyond.

For answering the first of our evaluative questions, *How fully has the poem's purpose been accomplished?* there are no easy yardsticks that we can apply. We cannot ask, Is the poem melodious? Does it have smooth meter? Does it use good grammar? Does it contain figures of speech? Are

---

*As indicated in the footnote on page 23, some objection has been made to the use of the term "purpose" in literary criticism. For the two criteria suggested above may be substituted these two: (1) How thoroughly are the materials of the poem integrated or unified? (2) How many and how diverse are the materials that it integrates? Thus a poem becomes successful in proportion to the tightness of its organization—that is, according to the degree to which all its elements work together and require each other to produce the total effect—and it becomes great in proportion to its scope—that is, according to the amount and diversity of the material it amalgamates into unity.

†Throughout this discussion the term "qualified reader" is of utmost importance. By a qualified reader we mean briefly a person with considerable experience of literature and considerable experience of life: a person of intelligence, sensitivity, and knowledge. Without these qualities a person is no more qualified to judge literature than would be a color-blind man to judge painting, or a tone-deaf man to judge music, or a man who had never seen a horse before to judge a horse.

the rimes perfect? Excellent poems exist without any of these attributes. We can judge any element in a poem only as it contributes or fails to contribute to the achievement of the central purpose; and we can judge the total poem only as these elements work together to form an integrated whole. But we can at least attempt a few generalizations. In a perfect poem there are no excess words, no words that do not bear their full weight in contributing to the total meaning, and no words just to fill out the meter. Each word is the best word for expressing the total meaning: there are no inexact words forced by the rime scheme or the metrical pattern. The word order is the best order for expressing the author's total meaning; distortions or departures from normal order are for emphasis or some other meaningful purpose. The diction, the images, and the figures of speech are fresh, not trite (except, of course, when the poet uses trite language deliberately for purposes of irony). There are no clashes between the sound of the poem and its sense, or its form and its content; and in general the poet uses both sound and pattern in such a way as to support his meaning. The organization of the poem is the best possible organization: images and ideas are so effectively arranged that any rearrangement would be harmful to the poem. We will always remember, however, that a good poem may have flaws. We should never damn a poem for its flaws if these flaws are amply compensated for by positive excellence.

If a poem is to have true excellence, it must be in some sense a "new" poem; it must exact a fresh response from the qualified reader – make him respond in a new way. It will not be merely imitative of previous literature nor appeal to stock, preestablished ways of thinking and feeling that in some readers are automatically stimulated by words like *mother, baby, home, country, faith,* or *God,* as a coin put into a slot always gets an expected reaction.

And here, perhaps, may be discussed the kinds of poems that most frequently "fool" poor readers (and occasionally a few good ones) and achieve sometimes a tremendous popularity without winning the respect of most good readers. These poems are found pasted in great numbers in the scrapbooks of sweet old ladies and appear in anthologies entitled *Poems of Inspiration, Poems of Courage,* or *Heart-Throbs.* The people who write such poems and the people who like them are often the best of people, but they are not poets or lovers of poetry in any genuine sense. They are lovers of conventional ideas or sentiments or feelings, which they like to see expressed with the adornment of rime and meter, and which, when so expressed, they respond to in predictable ways.

Of the several varieties of inferior poetry, we shall concern ourselves with three: the sentimental, the rhetorical, and the purely didactic. All three are perhaps unduly dignified by the name of poetry. They might more aptly be described as verse.

SENTIMENTALITY is indulgence in emotion for its own sake, or expression of more emotion than an occasion warrants. A sentimental *person* is gushy, stirred to tears by trivial or inappropriate causes; he weeps at all weddings and all funerals; he is made ecstatic by manifestations of young love; he clips locks of hair, gilds baby shoes, and talks baby talk; he grows compassionate over hardened criminals when he hears of their being punished. His opposite is the callous or unfeeling person. The ideal is the person who responds sensitively on appropriate occasions and feels deeply on occasions that deserve deep feeling, but who has nevertheless a certain amount of emotional reserve, a certain command over his feelings. Sentimental *literature* is *"tear-jerking"* literature. It aims primarily at stimulating the emotions directly rather than at communicating experience truly and freshly; it depends on trite and well-tried formulas for exciting emotion; it revels in old oaken buckets; rocking chairs, mother love, and the pitter-patter of little feet; it oversimplifies; it is unfaithful to the full complexity of human experience. In our book the best example of sentimental verse is the first seven lines of the anonymous "Love" (page 164). If this verse had ended as it began, it would have been pure sentimentalism. The eighth line redeems it by making us realize that the writer is not serious and thus transfers the piece from the classification of sentimental verse to that of humorous verse. In fact, the writer is poking fun at sentimentality by showing that in its most maudlin form it is characteristic of drunks.

RHETORICAL poetry uses a language more glittering and high flown than its substance warrants. It offers a spurious vehemence of language – language without a corresponding reality of emotion or thought underneath. It is oratorical, overelegant, artificially eloquent. It is superficial and, again, often basically trite. It loves rolling phrases like "from the rocky coast of Maine to the sun-washed shores of California" and "our heroic dead" and "Old Glory." It deals in generalities. At its worst it is bombast. In this book an example is offered by the two lines quoted from the play-within-a-play in Shakespeare's *A Midsummer Night's Dream:*

> Whereat with blade, with bloody, blameful blade,
> He bravely broached his boiling bloody breast.

Another example may be found in the player's recitation in *Hamlet* (in Act II, scene 2):

> Out, out, thou strumpet Fortune! All you gods,
> In general synod take away her power,
> Break all the spokes and fellies from her wheel,
> And bowl the round nave down the hill of heaven
> As low as to the fiends!

DIDACTIC poetry has as a primary purpose to teach or preach. It is probable that all the very greatest poetry teaches in subtle ways, without being expressly didactic; and much expressly didactic poetry ranks high in poetic excellence: that is, it accomplishes its teaching without ceasing to be poetry. But when the didactic purpose supersedes the poetic purpose, when the poem communicates information or moral instruction only, then it ceases to be didactic poetry and becomes didactic verse. Such verse appeals to people who go to poetry primarily for noble thoughts or inspiring lessons and like them prettily expressed. It is recognizable often by the flatness of its diction, the poverty of its imagery and figurative language, its emphasis on moral platitudes, its lack of poetic freshness. It is either very trite or has little to distinguish it from informational prose except rime or meter. Bryant's "To a Waterfowl" (page 143) is an example of didactic *poetry*. The familiar couplet

> Early to bed and early to rise,
> Makes a man healthy, wealthy, and wise

is more aptly characterized as didactic *verse*.

Undoubtedly, so far in this chapter, we have spoken too categorically, have made our distinctions too sharp and definite. All poetic excellence is a matter of degree. There are no absolute lines between sentimentality and true emotion, artificial and genuine eloquence, didactic verse and didactic poetry. Though the difference between extreme examples is easy to recognize, subtler discriminations are harder to make. But a primary distinction between the educated man and the ignorant man is the ability to make value judgments.

A final caution to students. In making judgments on literature, always be honest. Do not pretend to like what you really do not like. Do not be afraid to admit a liking for what you do like. A genuine enthusiasm for the second-rate is much better than false enthusiasm or no enthusiasm at all. Be neither hasty nor timorous in making your judgments. When you have attentively read a poem and thoroughly considered it, decide what you think. Do not hedge, equivocate, or try to find out others' opinions before forming your own. Having formed an opinion and expressed it, do not allow it to petrify. Compare your opinion *then* with the opinions of others; allow yourself to change it when convinced of its error: in this way you learn. Honesty, courage, and humility are the necessary moral foundations for all genuine literary judgment.

In the poems for comparison in this chapter, the distinction to be made is not always between black and white; it may be between varying degrees of poetic merit.

EXERCISE

1. Poetry is not so much a thing as a quality; it exists in varying degrees in different specimens of language. Though we cannot always say definitely, "This is poetry; that is not," we can often say, "This is more poetical than that." Rank the following passages from most poetical to least poetical or not poetical at all.

   a. Why should we be in such desperate haste to succeed and in such desperate enterprises? If a man does not keep pace with his companions, perhaps it is because he hears a different drummer. Let him step to the music which he hears, however measured or far away.

   b. $(x - 12) (x - 2) = x^2 - 14x + 24.$

   c. Thirty days hath September,
      April, June, and November.
      All the rest have thirty-one,
      Except February alone,
      To which we twenty-eight assign,
      Till leap year makes it twenty-nine.

   d. "Meeting at Night" (page 51).

   e. Thus, through the serene tranquilities of the tropical sea, among waves whose handclappings were suspended by exceeding rapture, Moby Dick moved on, still withholding from sight the full terrors of his submerged trunk, entirely hiding the wrenched hideousness of his jaw. But soon the fore part of him slowly rose from the water; for an instant his whole marbleized body formed a high arch, like Virginia's Natural Bridge, and warningly waving his bannered flukes in the air, the grand god revealed himself, sounded, and went out of sight. Hoveringly halting, and dipping on the wing, the white sea fowls longingly lingered over the agitated pool that he left.

f. Nature in the abstract is the aggregate of the powers and properties of all
    things. Nature means the sum of all phenomena, together with the causes
    which produce them; including not only all that happens, but all that is
    capable of happening; the unused capabilities of causes being as much a
    part of the idea of Nature, as those which take effect.

*   *   *   *   *

LOITERING WITH A VACANT EYE

Loitering with a vacant eye
Along the Grecian gallery,
And brooding on my heavy ill,
I met a statue standing still.
Still in marble stone stood he,   5
And steadfastly he looked at me.
"Well met," I thought the look would say,
"We both were fashioned far away;
We neither knew, when we were young,
These Londoners we live among."   10

Still he stood and eyed me hard,
An earnest and a grave regard:
"What, lad, drooping with your lot?
I too would be where I am not.
I too survey that endless line   15
Of men whose thoughts are not as mine.
Years, ere you stood up from rest,
On my neck the collar prest;
Years, when you lay down your ill,
I shall stand and bear it still.   20
Courage, lad, 'tis not for long:
Stand, quit you like stone, be strong."
So I thought his look would say;
And light on me my trouble lay,
And I stept out in flesh and bone   25
Manful like the man of stone.

BE STRONG

Be strong!
We are not here to play, – to dream, to drift.
We have hard work to do and loads to lift.
Shun not the struggle, – face it: 'tis God's gift.

Be strong!   5
Say not the days are evil. Who's to blame?
And fold the hands and acquiesce, – O shame!
Stand up, speak out, and bravely, in God's name.

Be strong!
It matters not how deep intrenched the wrong,   10
How hard the battle goes, the day how long;
Faint not, – fight on! Tomorrow comes the song.

QUESTIONS

1. The "Grecian gallery" (2), in the first poem of this pair, is a room in the British Museum in London. Who is the speaker? Who is the speaker in the second poem?
2. Which is the superior poem? Discuss.

A PRAYER IN SPRING

Oh, give us pleasure in the flowers today;
And give us not to think so far away
As the uncertain harvest; keep us here
All simply in the springing of the year.

Oh, give us pleasure in the orchard white,   5
Like nothing else by day, like ghosts by night;
And make us happy in the happy bees,
The swarm dilating round the perfect trees.

And make us happy in the darting bird
That suddenly above the bees is heard,   10
The meteor that thrusts in with needle bill,
And off a blossom in mid air stands still.

For this is love and nothing else is love,
The which it is reserved for God above
To sanctify to what far ends He will,   15
But which it only needs that we fulfill.

PRAY IN MAY

Today the birds are singing and
The grass and leaves are green,

And all the gentle earth presents
A bright and sunny scene.
It is the merry month of May   5
When flowers bloom once more,
And there are hopes and happy dreams
And promises in store.
What time could be more wisely spent
Than this the first of May   10
To say that we are thankful for
Our blessings every day?
To give our gratitude to God
In humbleness and prayer
And offer deeds of charity   15
As incense in the air?
Then let us love our neighbor and
Our rich and fruitful sod,
And let us go to church today
And thank almighty God.   20

QUESTION

1. Which poem treats its subject with greater truth, freshness, and technical
   skill?

GOD'S WILL FOR YOU AND ME

Just to be tender, just to be true,
Just to be glad the whole day through,
Just to be merciful, just to be mild,
Just to be trustful as a child,
Just to be gentle and kind and sweet,   5
Just to be helpful with willing feet,
Just to be cheery when things go wrong,
Just to drive sadness away with a song,
Whether the hour is dark or bright,
Just to be loyal to God and right,   10
Just to believe that God knows best,
Just in his promises ever to rest —
Just to let love be our daily key,
That is God's will for you and me.

PIED BEAUTY

Glory be to God for dappled things –
    For skies of couple-color as a brinded cow;
        For rose-moles all in stipple upon trout that swim;
Fresh-firecoal chestnut-falls; finches' wings;
    Landscape plotted and pieced – fold, fallow and plow;   5
        And all trades, their gear and tackle and trim.

All things counter, original, spare, strange;
    Whatever is fickle, freckled (who knows how?)
        With swift, slow; sweet, sour; adazzle, dim;
He fathers-forth whose beauty is past change: 10
        Praise him.

QUESTION

1. Which is the superior poem? Explain in full.

A POISON TREE

I was angry with my friend:
I told my wrath, my wrath did end.
I was angry with my foe:
I told it not, my wrath did grow.

And I watered it in fears,   5
Night and morning with my tears;
And I sunned it with smiles,
And with soft deceitful wiles.

And it grew both day and night
Till it bore an apple bright;   10
And my foe beheld it shine,
And he knew that it was mine,

And into my garden stole
When the night had veiled the pole:
In the morning glad I see   15
My foe outstretched beneath the tree.

THE MOST VITAL THING IN LIFE

When you feel like saying something
    That you know you will regret,
Or keenly feel an insult
    Not quite easy to forget,
That's the time to curb resentment   5
    And maintain a mental peace,
For when your mind is tranquil
    All your ill-thoughts simply cease.

It is easy to be angry
    When defrauded or defied,   10
To be peeved and disappointed
    If your wishes are denied;
But to win a worthwhile battle
    Over selfishness and spite,
You must learn to keep strict silence   15
    Though you know you're in the right.

So keep your mental balance
    When confronted by a foe,
Be it enemy in ambush
    Or some danger that you know.   20
If you are poised and tranquil
    When all around is strife,
Be assured that you have mastered
    The most vital thing in life.

QUESTION

1. Which poem has more poetic merit? Explain.

IF I CAN STOP ONE HEART FROM BREAKING

If I can stop one heart from breaking,
I shall not live in vain;
If I can ease one life the aching,
Or cool one pain,

Or help one fainting robin
Unto his nest again,
I shall not live in vain.

DEATH IS A DIALOGUE

Death is a dialogue between
The spirit and the dust.
"Dissolve," says Death. The Spirit, "Sir,
I have another trust."

Death doubts it, argues from the ground.
The Spirit turns away,
Just laying off, for evidence,
An overcoat of clay.

QUESTION

1. Both of these poems are by the American poet Emily Dickinson. Which more
   surely testifies to her poetic power? Why?

ON A DEAD CHILD

Man proposes, God in His time disposes,
    And so I wandered up to where you lay,
A little rose among the little roses,
    And no more dead than they.

It seemed your childish feet were tired of straying,   5
    You did not greet me from your flower-strewn bed,
Yet still I knew that you were only playing –
    Playing at being dead.

I might have thought that you were really sleeping,
    So quiet lay your eyelids to the sky,   10
So still your hair, but surely you were weeping;
    And so I did not cry.

God knows, and in His proper time disposes,
    And so I smiled and gently called your name,
Added my rose to your sweet heap of roses,   15
    And left you to your game.

BELLS FOR JOHN WHITESIDE'S DAUGHTER

There was such speed in her little body,
And such lightness in her footfall,
It is no wonder her brown study
Astonishes us all.

Her wars were bruited in our high window.   5
We looked among orchard trees and beyond
Where she took arms against her shadow,
Or harried unto the pond

The lazy geese, like a snow cloud
Dripping their snow on the green grass,   10
Tricking and stopping, sleepy and proud,
Who cried in goose, Alas,

For the tireless heart within the little
Lady with rod that made them rise
From their noon apple-dreams and scuttle   15
Goose-fashion under the skies!

But now go the bells, and we are ready,
In one house we are sternly stopped
To say we are vexed at her brown study,
Lying so primly propped.   20

QUESTION

1. Which is the sentimental poem? Which is the honest one? Explain.

THE SEND-OFF

Down the close, darkening lanes they sang their way
To the siding-shed,
And lined the train with faces grimly gay.

Their breasts were stuck all white with wreath and spray
As men's are, dead.   5

Dull porters watched them, and a casual tramp
Stood staring hard,
Sorry to miss them from the upland camp.
Then, unmoved, signals nodded, and a lamp
Winked to the guard.   10

So secretly, like wrongs hushed-up, they went.
They were not ours:
We never heard to which front these were sent.

Nor there if they yet mock what women meant
Who gave them flowers.   15

Shall they return to beatings of great bells
In wild train-loads?
A few, a few, too few for drums and yells,
May creep back, silent, to village wells
Up half-known roads.   20

CHA TILL MACCRUIMEIN

The pipes in the street were playing bravely,
    The marching lads went by,
With merry hearts and voices singing
    My friends marched out to die;
But I was hearing a lonely pibroch   5
    Out of an older war,
"Farewell, farewell, farewell, MacCrimmon,
    MacCrimmon comes no more."

And every lad in his heart was dreaming
    Of honor and wealth to come,   10
And honor and noble pride were calling
    To the tune of the pipes and drum;
But I was hearing a woman singing
    On dark Dunvegan shore,
"In battle or peace, with wealth or honor,   15
    MacCrimmon comes no more."

And there in front of the men were marching,
    With feet that made no mark,
The grey old ghosts of the ancient fighters
    Come back again from the dark;   20
And in front of them all MacCrimmon piping
    A weary tune and sore,
"On the gathering day, for ever and ever,
    MacCrimmon comes no more."

QUESTIONS

1. Vocabulary: *pibroch* (5).
2. The first poem was written by an English poet, the second by a Scottish one; both poets were killed in World War I. "Cha Till Maccruimein" is Gaelic and means "MacCrimmon comes no more." The MacCrimmons were a famous

race of hereditary pipers from the Isle of Skye. One of them, when his clan was about to leave on a dangerous expedition, composed a lament in which he accurately prophesied his own death in the coming fight. According to Sir Walter Scott, emigrants from the West Highlands and Western Isles usually left their native shore to the accompaniment of this strain. Compare these two poems as to subject and purpose. Taking into account their rhythm, imagery, freshness, and emotional content, decide which is the superior poem.*

LITTLE BOY BLUE

> The little toy dog is covered with dust,
>> But sturdy and staunch he stands;
> And the little toy soldier is red with rust,
>> And his musket moulds in his hands.
> Time was when the little toy dog was new,   5
>> And the soldier was passing fair;
> And that was the time when our Little Boy Blue
>> Kissed them and put them there.
>
> "Now, don't you go till I come," he said,
>> "And don't you make any noise!"   10
> So, toddling off to his trundle-bed,
>> He dreamt of the pretty toys;
> And, as he was dreaming, an angel song
>> Awakened our Little Boy Blue—
> Oh! the years are many, the years are long,   15
>> But the little toy friends are True!
>
> Ay, faithful to Little Boy Blue they stand
>> Each in the same old place—
> Awaiting the touch of a little hand,
>> The smile of a little face;   20
> And they wonder, as waiting the long years through
>> In the dust of that little chair,
> What has become of our Little Boy Blue,
>> Since he kissed them and put them there.

*For this pairing I am indebted to Denys Thompson, *Reading and Discrimination,* rev. ed. (London: Chatto & Windus, 1954).

THE TOYS

My little Son, who looked from thoughtful eyes
And moved and spoke in quiet grown-up wise,
Having my law the seventh time disobeyed,
I struck him, and dismissed
With hard words and unkissed,   5
His Mother, who was patient, being dead.
Then, fearing lest his grief should hinder sleep,
I visited his bed,
But found him slumbering deep,
With darkened eyelids, and their lashes yet   10
From his late sobbing wet.
And I, with moan,
Kissing away his tears, left others of my own;
For, on a table drawn beside his head,
He had put, within his reach,   15
A box of counters and a red-veined stone,
A piece of glass abraded by the beach,
And six or seven shells,
A bottle with bluebells,
And two French copper coins, ranged there with careful art,   20
To comfort his sad heart.
So when that night I prayed
To God, I wept, and said:
Ah, when at last we lie with trancèd breath,
Not vexing Thee in death,   25
And thou rememberest of what toys
We made our joys,
How weakly understood
Thy great commanded good,
Then, fatherly not less   30
Than I whom Thou has moulded from the clay,
Thou'lt leave Thy wrath, and say,
"I will be sorry for their childishness."

QUESTION

1. One of these poems has an obvious appeal for the beginning reader. The other
   is likely to have more meaning for the mature reader. Try to explain in terms
   of sentimentality and honesty.

16 Good Poetry And Great

I
f a poem has successfully met the test in the question, *How fully has it accomplished its purpose?* we are ready to subject it to our second question, *How important is its purpose?*

Great poetry must, of course, be good poetry. Noble intent alone cannot redeem a work that does not measure high on the scale of accomplishment; otherwise the sentimental and purely didactic verse of much of the last chapter would stand with the world's masterpieces. But once a work has been judged as successful on the scale of execution, its final standing will depend on its significance of purpose.

Suppose, for instance, we consider three poems in our text: the limerick "There was a young lady of Niger" (page 220), Emily Dickinson's poem "It sifts from leaden sieves" (page 63), and Shakespeare's sonnet "That time of year" (page 222). Each of these would probably be judged by competent critics as highly successful in accomplishing what it sets out to do. The limerick tells its little story without an unnecessary word, with no "wrong" word, with no distortion of normal sentence order forced by exigencies of meter or rime; the limerick form is ideally suited to the author's humorous purpose; and the manner in which the story is told, with its understatement, its neat shift in position of the lady and her smile, is economical and delicious. Yet we should hardly call this poetry at all: it does not really communicate experience, nor does it attempt to. It attempts merely to relate a brief anecdote humorously and effectively. On the other hand, Emily Dickinson's poem *is* poetry, and very good poetry. It appeals richly to our senses and to our imaginations, and it succeeds excellently in its purpose: to convey the appearance and the quality of falling and newly fallen snow as well as a sense of the magic and the mystery of nature. Yet, when we compare this excellent poem with Shakespeare's, we again see important differences. Although the first poem engages the senses and the imagination and may affect us with wonder and cause us to meditate on nature, it does not deeply engage the emotions or the intellect. It does not come as close to the core of human living and suffering as does Shakespeare's sonnet. In fact, it is concerned primarily with that staple of small talk, the weather. On the other hand, Shakespeare's sonnet is concerned with the universal human tragedy of growing old, with approaching death, and with love. Of these three selections, then, Shakespeare's is the greatest. It "says" more than Emily Dickinson's poem or the limerick; it communicates a richer experience; it successfully accomplishes a more significant purpose. The discriminating reader will get from it a deeper enjoyment, because he has been nourished as well as delighted.

Great poetry engages the whole man in his response – senses, imagination, emotion, intellect; it does not touch him merely on one or two sides of his nature. Great poetry seeks not merely to entertain the reader, but to bring him – along with pure pleasure – fresh insights, or renewed insights, and important insights, into the nature of human experience. Great poetry, we might say, gives its reader a broader and deeper understanding of life, of his fellow men, and of himself, always with the qualification, of course, that the kind of insight literature gives is not necessarily the kind that can be summed up in a simple "lesson" or "moral." It is *knowledge – felt* knowledge, *new* knowledge – of the complexities of human nature and of the tragedies and sufferings, the excitements and joys, that characterize human experience.

Is Shakespeare's sonnet a *great* poem? It is, at least, a great *sonnet*. Greatness, like goodness, is relative. If we compare any of Shakespeare's sonnets with his greatest plays – *Macbeth, Othello, Hamlet, King Lear* – another big difference appears. What is undertaken and accomplished in these tragedies is enormously greater, more difficult, and more complex than could ever be undertaken or accomplished in a single sonnet. Greatness in literature, in fact, cannot be entirely dissociated from size. In literature, as in basketball and football, a good big man is better than a good little man. The greatness of a poem is in proportion to the range and depth and intensity of experience that it brings to us: its amount of life. Shakespeare's plays offer us a multiplicity of life and a depth of living that could never be compressed into the fourteen lines of a sonnet. They organize a greater complexity of life and experience into unity.

Yet, after all, we have provided no easy yardsticks or rule-of-thumb measures for literary judgment. There are no mechanical tests. The final measuring rod can be only the responsiveness, the maturity, the taste and discernment of the cultivated reader. Such taste and discernment are partly a native endowment, partly the product of maturity and experience, partly the achievement of conscious study, training, and intellectual effort. They cannot be achieved suddenly or quickly; they can never be achieved in perfection. The pull is a long and a hard one. But success, even relative success, brings enormous rewards in enrichment and command of life.

*   *   *   *   *

THE DEATH OF THE HIRED MAN

Mary sat musing on the lamp-flame at the table
Waiting for Warren. When she heard his step,
She ran on tip-toe down the darkened passage
To meet him in the doorway with the news
And put him on his guard. "Silas is back."   5
She pushed him outward with her through the door
And shut it after her. "Be kind" she said.
She took the market things from Warren's arms
And set them on the porch, then drew him down
To sit beside her on the wooden steps.   10

"When was I ever anything but kind to him?
But I'll not have the fellow back," he said.
"I told him so last haying, didn't I?
If he left then, I said, that ended it.
What good is he? Who else will harbor him   15
At his age for the little he can do?
What help he is there's no depending on.
Off he goes always when I need him most.
He thinks he ought to earn a little pay,
Enough at least to buy tobacco with,   20
So he won't have to beg and be beholden.
'All right,' I say, 'I can't afford to pay
Any fixed wages, though I wish I could.'

'Someone else can.' 'Then someone else will have to.'
I shouldn't mind his bettering himself   25
If that was what it was. You can be certain,
When he begins like that, there's someone at him
Trying to coax him off with pocket-money –
In haying time, when any help is scarce.
In winter he comes back to us. I'm done."   30

"Sh! not so loud: he'll hear you," Mary said.

"I want him to: he'll have to soon or late."

"He's worn out. He's asleep beside the stove.
When I came up from Rowe's I found him here,
Huddled against the barn-door fast asleep,   35
A miserable sight, and frightening, too –
You needn't smile – I didn't recognize him –
I wasn't looking for him – and he's changed.
Wait till you see."

                    "Where did you say he'd been?"

"He didn't say, I dragged him to the house,   40
And gave him tea and tried to make him smoke.
I tried to make him talk about his travels.
Nothing would do: he just kept nodding off."

"What did he say? Did he say anything?"

"But little."

                    "Anything? Mary, confess   45
He said he'd come to ditch the meadow for me."

"Warren!"

                    "But did he? I just want to know."

"Of course he did. What would you have him say?
Surely you wouldn't grudge the poor old man
Some humble way to save his self-respect.   50
He added, if you really care to know,
He meant to clear the upper pasture, too.
That sounds like something you have heard before?
Warren, I wish you could have heard the way

He jumbled everything. I stopped to look   55
Two or three times – he made me feel so queer –
To see if he was talking in his sleep.
He ran on Harold Wilson – you remember –
The boy you had in haying four years since.
He's finished school, and teaching in his college.   60
Silas declares you'll have to get him back.
He says they two will make a team for work:
Between them they will lay this farm as smooth!
The way he mixed that in with other things.
He thinks young Wilson a likely lad, though daft   65
On education – you know how they fought
All through July under the blazing sun,
Silas up on the cart to build the load,
Harold along beside to pitch it on."

"Yes, I took care to keep well out of earshot."   70

"Well, those days trouble Silas like a dream.
You wouldn't think they would. How some things linger!
Harold's young college boy's assurance piqued him.
After so many years he still keeps finding
Good arguments he sees he might have used.   75
I sympathize. I know just how it feels
To think of the right thing to say too late.
Harold's associated in his mind with Latin.
He asked me what I thought of Harold's saying
He studied Latin like the violin   80
Because he liked it – that an argument!
He said he couldn't make the boy believe
He could find water with a hazel prong –
Which showed how much good school had ever done him.
He wanted to go over that. But most of all   85
He thinks if he could have another chance
To teach him how to build a load of hay – "

"I know, that's Silas' one accomplishment.
He bundles every forkful in its place,
And tags and numbers it for future reference,   90
So he can find and easily dislodge it
In the unloading. Silas does that well.

He takes it out in bunches like big birds' nests.
You never see him standing on the hay
He's trying to lift, straining to lift himself." 95

"He thinks if he could teach him that, he'd be
Some good perhaps to someone in the world.
He hates to see a boy the fool of books.
Poor Silas, so concerned for other folk,
And nothing to look backward to with pride, 100
And nothing to look forward to with hope,
So now and never any different.

Part of a moon was falling down the west,
Dragging the whole sky with it to the hills.
Its light poured softly in her lap. She saw it 105
And spread her apron to it. She put out her hand
Among the harp-like morning-glory strings,
Taut with the dew from garden bed to eaves,
As if she played unheard some tenderness
That wrought on him beside her in the night. 110
"Warren," she said, "he has come home to die:
You needn't be afraid he'll leave you this time."

"Home," he mocked gently.

                              "Yes, what else but home?
It all depends on what you mean by home.
Of course he's nothing to us, any more 115
Than was the hound that came a stranger to us
Out of the woods, worn out upon the trail."

"Home is the place where, when you have to go there,
They have to take you in."

                              "I should have called it
Something you somehow haven't to deserve." 120

Warren leaned out and took a step or two,
Picked up a little stick, and brought it back
And broke it in his hand and tossed it by.
"Silas has better claim on us you think
Than on his brother? Thirteen little miles 125
As the road winds would bring him to his door.

Silas has walked that far no doubt today.
Why doesn't he go there? His brother's rich,
A somebody – director in the bank."

"He never told us that."

                    "We know it though."   130

"I think his brother ought to help, of course.
I'll see to that if there is need. He ought of right
To take him in, and might be willing to –
He may be better than appearances.
But have some pity on Silas. Do you think   135
If he had any pride in claiming kin
Or anything he looked for from his brother,
He'd keep so still about him all this time?"

"I wonder what's between them."

                         "I can tell you.
Silas is what he is – we wouldn't mind him –   140
But just the kind that kinsfolk can't abide.
He never did a thing so very bad.
He don't know why he isn't quite as good
As anybody. Worthless though he is,
He won't be made ashamed to please his brother."   145

"*I* can't think Si ever hurt anyone."

"No, but he hurt my heart the way he lay
And rolled his old head on that sharp-edged chair-back.
He wouldn't let me put him on the lounge.
You must go in and see what you can do.   150
I made the bed up for him there tonight.
You'll be surprised at him – how much he's broken.
His working days are done; I'm sure of it."

"I'd not be in a hurry to say that."

"I haven't been. Go, look, see for yourself.   155
But, Warren, please remember how it is:
He's come to help you ditch the meadow.
He has a plan. You mustn't laugh at him.
He may not speak of it, and then he may.

I'll sit and see if that small sailing cloud   160
Will hit or miss the moon."

                    It hit the moon.
Then there were three there, making a dim row,
The moon, the little silver cloud, and she.

Warren returned – too soon, it seemed to her,
Slipped to her side, caught up her hand and waited.   165

"Warren?" she questioned.

                    "Dead," was all he answered.

                                        Robert Frost (1874–1963)

QUESTIONS

1. Vocabulary: *beholden* (21), *piqued* (73).
2. What kind of person is Silas? Characterize him as fully as possible, showing, especially, what is revealed about his character by his relationships with Harold Wilson, with his brother, and with Warren and Mary.
3. Characterize Warren and Mary. Are they basically unlike in their natures and attitudes, or not really too far apart? Can you suggest reasons why Warren should at first be less solicitous than Mary?
4. Define as precisely as possible the moral problem faced by Warren and Mary. How would Warren finally have answered it (if an answer had not been made unnecessary)? Give reasons for your answer.
5. Is the poem written in free verse or blank verse? How would you describe its rhythm and language?

THE LOVE SONG OF J. ALFRED PRUFROCK

> *S'io credesse che mia risposta fosse*
> *A persona che mai tornasse al mondo,*
> *Questa fiamma staria senza piu scosse.*
> *Ma perciocche giammai di questo fondo*
> *Non torno vivo alcun, s'i'odo il vero,*
> *Senza tema d'infamia ti rispondo.*

Let us go then, you and I,
When the evening is spread out against the sky
Like a patient etherized upon a table;
Let us go, through certain half-deserted streets,

The muttering retreats 5
Of restless nights in one-night cheap hotels
And sawdust restaurants with oyster-shells:
Streets that follow like a tedious argument
Of insidious intent
To lead you to an overwhelming question . . . 10
Oh, do not ask, "What is it?"
Let us go and make our visit.

In the room the women come and go
Talking of Michelangelo.

The yellow fog that rubs its back upon the window-panes, 15
The yellow smoke that rubs its muzzle on the window-panes
Licked its tongue into the corners of the evening,
Lingered upon the pools that stand in drains,
Let fall upon its back the soot that falls from chimneys,
Slipped by the terrace, made a sudden leap, 20
And seeing that it was a soft October night,
Curled once about the house, and fell asleep.

And indeed there will be time
For the yellow smoke that slides along the street,
Rubbing its back upon the window-panes; 25
There will be time, there will be time
To prepare a face to meet the faces that you meet;
There will be time to murder and create,
And time for all the works and days of hands
That lift and drop a question on your plate; 30
Time for you and time for me,
And time yet for a hundred indecisions,
And for a hundred visions and revisions,
Before the taking of a toast and tea.

In the room the women come and go 35
Talking of Michelangelo.

And indeed there will be time
To wonder, "Do I dare?" and, "Do I dare?"
Time to turn back and descend the stair,
With a bald spot in the middle of my hair — 40
(They will say: "How his hair is growing thin!")

My morning coat, my collar mounting firmly to the chin,
My necktie rich and modest, but asserted by a simple pin –
(They will say: "But how his arms and legs are thin!")
Do I dare   45
Disturb the universe?
In a minute there is time
For decisions and revisions which a minute will reverse.

    For I have known them all already, known them all: –
Have known the evenings, mornings, afternoons,   50
I have measured out my life with coffee spoons;
I know the voices dying with a dying fall
Beneath the music from a farther room.
      So how should I presume?

    And I have known the eyes already, known them all –   55
The eyes that fix you in a formulated phrase,
And when I am formulated, sprawling on a pin,
When I am pinned and wriggling on the wall,
Then how should I begin
To spit out all the butt-ends of my days and ways   60
      And how should I presume?

    And I have known the arms already, known them all –
Arms that are braceleted and white and bare
(But in the lamplight, downed with light brown hair!)
Is it perfume from a dress   65
That makes me so digress?
Arms that lie along a table, or wrap about a shawl.
      And should I then presume?
      And how should I begin?

          *   *   *

Shall I say, I have gone at dusk through narrow streets   70
And watched the smoke that rises from the pipes
Of lonely men in shirt-sleeves, leaning out of windows? . . .

    I should have been a pair of ragged claws
Scuttling across the floors of silent seas.

          *   *   *

And the afternoon, the evening, sleeps so peacefully!   75
Smoothed by long fingers,
Asleep . . . tired . . . or it malingers,
Stretched on the floor, here beside you and me.
Should I, after tea and cakes and ices,
Have the strength to force the moment to its crisis?   80
But though I have wept and fasted, wept and prayed,
Though I have seen my head (grown slightly bald) brought in
    upon a platter,
I am no prophet – and here's no great matter;
I have seen the moment of my greatness flicker,
And I have seen the eternal Footman hold my coat, and snicker,   85
And in short, I was afraid.

    And would it have been worth it, after all,
After the cups, the marmalade, the tea,
Among the porcelain, among some talk of you and me,
Would it have been worth while,   90
To have bitten off the matter with a smile,
To have squeezed the universe into a ball
To roll it toward some overwhelming question,
To say: "I am Lazarus, come from the dead,
Come back to tell you all, I shall tell you all" –   95
If one, settling a pillow by her head,
    Should say: "That is not what I meant at all.
    That is not it, at all."

    And would it have been worth it, after all,
Would it have been worth while,   100
After the sunsets and the dooryards and the sprinkled streets,
After the novels, after the teacups, after the skirts that trail
    along the floor –
And this, and so much more? –
It is impossible to say just what I mean!
But as if a magic lantern threw the nerves in patterns on a screen: 105
Would it have been worth while
If one, settling a pillow or throwing off a shawl,
And turning toward the window, should say:
    "That is not it at all,
    That is not what I meant, at all."   110

                    *   *   *

No! I am not Prince Hamlet, nor was meant to be;
Am an attendant lord, one that will do
To swell a progress, start a scene or two,
Advise the prince; no doubt, an easy tool,
Deferential, glad to be of use,   115
Politic, cautious, and meticulous:
Full of high sentence, but a bit obtuse;
At times, indeed, almost ridiculous –
Almost, at times, the Fool.

    I grow old . . . I grow old . . .   120
I shall wear the bottoms of my trousers rolled.°   cuffed

    Shall I part my hair behind? Do I dare to eat a peach?
I shall wear white flannel trousers, and walk upon the beach.
I have heard the mermaids singing, each to each.

    I do not think that they will sing to me.   125

    I have seen them riding seaward on the waves
Combing the white hair of the waves blown back
When the wind blows the water white and black.

    We have lingered in the chambers of the sea
By sea-girls wreathed with seaweed red and brown   130
Till human voices wake us, and we drown.

                         T. S. Eliot (1888–1965)

QUESTIONS

1. Vocabulary: *insidious* (9), *Michelangelo* (14), *muzzle* (16), *malingers* (77), *progress* (113), *deferential* (115), *politic* (116), *meticulous* (116), *sentence* (117).
2. This poem may be for you the most difficult in the book, because it uses a "stream of consciousness" technique (that is, presents the apparently random thoughts going through a person's head within a certain time interval), in which the transitional links are psychological rather than logical, and also because it uses allusions you may be unfamiliar with. Even though you do not at first understand the poem in detail, you should be able to get from it a quite accurate picture of Prufrock's character and personality. What kind of person is he? (Answer this as fully as possible.) From what class of society is he? What one line especially well sums up the nature of his past life? A brief initial orientation may be helpful: Prufrock is apparently on his way, at the beginning of the poem, to a late afternoon tea, at which he wishes (or does he?) to make a declaration of love to some lady who will be present. The "you and I" of the first line are divided parts of Prufrock's own nature, for he is

undergoing internal conflict. Does he make the declaration? Why not? Where does the climax of the poem come? If the first half of the poem (up to the climax) is devoted to Prufrock's effort to prepare himself psychologically to make the declaration (or to postpone such effort), what is the latter half (after the climax) devoted to?

3. There are a number of striking or unusual figures of speech in the poem. Most of them in some way reflect Prufrock's own nature or his desires or fears. From this point of view discuss lines 2–3; 15–22 and 75–78; 57–58; 73–74; and 124–31. What figure of speech is lines 73–74? In what respect is the title ironical?

4. The poem makes an extensive use of literary allusion. The Italian epigraph is a passage from Dante's *Inferno* in which a man in Hell tells a visitor that he would never tell his story if there were a chance that it would get back to living ears. In line 29 the phrase "works and days" is the title of a long poem – a description of agricultural life and a call to toil – by the early Greek poet Hesiod. Line 52 echoes the opening speech of Shakespeare's *Twelfth Night*. The prophet of lines 81–83 is John the Baptist, whose head was delivered to Salome by Herod as a reward for her dancing (Matthew 14:1–11, and Oscar Wilde's play *Salome*). Line 92 echoes the closing six lines of Marvell's "To His Coy Mistress" (page 75). Lazarus (94–95) may be either the beggar Lazarus (of Luke 16) who was not permitted to return from the dead to warn the brothers of a rich man about Hell or the Lazarus (of John 11) whom Christ raised from death or both. Lines 111–19 allude to a number of characters from Shakespeare's *Hamlet:* Hamlet himself, the chamberlain Polonius, and various minor characters including probably Rosencrantz, Guildenstern, and Osric. "Full of high sentence" (117) echoes Chaucer's description of the Clerk of Oxford in the Prologue to *The Canterbury Tales*. Relate as many of these allusions as you can to the character of Prufrock. How is Prufrock particularly like Hamlet, and how is he unlike him? Contrast Prufrock with the speaker in "To His Coy Mistress."

5. This poem and "The Death of the Hired Man" are dramatic in structure. Frost's poem (though it has a slight narrative element) is largely a dialogue between two characters who speak in their own voices; Eliot's is a highly allusive soliloquy or interior monologue. In what ways do their dramatic structures facilitate what they have to say?

OUT OF THE CRADLE ENDLESSLY ROCKING

Out of the cradle endlessly rocking,
Out of the mocking-bird's throat, the musical shuttle,
Out of the Ninth-month midnight,
Over the sterile sands and the fields beyond where the child leaving his bed
    wandered alone, bareheaded, barefoot,

Down from the showered halo,   5
Up from the mystic play of shadows twining and twisting as if they were
    alive,
Out from the patches of briers and blackberries,
From the memories of the bird that chanted to me,
From your memories sad brother, from the fitful risings and fallings I
    heard,
From under that yellow half-moon late-risen and swollen as if with tears, 10
From those beginning notes of yearning and love there in the mist,
From the thousand responses of my heart never to cease,
From the myriad thence aroused words,
From the word stronger and more delicious than any,
From such as now they start the scene revisiting,   15
As a flock, twittering, rising, or overhead passing,
Borne hither, ere all eludes me, hurriedly,
A man, yet by these tears a little boy again,
Throwing myself on the sand, confronting the waves,
I, chanter of pains and joys, uniter of here and hereafter,   20
Taking all hints to use them, but swiftly leaping beyond them,
A reminiscence sing.

Once Paumanok,
When the lilac-scent was in the air and Fifth-month grass was growing,
Up this seashore in some briers,   25
Two feathered guests from Alabama, two together,
And their nest, and four light-green eggs spotted with brown,
And every day the he-bird to and fro near at hand,
And every day the she-bird crouched on her nest, silent, with bright eyes,
And every day I, a curious boy, never too close, never disturbing them, 30
Cautiously peering, absorbing, translating.

Shine! shine! shine!
Pour down your warmth, great sun!
While we bask, we two together,

Two together!   35
Winds blow south, or winds blow north,
Day come white, or night come black,
Home, or rivers and mountains from home,
Singing all time, minding no time,
While we two keep together.   40

Till of a sudden,
May-be killed, unknown to her mate,
One forenoon the she-bird crouched not on the nest,
Nor returned that afternoon, nor the next,
Nor ever appeared again.   45

And thenceforward all summer in the sound of the sea,
And at night under the full of the moon in calmer weather,
Over the hoarse surging of the sea,
Or flitting from brier to brier by day,
I saw, I heard at intervals the remaining one, the he-bird,   50
The solitary guest from Alabama.

Blow! blow! blow!
Blow up sea-winds along Paumanok's shore;
I wait and I wait till you blow my mate to me.

Yes, when the stars glistened,   55
All night long on the prong of a moss-scalloped stake,
Down almost amid the slapping waves,
Sat the lone singer wonderful causing tears.

He called on his mate,
He poured forth the meanings which I of all men know.   60

Yes my brother I know,
The rest might not, but I have treasured every note,
For more than once dimly down to the beach gliding,
Silent, avoiding the moonbeams, blending myself with the shadows,
Recalling now the obscure shapes, the echoes, the sounds and sights after
    their sorts,   65
The white arms out in the breakers tirelessly tossing,
I, with bare feet, a child, the wind wafting my hair,
Listened long and long.

Listened to keep, to sing, now translating the notes,
Following you my brother.   70

Soothe! soothe! soothe!
Close on its wave soothes the wave behind,
And again another behind embracing and lapping, every one close,
But my love soothes not me, not me.

Low hangs the moon, it rose late, 75
It is lagging – O I think it is heavy with love, with love.

O madly the sea pushes upon the land,
With love, with love.

O night! do I not see my love fluttering out among the breakers?
What is that little black thing I see there in the white? 80

Loud! loud! loud!
Loud I call to you, my love!
High and clear I shoot my voice over the waves,
Surely you must know who is here, is here,
You must know who I am, my love. 85

Low-hanging moon!
What is that dusky spot in your brown yellow?
O it is the shape, the shape of my mate!
O moon do not keep her from me any longer.

Land! land! O land! 90
Whichever way I turn, O I think you could give me my mate back again if you only would,
For I am almost sure I see her dimly whichever way I look.

O rising stars!
Perhaps the one I want so much will rise, will rise with some of you.

O throat! O trembling throat! 95
Sound clearer through the atmosphere!
Pierce the woods, the earth,
Somewhere listening to catch you must be the one I want.

Shake out carols!
Solitary here, the night's carols! 100
Carols of lonesome love! death's carols!
Carols under that lagging, yellow, waning moon!
O under that moon where she droops almost down into the sea!
O reckless despairing carols.

But soft! sink low! 105
Soft, let me just murmur,
And do you wait a moment you husky-noised sea,
For somewhere I believe I heard my mate responding to me,

So faint, I must be still, be still to listen,
But not altogether still, for then she might not come immediately to me.   110

Hither my love!
Here I am! Here!
With this just-sustained note I announce myself to you,
This gentle call is for you my love, for you.

Do not be decoyed elsewhere,   115
That is the whistle of the wind, it is not my voice,
That is the fluttering, the fluttering of the spray,
Those are the shadows of leaves.

O darkness! O in vain!
O I am very sick and sorrowful.   120

O brown halo in the sky near the moon, drooping upon the sea!
O troubled reflection in the sea!
O throat! O throbbing heart!
And I singing uselessly, uselessly all the night.

O past! O happy life! O songs of joy!   125
In the air, in the woods, over fields,
Loved! loved! loved! loved! loved!
But my mate no more, no more with me!
We two together no more.

The aria sinking,   130
All else continuing, the stars shining,
The winds blowing, the notes of the bird continuous echoing,
With angry moans the fierce old mother incessantly moaning,
On the sands of Paumanok's shore gray and rustling,
The yellow half-moon enlarged, sagging down, drooping, the face of the
    sea almost touching,   135
The boy ecstatic, with his bare feet the waves, with his hair the atmosphere
    dallying,
The love in the heart long pent, now loose, now at last tumultuously
    bursting,
The aria's meaning, the ears, the soul, swiftly depositing,
The strange tears down the cheeks coursing,
The colloquy there, the trio, each uttering,   140
The undertone, the savage old mother incessantly crying,

To the boy's soul's questions sullenly timing, some drowned secret hissing,
To the outsetting bard.

Demon or bird! (said the boy's soul,)
Is it indeed toward your mate you sing? or is it really to me?   145
For I, that was a child, my tongue's use sleeping, now I have heard you,
Now in a moment I know what I am for, I awake,
And already a thousand singers, a thousand songs, clearer, louder and more
    sorrowful than yours,
A thousand warbling echoes have started to life within me, never to die.

O you singer solitary, singing by yourself, projecting me,   150
O solitary me listening, never more shall I cease perpetuating you,
Never more shall I escape, never more the reverberations,
Never more the cries of unsatisfied love be absent from me,
Never again leave me to be the peaceful child I was before what there in
    the night,
By the sea under the yellow and sagging moon,   155
The messenger there aroused, the fire, the sweet hell within,
The unknown want, the destiny of me.

O give me the clue! (it lurks in the night here somewhere,)
O if I am to have so much, let me have more!

A word then, (for I will conquer it,)   160
The word final, superior to all,
Subtle, sent up – what is it? – I listen;
Are you whispering it, and have been all the time, you sea-waves?
Is that it from your liquid rims and wet sands?

Whereto answering, the sea,   165
Delaying not, hurrying not,
Whispered me through the night, and very plainly before daybreak,
Lisped to me the low and delicious word death,
And again death, death, death, death,
Hissing melodious, neither like the bird nor like my aroused child's
    heart,   170
But edging near as privately for me rustling at my feet,
Creeping thence steadily up to my ears and laving me softly all over
Death, death, death, death, death.

Which I do not forget,
But fuse the song of my dusky demon and brother,   175

That he sang to me in the moonlight on Paumanok's gray beach,
With the thousand responsive songs at random,
My own songs awaked from that hour,
And with them the key, the word up from the waves,
The word of the sweetest song and all songs,   180
That strong and delicious word which, creeping to my feet,
(Or like some old crone rocking the cradle, swathed in sweet garments,
    bending aside,)
The sea whispered me.

Walt Whitman (1819–1892)

QUESTIONS

1. The first twenty-two lines of the poem form a single sentence. What is its subject, its verb, its direct object? How do the various prepositional phrases with which the poem begins relate grammatically to this sentence? How do these first twenty-two lines relate to the rest of the poem?

2. Who is the speaker? What does his "reminiscence" (22) concern? What is the occasion for his reminiscence (lines 15–19)? Of what particular significance to his life was the incident he recounts (lines 11–13, 143, 146–157, 178)?

3. Are the following terms literal or metaphorical: "the cradle endlessly rocking" (1), "sad brother" (9), "the fierce old mother" (133), "old crone" (182)? What do they represent? Who is the "child" (4)? What is "the word stronger and more delicious than any" (14)? What are the "two feathered guests from Alabama" (26)? Who are the three chief "characters" of the poem – i.e., "the trio" (140)? (Read the whole poem before you answer.)

4. Paumanok (23) is the Indian name for Long Island, where Walt Whitman grew up. Does this knowledge help to identify the speaker? The word "demon" (144, 175), sometimes spelled *daemon,* does not have here its modern meaning of a devil or wicked spirit. Look it up in a good dictionary. What meanings are applicable? Does the bird become in any sense symbolical?

5. Where does the speaker's "reminiscence" begin? Where does it end? How much time is covered by the experience it relates? Why does the incident concerning the birds make such an impact on the speaker?

6. Why is the impact of the experience not complete for the speaker until the sea utters the word "death," and why is that word called "delicious" (168)? (To answer this question fully requires a knowledge of Whitman's other poetry, but hints are given here, as in line 20. Also, of what significance is it that the word is uttered by the sea, which is also referred to as a "mother" rocking a "cradle"? Does the sea have any symbolical value?)

7. This poem is written in free verse (without meter) and it also dispenses with rime. The line lengths vary from quite long to very short. Is it rhythmical or unrhythmical? What elements of order and patterning do you find in it? Examine lines 1–22, for instance, or lines 130–143. What generalizations can you make about how the lines begin? How they end? Can you find examples of alliteration and assonance in the poem? Of onomatopoeia or onomatopoetic effects?

8. Why are some sections of the poem printed in italics? How do they differ from the other sections? What purpose do the repetitions in these sections serve?

EXERCISES

In the following exercises, use both scales of poetic measurement – perfection and significance of accomplishment.

1. Considering such matters as economy and richness of poetic communication, inevitability of organization, and the complexity and maturity of the attitude or philosophy expressed, decide whether "Barter" (page 138) or "Stopping by Woods on a Snowy Evening (page 138) is the superior poem.

2. Which of the ballads "Sir Patrick Spens" (page 12) and "Edward" (page 230) is superior as judged by the power and complexity of its poetic achievement and the human significance of its result?

3. Rank the following short poems and explain the reasons for your ranking:
   a. "Scylla Toothless (page 112), "The Span of Life" (page 205).
   b. "Fog" (page 99), "In the Garden" (page 135), "The Death of the Ball Turret Gunner" (page 322).
   c. "The Coming of Wisdom with Time" (page 156), "The Turtle" (page 166), "Splinter" (page 201).
   d. "Wind and Silver" (page 100), "The Dark Hills" (page 213).

4. The following poems are all on seasons of the year. Rank them on a scale of poetic accomplishment: "Winter" (page 6), "To Autumn" (page 58), "Spring" (page 11).

5. "The Man He Killed" (page 21) and "Naming of Parts" (page 44) both treat the subject of war. Which is the superior poem?

6. "A Valediction: Forbidding Mourning" (page 74), "To Lucasta, Going to the Wars" (page 102), and "The 'Je Ne Sais Quoi' " (page 190) all in one way or another treat the subject of love. Evaluate and rank them.

7. Rank the following poems by Robert Browning in order of their excellence and defend your ranking: "Meeting at Night" and "Parting at Morning" (considered as one poem) (pages 51–52), "My Star" (page 82), "My Last Duchess" (page 119).

8. Bryant's "To a Waterfowl" and Frost's "Design" (pages 143–44) have a similar subject. Which is the greater poem? Why?

9. Herrick's "To the Virgins, to Make Much of Time" (page 88) and Marvell's "To His Coy Mistress" (page 75) are both *carpe diem* poems of acknowledged excellence. Which achieves the more complex unity?

10. Each of the following pairs is written by a single author. Pick the poem of each pair that you think represents the higher poetic accomplishment and explain why.

 a. "Nature the gentlest mother is" and "What mystery pervades a well!" (pages 141–42).

 b. "Virtue" (page 188), "A Wreath" (page 228).

 c. "When green buds hang in the elm" (page 43), "Eight O'Clock" (page 214).

 d. "Fire and Ice" (page 92), "Dust of Snow" (page 99).

 e. "Dover Beach" and "To Marguerite" (pages 280–82).

 f. "I gave myself to him" (page 27), "Heart! We will forget him!" (page 106).

 g. "Adam's Curse" and "Sailing to Byzantium" (pages 354–56).

 h. "Departmental" (page 116), "Mending Wall" (page 310).

 i. "All day I hear" (page 214), "I hear an army" (page 175).

 j. "Bereft" (page 62), "Acquainted with the Night" (page 309).

 k. "On moonlit heath and lonesome bank" (page 54), "Oh who is that young sinner" (page 193).

 l. "Stopping by Woods on a Snowy Evening" (page 138), "The Aim Was Song" (page 198).

 m. "I like to see it lap the miles" (page 209), "Because I could not stop for death" (page 302).

 n. "The Lamb" and "The Tiger" (pages 284–85).

 o. "Had I the Choice" (page 197), "A Noiseless Patient Spider" (page 349).

 p. "Pike" and "Wind" (pages 319–21).

II Poems for Further Reading

MORNING SONG FROM "SENLIN"

It is morning, Senlin says, and in the morning
When the light drips through the shutters like the dew,
I arise, I face the sunrise,
And do the things my fathers learned to do.
Stars in the purple dusk above the rooftops   5
Pale in a saffron mist and seem to die,
And I myself on a swiftly tilting planet
Stand before a glass and tie my tie.

Vine leaves tap my window,
Dew-drops sing to the garden stones,   10
The robin chirps in the chinaberry tree
Repeating three clear tones.

It is morning. I stand by the mirror
And tie my tie once more.
While waves far off in a pale rose twilight   15
Crash on a coral shore.
I stand by a mirror and comb my hair:
How small and white my face! —
The green earth tilts through a sphere of air
And bathes in a flame of space.   20

There are houses hanging above the stars
And stars hung under a sea.
And a sun far off in a shell of silence
Dapples my walls for me.

It is morning, Senlin says, and in the morning   25
Should I not pause in the light to remember god?
Upright and firm I stand on a star unstable,
He is immense and lonely as a cloud.
I will dedicate this moment before my mirror
To him alone, for him I will comb my hair.   30
Accept these humble offerings, cloud of silence!
I will think of you as I descend the stair.

Vine leaves tap my window,
The snail-track shines on the stones,
Dew-drops flash from the chinaberry tree   35
Repeating two clear tones.

It is morning, I awake from a bed of silence,
Shining I rise from the starless waters of sleep.
The walls are about me still as in the evening,
I am the same, and the same name still I keep.   40
The earth revolves with me, yet makes no motion,
The stars pale silently in a coral sky.
In a whistling void I stand before my mirror,
Unconcerned, and tie my tie.

There are horses neighing on far-off hills   45
Tossing their long white manes,
And mountains flash in the rose-white dusk,
Their shoulders black with rains.
It is morning. I stand by the mirror
And surprise my soul once more;   50
The blue air rushes above my ceiling,
There are suns beneath my floor.

. . . It is morning, Senlin says, I ascend from darkness
And depart on the winds of space for I know not where,
My watch is wound, a key is in my pocket,   55
And the sky is darkened as I descend the stair.

There are shadows across the windows, clouds in heaven,
And a god among the stars; and I will go
Thinking of him as I might think of daybreak
And humming a tune I know.   60

Vine leaves tap at the window,
Dew-drops sing to the garden stones,
The robin chirps in the chinaberry tree
Repeating three clear tones.

Conrad Aiken (b. 1889)

THE LAST WAR

The first country to die was normal in the evening,
Ate a good but plain dinner, chatted with some friends
Over a glass, and went to bed soon after ten;
And in the morning was found disfigured and dead.
   That was a lucky one.   5

At breakfast the others heard about it, and kept
Their eyes on their plates. Who was guilty? No one knew,
But by lunch-time three more would never eat again.
The rest appealed for frankness, quietly cocked their guns,
   Declared "This can't go on."   10

They were right. Only the strongest turned up for tea:
The old ones with the big estates hadn't survived
The slobbering blindfold violence of the afternoon.
One killer or many? Was it a gang, or all-against-all?
   Somebody must have known.   15

But each of them sat there watching the others, until
Night came and found them anxious to get it over.
Then the lights went out. A few might have lived, even then;
Innocent, they thought (at first) it still mattered what
   You had or hadn't done.   20

They were wrong. One had been lenient with his servants;
Another ran an island brothel, but rarely left it;
The third owned a museum, the fourth a remarkable gun;
The name of the fifth was quite unknown, but in the end
   What was the difference? None.   25

Homicide, pacifist, crusader, cynic, gentile, jew
Staggered about moaning, shooting into the dark.
Next day, to tidy up as usual, the sun came in
When they and their ammunition were all used up,
      And found himself alone.   30

Upset, he looked them over, to separate, if he could,
The assassins from the victims, but every face
Had taken on the flat anonymity of pain;
And soon they'll all smell alike, he thought, and felt sick,
      And went to bed at noon.   35

Kingsley Amis (b. 1922)

DOVER BEACH

The sea is calm tonight,
The tide is full, the moon lies fair
Upon the straits; – on the French coast the light
Gleams and is gone; the cliffs of England stand,
Glimmering and vast, out in the tranquil bay.   5
Come to the window, sweet is the night-air!
Only, from the long line of spray
Where the sea meets the moon-blanched land,
Listen! you hear the grating roar
Of pebbles which the waves draw back, and fling.   10
At their return, up the high strand,
Begin, and cease, and then again begin,
With tremulous cadence slow, and bring
The eternal note of sadness in.

Sophocles long ago   15
Heard it on the Aegean, and it brought
Into his mind the turbid ebb and flow
Of human misery; we
Find also in the sound a thought,
Hearing it by this distant northern sea.   20

The Sea of Faith
Was once, too, at the full, and round earth's shore

Lay like the folds of a bright girdle furled.
But now I only hear
Its melancholy, long, withdrawing roar,   25
Retreating, to the breath
Of the night-wind, down the vast edges drear
And naked shingles° of the world.   pebbled beaches

Ah, love, let us be true
To one another! for the world, which seems   30
To lie before us like a land of dreams,
So various, so beautiful, so new,
Hath really neither joy, nor love, nor light,
Nor certitude, nor peace, nor help for pain;
And we are here as on a darkling plain   35
Swept with confused alarms of struggle and flight,
Where ignorant armies clash by night.

Matthew Arnold (1822–1888)

TO MARGUERITE

Yes! in the sea of life enisled,
With echoing straits between us thrown,
Dotting the shoreless watery wild,
We mortal millions live *alone*.
The islands feel the enclasping flow   5
And then their endless bounds they know.

But when the moon their hollows lights,
And they are swept by balms of spring,
And in their glens, on starry nights,
The nightingales divinely sing;   10
And lovely notes, from shore to shore,
Across the sounds and channels pour –

Oh! then a longing like despair
Is to their farthest caverns sent;
For surely once, they feel, we were   15
Parts of a single continent!
Now round us spreads the watery plain –
Oh might our marges meet again!

Who ordered that their longing's fire
Should be, as soon as kindled, cooled? 20
Who renders vain their deep desire? –
A God, a God their severance ruled!
And bade betwixt their shores to be
The unplumbed, salt, estranging sea.

Matthew Arnold (1822–1888)

"O WHERE ARE YOU GOING?"

"O where are you going?" said reader to rider,
"That valley is fatal when furnaces burn,
Yonder's the midden whose odours will madden,
That gap is the grave where the tall return."

"O do you imagine," said fearer to farer, 5
"That dusk will delay on your path to the pass,
Your diligent looking discover the lacking
Your footsteps feel from granite to grass?"

"O what was that bird," said horror to hearer,
"Did you see that shape in the twisted trees? 10
Behind you swiftly the figure comes softly,
The spot on your skin is a shocking disease?"

"Out of this house" – said rider to reader,
"Yours never will" – said farer to fearer,
"They're looking for you" – said hearer to horror, 15
As he left them there, as he left them there.

W. H. Auden (1907–1973)

ON READING POEMS TO A SENIOR CLASS AT SOUTH HIGH

Before
I opened my mouth
I noticed them sitting there
as orderly as frozen fish
in a package. 5

Slowly water began to fill the room
though I did not notice it

till it reached
my ears

and then I heard the sounds   10
of fish in an aquarium

and I knew that though I had
tried to drown them
with my words
that they had only opened up   15
like gills for them
and let me in.

Together we swam around the room
like thirty tails whacking words
till the bell rang   20
puncturing
a hole in the door

where we all leaked out

They went to another class
I suppose and I home   25

where Queen Elizabeth
my cat met me
and licked my fins
till they were hands again.

D. C. Berry (b. 1947)

THE LITTLE BLACK BOY

My mother bore me in the southern wild,
And I am black, but O! my soul is white;
White as an angel is the English child:
But I am black, as if bereaved of light.

My mother taught me underneath a tree,   5
And sitting down before the heat of day,
She took me on her lap and kissèd me,
And pointing to the east, began to say:

"Look on the rising sun: there God does live,
And gives his light, and gives his heat away;   10

And flowers and trees and beasts and men receive
Comfort in morning, joy in the noon day.

"And we are put on earth a little space
That we may learn to bear the beams of love;
And these black bodies and this sunburnt face   15
Is but a cloud, and like a shady grove.

"For when our souls have learned the heat to bear,
The cloud will vanish; we shall hear his voice,
Saying: 'Come out from the grove, my love and care,
And round my golden tent like lambs rejoice.' "   20

Thus did my mother say, and kissèd me;
And thus I say to little English boy:
When I from black and he from white cloud free,
And round the tent of God like lambs we joy,

I'll shade him from the heat till he can bear   25
To lean in joy upon our father's knee;
And then I'll stand and stroke his silver hair,
And be like him, and he will then love me.

William Blake (1757–1827)

THE LAMB

    Little Lamb, who made thee?
    Dost thou know who made thee?
By the stream and o'er the mead;
Gave thee clothing of delight,   5
Softest clothing wooly bright;
Gave thee such a tender voice,
Making all the vales rejoice!
    Little Lamb, who made thee?
    Dost thou know who made thee?   10

    Little Lamb, I'll tell thee,
    Little Lamb, I'll tell thee!
He is callèd by thy name,
For he calls himself a Lamb;
He is meek and he is mild,   15
He became a little child;
I a child and thou a lamb,

We are callèd by his name.
    Little Lamb, God bless thee.
    Little Lamb, God bless thee.   20

William Blake (1757–1827)

THE TIGER

Tiger! Tiger! burning bright
In the forests of the night,
What immortal hand or eye
Could frame thy fearful symmetry?

In what distant deeps or skies   5
Burnt the fire of thine eyes?
On what wings dare he aspire?
What the hand dare seize the fire?

And what shoulder, and what art,
Could twist the sinews of thy heart?   10
And when thy heart began to beat,
What dread hand forged thy dread feet?

What the hammer? what the chain?
In what furnace was thy brain?
What the anvil? what dread grasp   15
Dare its deadly terrors clasp?

When the stars threw down their spears,
And watered heaven with their tears,
Did he smile his work to see?
Did he who made the Lamb make thee?   20

Tiger! Tiger! burning bright
In the forests of the night,
What immortal hand or eye,
Dare frame thy fearful symmetry?

William Blake (1757–1827)

THE GARDEN OF LOVE

I went to the Garden of Love,
And saw what I never had seen:
A Chapel was built in the midst,
Where I used to play on the green.

And the gates of this Chapel were shut,   5
And "Thou shalt not" writ over the door;
So I turned to the Garden of Love
That so many sweet flowers bore;

And I saw it was filled with graves,
And tomb-stones where flowers should be;   10
And Priests in black gowns were walking their rounds,
And binding with briars my joys and desires.

William Blake (1757–1827)

SOUTHERN MANSION

Poplars are standing there still as death
And ghosts of dead men
Meet their ladies walking
Two by two beneath the shade
And standing on the marble steps.   5

There is a sound of music echoing
Through the open door
And in the field there is
Another sound tinkling in the cotton:
Chains of bondmen dragging on the ground.   10

The years go back with an iron clank,
A hand is on the gate,
A dry leaf trembles on the wall.
Ghosts are walking.
They have broken roses down   15
And poplars stand there still as death.

Arna Bontemps (1902–1973)

PARANOIA

When you drive on the freeway, cars follow you.

Someone opens your mail, two hands
that come out of your shirt-sleeves.

Your dog looks at you, he does not like you.

At the driving test the cop is tired. He has sat up   5
all night, screening your dreams.

If you go to the zoo, be sure to take your passport.

Everywhere you go, the dog goes with you. Beautiful women
come up to you and ask for the dog's telephone number.

You go to teach; everyone who passes you in the corridor   10
knows you never finished *Tristram Shandy.*
You are the assistant professor no one associates with.

At the yoga class you finally get
into the lotus position.
You are carried home.   15

When you close your eyes in meditation, all you see is breasts.

When you turn the refrigerator to defrost, the TV drips.

Across the street, the pigeons call softly to each other
like the FBI on a stakeout.

When you walk to the post office and see the flag at half-mast   20
you know you have died.

Michael Dennis Browne (b. 1940)

ANDREA DEL SARTO
(Called "The Faultless Painter")

> But do not let us quarrel any more,
> No, my Lucrezia; bear with me for once:
> Sit down and all shall happen as you wish.

ANDREA DEL SARTO. Andrea del Sarto (1486–1531), a Florentine painter, was three years
younger than Raphael ("the Urbinate," line 105), eleven years younger than Michelangelo
("Agnolo," line 130), and thirty-four years younger than Leonardo da Vinci ("Leonard,"
line 263). In 1517 he married a widow, Lucrezia, and in 1518 was invited to France to paint
at the Court of Francis I, but stayed only a year, being pressed by Lucrezia to return to
Italy, where he misused funds entrusted him to buy art works for Francis, and bought
instead a house for Lucrezia. Browning got his facts for Andrea's life from *Lives of the
Painters* by George Vasari (106), a pupil of Andrea's. Andrea was of humble parentage,
the son of a tailor *(sarto),* hence called *del Sarto.*   15. *Fiesole:* suburb on a hill overlooking
Florence.   57. *cartoon:* a preliminary drawing for a painting.   93. *Morello:* mountain
north of Florence.

You turn your face, but does it bring your heart?
I'll work then for your friend's friend, never fear,   5
Treat his own subject after his own way,
Fix his own time, accept too his own price,
And shut the money into this small hand
When next it takes mine. Will it? tenderly?
Oh, I'll content him, – but to-morrow, Love!   10
I often am much wearier than you think,
This evening more than usual, and it seems
As if – forgive now – should you let me sit
Here by the window with your hand in mine
And look a half-hour forth on Fiesole,   15
Both of one mind, as married people use,
Quietly, quietly the evening through,
I might get up to-morrow to my work
Cheerful and fresh as ever. Let us try.
To-morrow, how you shall be glad for this!   20
Your soft hand is a woman of itself,
And mine the man's bared breast she curls inside.
Don't count the time lost, either; you must serve
For each of the five pictures we require:
It saves a model. So! keep looking so –   25
My serpentining beauty, rounds on rounds!
– How could you ever prick those perfect ears,
Even to put the pearl there! oh, so sweet –
My face, my moon, my everybody's moon,
Which everybody looks on and calls his,   30
And, I suppose, is looked on by in turn,
While she looks – no one's: very dear, no less.
You smile? why, there's my picture ready made,
There's what we painters call our harmony!
A common grayness silvers everything, –   35
All in a twilight, you and I alike
– You, at the point of your first pride in me
(That's gone you know), – but I, at every point;
My youth, my hope, my art, being all toned down
To yonder sober pleasant Fiesole.   40
There's the bell clinking from the chapel-top;
That length of convent-wall across the way
Holds the trees safer, huddled more inside;

The last monk leaves the garden; days decrease,
And autumn grows, autumn in everything.   45
Eh? the whole seems to fall into a shape
As if I saw alike my work and self
And all that I was born to be and do,
A twilight-piece. Love, we are in God's hand.
How strange now, looks the life he makes us lead;   50
So free we seem, so fettered fast we are!
I feel he laid the fetter: let it lie!
This chamber for example – turn your head –
All that's behind us! You don't understand
Nor care to understand about my art,   55
But you can hear at least when people speak:
And that cartoon, the second from the door
– It is the thing, Love! so such things should be –
Behold Madonna! – I am bold to say.
I can do with my pencil what I know,   60
What I see, what at bottom of my heart
I wish for, if I ever wish so deep –
Do easily, too – when I say, perfectly,
I do not boast, perhaps: yourself are judge
Who listened to the Legate's talk last week,   65
And just as much they used to say in France.
At any rate 'tis easy, all of it!
No sketches first, no studies, that's long past:
I do what many dream of all their lives
– Dream? strive to do, and agonize to do,   70
And fail in doing. I could count twenty such
On twice your fingers, and not leave this town,
Who strive – you don't know how the others strive
To paint a little thing like that you smeared
Carelessly passing with your robes afloat, –   75
Yet do much less, so much less, Someone says,
(I know his name, no matter) – so much less!
Well, less is more, Lucrezia: I am judged.
There burns a truer light of God in them,
In their vexed beating stuffed and stopped-up brain,   80
Heart, or whate'er else, than goes on to prompt
This low-pulsed forthright craftman's hand of mine.
Their works drop groundward, but themselves, I know,

Reach many a time a heaven that's shut to me,
Enter and take their place there sure enough,   85
Though they come back and cannot tell the world.
My works are nearer heaven, but I sit here.
The sudden blood of these men! at a word—
Praise them, it boils, or blame them, it boils too.
I, painting from myself and to myself,   90
Know what I do, am unmoved by men's blame
Or their praise either. Somebody remarks
Morello's outline there is wrongly traced,
His hue mistaken; what of that? or else,
Rightly traced and well ordered; what of that?   95
Speak as they please, what does the mountain care?
Ah, but a man's reach should exceed his grasp,
Or what's a heaven for? All is silver-gray
Placid and perfect with my art: the worse!
I know both what I want and what might gain;   100
And yet how profitless to know, to sigh
"Had I been two, another and myself,
Our head would have o'erlooked the world!" No doubt.
Yonder's a work now, of that famous youth
The Urbinate who died five years ago.   105
('Tis copied, George Vasari sent it me.)
Well, I can fancy how he did it all,
Pouring his soul, with kings and popes to see,
Reaching, that heaven might so replenish him,
Above and through his art—for it gives way;   110
That arm is wrongly put—and there again—
A fault to pardon in the drawing's lines,
Its body, so to speak: its soul is right,
He means right—that, a child may understand.
Still, what an arm! and I could alter it: 115
But all the play, the insight and the stretch—
Out of me, out of me! And wherefore out?
Had you enjoined them on me, given me soul,
We might have risen to Rafael, I and you!
Nay, Love, you did give all I asked, I think—   120
More than I merit, yes, by many times.
But had you—oh, with the same perfect brow,
And perfect eyes, and more than perfect mouth,

And the low voice my soul hears, as a bird
The fowler's pipe, and follows to the snare –   125
Had you, with these the same, but brought a mind!
Some women do so. Had the mouth there urged
"God and the glory! never care for gain.
The present by the future, what is that?
Live for fame, side by side with Agnolo!   130
Rafael is waiting: up to God, all three!"
I might have done it for you. So it seems:
Perhaps not. All is as God overrules.
Beside, incentives come from the soul's self;
The rest avail not. Why do I need you?   135
What wife had Rafael, or has Agnolo?
In this world, who can do a thing, will not;
And who would do it, cannot, I perceive:
Yet the will's somewhat – somewhat, too, the power –
And thus we half-men struggle. At the end,   140
God, I conclude, compensates, punishes.
'Tis safer for me, if the award be strict,
That I am something underrated here,
Poor this long while, despised, to speak the truth.
I dared not, do you know, leave home all day,   145
For fear of chancing on the Paris lords.
The best is when they pass and look aside;
But they speak sometimes; I must bear it all.
Well may they speak! That Francis, that first time,
And that long festal year at Fontainebleau!   150
I surely then could sometimes leave the ground,
Put on the glory, Rafael's daily wear,
In that humane great monarch's golden look, –
One finger in his beard or twisted curl
Over his mouth's good mark that made the smile,   155
One arm about my shoulder, round my neck,
The jingle of his gold chain in my ear,
I painting proudly with his breath on me,
All his court round him, seeing with his eyes,
Such frank French eyes, and such a fire of souls   160
Profuse, my hand kept plying by those hearts, –
And, best of all, this, this, this face beyond,
This in the background, waiting on my work,

To crown the issue with a last reward!
A good time, was it not, my kingly days?   165
And had you not grown restless . . . but I know –
'Tis done and past; 'twas right, my instinct said;
Too live the life grew, golden and not gray,
And I'm the weak-eyed bat no sun should tempt
Out of the grange whose four walls make his world.   170
How could it end in any other way?
You called me, and I came home to your heart.
The triumph was, – to reach and stay there; since
I reached it ere the triumph, what is lost?
Let my hands frame your face in your hair's gold,   175
You beautiful Lucrezia that are mine!
"Rafael did this, Andrea painted that;
The Roman's is the better when you pray,
But still the other's Virgin was his wife" –
Men will excuse me. I am glad to judge   180
Both pictures in your presence; clearer grows
My better fortune, I resolve to think.
For, do you know, Lucrezia, as God lives,
Said one day Agnolo, his very self,
To Rafael . . . I have known it all these years . . .   185
(When the young man was flaming out his thoughts
Upon a palace-wall for Rome to see,
Too lifted up in heart because of it),
"Friend, there's a certain sorry little scrub
Goes up and down our Florence, none cares how,   190
Who, were he set to plan and execute
As you are, pricked on by your popes and kings,
Would bring the sweat into that brow of yours!"
To Rafael's! – And indeed the arm is wrong.
I hardly dare . . . yet, only you to see,   195
Give the chalk here – quick, thus the line should go!
Ay, but the soul! he's Rafael! rub it out!
Still, all I care for, if he spoke the truth,
(What he? why, who but Michel Agnolo?
Do you forget already words like those?)   200
If really there was such a chance, so lost, –
Is, whether you're – not grateful – but more pleased.
Well, let me think so. And you smile indeed!

This hour has been an hour! Another smile?
If you would sit thus by me every night   205
I should work better, do you comprehend?
I mean that I should earn more, give you more.
See, it is settled dusk now; there's a star;
Morello's gone, the watch-lights show the wall,
The cue-owls speak the name we call them by.   210
Come from the window, love, – come in, at last
Inside the melancholy little house
We built to be so gay with. God is just.
King Francis may forgive me: oft at nights
When I look up from painting, eyes tired out,   215
The walls become illumined, brick from brick
Distinct, instead of mortar, fierce bright gold,
That gold of his I did cement them with!
Let us but love each other. Must you go?
That Cousin here again? he waits outside?   220
Must see you – you, and not with me? Those loans?
More gaming debts to pay? you smiled for that?
Well, let smiles buy me! have you more to spend?
While hand and eye and something of a heart
Are left me, work's my ware, and what's it worth?   225
I'll pay my fancy. Only let me sit
The gray remainder of the evening out,
Idle, you call it, and muse perfectly
How I could paint, were I but back in France,
One picture, just one more – the Virgin's face,   230
Not yours this time! I want you at my side
To hear them – that is, Michel Agnolo –
Judge all I do and tell you of its worth.
Will you? To-morrow, satisfy your friend.
I take the subjects for his corridor,   235
Finish the portrait out of hand – there, there,
And throw him in another thing or two
If he demurs; the whole should prove enough
To pay for this same Cousin's freak. Beside,
What's better and what's all I care about,   240
Get you the thirteen scudi for the ruff!
Love, does that please you? Ah, but what does he,
The Cousin! what does he to please you more?

I am grown peaceful as old age to-night.
I regret little, I would change still less.   245
Since there my past life lies, why alter it?
The very wrong to Francis! – it is true
I took his coin, was tempted and complied,
And built this house and sinned, and all is said.
My father and my mother died of want.   250
Well, had I riches of my own? you see
How one gets rich! Let each one bear his lot.
They were born poor, lived poor, and poor they died:
And I have labored somewhat in my time
And not been paid profusely. Some good son   255
Paint my two hundred pictures – let him try!
No doubt, there's something strikes a balance. Yes,
You loved me quite enough, it seems to-night.
This must suffice me here. What would one have?
In heaven, perhaps, new chances, one more chance –   260
Four great walls in the New Jerusalem
Meted on each side by the angel's reed,
For Leonard, Rafael, Agnolo and me
To cover – the three first without a wife,
While I have mine! So – still they overcome   265
Because there's still Lucrezia, – as I choose.

Again the Cousin's whistle! Go, my Love.

Robert Browning (1812–1889)

THE SCIENTIST

"There's nothing mysterious about the skull."
He may have been suspicious of my request,
That being mainly a poet, I mainly guessed
There might be an esoteric chance to cull

Some succulent, unfamiliar word; that being   5
Mainly a woman, I now for his sake embraced
An object I held in fact in some distaste.
But he complied, his slender fingers freeing

(There must be a surgeon somewhere with stubby hands)
The latch that held a coil across "The suture   10

Between the parietals and occipital feature."
And gently, his flesh on the bone disturbed the bands

Which illustrated the way that "The mandible
Articulates with the temple next to the ear.
The nasal bone gives onto the maxilla here."   15
He laughed, "It's a bore, but it's not expendable;

"The features depend, if not for their shape, on the narrow
Cranium, formed of the commonest elements;
Weighing nine ounces, worth about fourteen cents;
Not even room for what you would call a marrow."   20

In words resembling these, he judged them dull;
The specimen, his detail, and my suggestion.
"The skin and the brain, of course, are another question,"
He said again, "but there's nothing to the skull."

And that must be so. The quick mind most demands a   25
Miracle in the covering or the core.
What lies between is shallow and functional fare:
My hand between this thought and the posturing stanza.

But his face belied us both. As he spoke his own
Eyes rhymed depth from the sockets of that example;   30
His jawline articulated with the temple
Over the words, and his fingers along the bone

Revealed his god in the praying of their plying.
So that, wonderfully, I justify his doubt:
Am moved, as woman to love, as poet to write,   35
By the mystery and the function of his denying.

Janet Burroway (b. 1936)

BADGER

When midnight comes a host of dogs and men
Go out and track the badger to his den,
And put a sack within the hole, and lie
Till the old grunting badger passes by.

He comes and hears – they let the strongest loose.   5
The old fox hears the noise and drops the goose.
The poacher shoots and hurries from the cry,
And the old hare half wounded buzzes by.
They get a forked stick to bear him down
And clap the dogs and take him to the town,   10
And bait him all the day with many dogs,
And laugh and shout and fright the scampering hogs.
He runs along and bites at all he meets:
They shout and hollo down the noisy streets.

He turns about to face the loud uproar   15
And drives the rebels to their very door.
The frequent stone is hurled where'er they go;
When badgers fight, then everyone's a foe.
The dogs are clapped and urged to join the fray;
The badger turns and drives them all away.   20
Though scarcely half as big, demure and small,
He fights with dogs for hours and beats them all.
The heavy mastiff, savage in the fray,
Lies down and licks his feet and turns away.
The bulldog knows his match and waxes cold,   25
The badger grins and never leaves his hold.
He drives the crowd and follows at their heels
And bites them through – the drunkard swears and reels.

The frighted women take the boys away,
The blackguard laughs and hurries on the fray.   30
He tries to reach the woods, an awkward race,
But sticks and cudgels quickly stop the chase.
He turns again and drives the noisy crowd
And beats the many dogs in noises loud.
He drives away and beats them every one,   35
And then they loose them all and set them on.
He falls as dead and kicked by dogs and men,
Then starts and grins and drives the crowd again;
Till kicked and torn and beaten out he lies
And leaves his hold and cackles, groans, and dies.   40

John Clare (1793–1864)

GOOD TIMES

My Daddy has paid the rent
and the insurance man is gone
and the lights is back on
and my uncle Brud has hit
for one dollar straight   5
and they is good times
good times
good times

My Mama has made bread
and Grampaw has come   10
and everybody is drunk
and dancing in the kitchen
and singing in the kitchen
oh these is good times
good times   15
good times

oh children think about the
good times

Lucille Clifton (b. 1936)

KUBLA KHAN

In Xanadu did Kubla Khan
A stately pleasure-dome decree:
Where Alph, the sacred river, ran
Through caverns measureless to man
    Down to a sunless sea.   5
So twice five miles of fertile ground
With walls and towers were girdled round:
And here were gardens bright with sinuous rills,
Where blossomed many an incense-bearing tree;
And here were forests ancient as the hills,   10
Enfolding sunny spots of greenery.

But oh! that deep romantic chasm which slanted
Down the green hill athwart a cedarn cover!

A savage place! as holy and enchanted
As e'er beneath a waning moon was haunted   15
By woman wailing for her demon-lover!
And from this chasm, with ceaseless turmoil seething,
As if this earth in fast thick pants were breathing,
A mighty fountain momently was forced:
Amid whose swift half-intermitted burst   20
Huge fragments vaulted like rebounding hail,
Or chaffy grain beneath the thresher's flail:
And 'mid these dancing rocks at once and ever
It flung up momently the sacred river.
Five miles meandering with a mazy motion   25
Through wood and dale the sacred river ran,
Then reached the caverns measureless to man,
And sank in tumult to a lifeless ocean:
And 'mid this tumult Kubla heard from far
Ancestral voices prophesying war!   30

    The shadow of the dome of pleasure
    Floated midway on the waves;
    Where was heard the mingled measure
    From the fountain and the caves.
It was a miracle of rare device,   35
A sunny pleasure-dome with caves of ice!

    A damsel with a dulcimer
    In a vision once I saw:
    It was an Abyssinian maid,
    And on her dulcimer she played,   40
    Singing of Mount Abora.
    Could I revive within me
    Her symphony and song,
    To such a deep delight, 'twould win me,
    That with music loud and long,   45
    I would build that dome in air,
    That sunny dome! those caves of ice!
    And all who heard should see them there,
    And all should cry, Beware! Beware!
    His flashing eyes, his floating hair!   50
    Weave a circle round him thrice,

And close your eyes with holy dread,
For he on honey-dew hath fed,
And drunk the milk of Paradise.

Samuel Taylor Coleridge (1772–1834)

SONG

Pious Selinda goes to prayers
    If I but ask the favor,
And yet the tender fool's in tears
    When she believes I'll leave her.

Would I were free from this restraint,
    Or else had hopes to win her;
Would she could make of me a saint,
    Or I of her a sinner.

William Congreve (1670–1729)

THE LISTENERS

"Is there anybody there?" said the Traveller,
    Knocking on the moonlit door;
And his horse in the silence champed the grasses
    Of the forest's ferny floor:
And a bird flew up out of the turret,   5
    Above the Traveller's head:
And he smote upon the door again a second time;
    "Is there anybody there?" he said.
But no one descended to the Traveller;
    No head from the leaf-fringed sill   10
Leaned over and looked into his grey eyes,
    Where he stood perplexed and still.
But only a host of phantom listeners
    That dwelt in the lone house then
Stood listening in the quiet of the moonlight   15
    To that voice from the world of men:
Stood thronging the faint moonbeams on the dark stair,
    That goes down to the empty hall,
Hearkening in an air stirred and shaken

By the lonely Traveller's call. 20
And he felt in his heart their strangeness,
    Their stillness answering his cry,
While his horse moved, cropping the dark turf,
    'Neath the starred and leafy sky;
For he suddenly smote on the door, even 25
    Louder, and lifted his head: –
"Tell them I came, and no one answered,
    That I kept my word," he said.
Never the least stir made the listeners,
    Though every word he spake 30
Fell echoing through the shadowiness of the still house
    From the one man left awake:
Ay, they heard his foot upon the stirrup,
    And the sound of iron on stone,
And how the silence surged softly backward, 35
    When the plunging hoofs were gone.

Walter de la Mare (1873–1956)

THE BEE

To the football coaches of Clemson College, 1942

One dot
Grainily shifting   we at roadside and
The smallest wings coming   along the rail fence out
Of the woods   one dot   of all that green. It now
Becomes flesh-crawling   then the quite still 5
Of stinging. I must live faster for my terrified
Small son   it is on him. Has come. Clings.

Old wingback, come
To life. If your knee action is high
Enough, the fat may fall in time   God damn 10
You, Dickey, *dig*   this is your last time to cut
And run   but you must give it everything you have
Left, for screaming near your screaming child is the sheer
Murder of California traffic: some bee hangs driving

Your child 15
Blindly onto the highway. Get there however

Is still possible. Long live what I badly did
At Clemson   and all of my clumsiest drives
For the ball   all of my trying to turn
The corner downfield   and my spindling explosions   20
Through the five-hole over tackle. O backfield

Coach Shag Norton,
Tell me as you never yet have told me
To get the lead out   scream whatever will get
The slow-motion of middle age off me   I cannot   25
Make it this way   I will have to leave
My feet   they are gone   I have him where
He lives   and down we go singing with screams into

The dirt,
Son-screams of fathers   screams of dead coaches turning   30
To approval   and from between us the bee rises screaming
With flight   grainily shifting   riding the rail fence
Back into the woods   traffic blasting past us
Unchanged, nothing heard through the air-
conditioning glass   we lying at roadside full   35

Of the forearm prints
Of roadrocks   strawberries on our elbows as from
Scrimmage with the varsity   now we can get
Up   stand   turn away from the highway   look straight
Into trees. See, there is nothing coming out   no   40
Smallest wing   no shift of a flight-grain   nothing
Nothing. Let us go in, son, and listen

For some tobacco-
mumbling voice in the branches   to say "That's
a little better,"   to our lives still hanging   45
By a hair. There is nothing to stop us   we can go
Deep   deeper   into elms, and listen to traffic die
Roaring, like a football crowd from which we have
Vanished. Dead coaches live in the air, son   live

In the ear   50
Like fathers, and *urge*   and *urge*. They want you better
Than you are. When needed, they rise and curse you   they scream
When something must be saved. Here, under this tree,

We can sit down. You can sleep, and I can try
To give back what I have earned by keeping us   55
Alive, and safe from bees: the smile of some kind

Of savior –
Of touchdowns, of fumbles, battles,
Lives. Let me sit here with you, son
As on the bench, while the first string takes back   60
Over, far away   and say with my silentest tongue, with the man-
creating bruises of my arms   with a live leaf a quick
Dead hand on my shoulder, "Coach Norton, I am your boy."

James Dickey (b. 1923)

BECAUSE I COULD NOT STOP FOR DEATH

Because I could not stop for Death,
He kindly stopped for me;
The carriage held but just ourselves
And Immortality.

We slowly drove; he knew no haste,   5
And I had put away
My labor and my leisure too,
For his civility.

We passed the school, where children strove,
At recess, in the ring,   10
We passed the fields of gazing grain,
We passed the setting sun,

Or rather, he passed us;
The dews drew quivering and chill;
For only gossamer, my gown;   15
My tippet, only tulle.
We paused before a house that seemed
A swelling of the ground;
The roof was scarcely visible.
The cornice, in the ground.   20

Since then, 'tis centuries, and yet
Feels shorter than the day

I first surmised the horses' heads
Were toward eternity.

Emily Dickinson (1830–1886)

I TASTE A LIQUOR NEVER BREWED

I taste a liquor never brewed,
From tankards scooped in pearl;
Not all the vats upon the Rhine
Yield such an alcohol!

Inebriate of air am I,   5
And debauchee of dew,
Reeling, through endless summer days,
From inns of molten blue.

When landlords turn the drunken bee
Out of the foxglove's door,   10
When butterflies renounce their drams,
I shall but drink the more!

Till seraphs swing their snowy hats,
And saints to windows run,
To see the little tippler   15
Leaning against the sun!

Emily Dickinson (1830–1886)

SONG: GO AND CATCH A FALLING STAR

Go and catch a falling star,
     Get with child a mandrake root,
Tell me where all past years are,
     Or who cleft the devil's foot,
Teach me to hear mermaids singing,   5
     Or to keep off envy's stinging,
               And find
               What wind
Serves to advance an honest mind.

SONG: 2. *mandrake:* supposed to resemble a human being because of its forked root.

If thou be'st born to strange sights,   10
    Things invisible to see,
Ride ten thousand days and nights,
    Till age snow white hairs on thee,
Thou, when thou return'st, wilt tell me
    All strange wonders that befell thee,   15
        And swear
        No where
Lives a woman true and fair.

If thou find'st one, let me know;
    Such a pilgrimage were sweet.   20
Yet do not; I would not go,
    Though at next door we might meet.
Though she were true when you met her,
    And last till you write your letter,
        Yet she   25
        Will be
False, ere I come, to two or three.

John Donne (1572–1631)

THE FLEA

Mark but this flea, and mark in this
How little that which thou deny'st me is;
It sucked me first, and now sucks thee,
And in this flea our two bloods mingled be;
Thou know'st that this cannot be said   5
A sin, nor shame, nor loss of maidenhead;
    Yet this enjoys before it woo,
    And pampered swells with one blood made of two,
    And this, alas, is more than we would do.

Oh stay, three lives in one flea spare,   10
Where we almost, yea more than married are.
This flea is you and I, and this
Our marriage bed, and marriage temple is;
Though parents grudge, and you, we are met
And cloistered in these living walls of jet.   15
    Though use make you apt to kill me,
    Let not to that, self-murder added be,
    And sacrilege, three sins in killing three.

Cruel and sudden, hast thou since
Purpled thy nail in blood of innocence?   20
Wherein could this flea guilty be,
Except in that drop which it sucked from thee?
Yet thou triumph'st and say'st that thou
Find'st not thyself, nor me the weaker now.
   'Tis true. Then learn how false fears be: 25
   Just so much honor, when thou yield'st to me,
   Will waste, as this flea's death took life from thee.

John Donne (1572 – 1631)

THE GOOD-MORROW

I wonder, by my troth, what thou and I
Did till we loved? were we not weaned till then,
But sucked on country pleasures childishly?
Or snorted we in the seven sleepers' den?
'Twas so; but this, all pleasures fancies be.   5
If ever any beauty I did see,
Which I desired, and got, 'twas but a dream of thee.

And now good-morrow to our waking souls,
Which watch not one another out of fear;
For love all love of other sights controls,   10
And makes one little room an everywhere.
Let sea-discoverers to new worlds have gone;
Let maps to other,° worlds on worlds have shown;   others
Let us possess one world; each hath one, and is one.

My face in thine eye, thine in mine appears,   15
And true plain hearts do in the faces rest;
Where can we find two better hemispheres
Without sharp north, without declining west?
Whatever dies was not mixed equally;
If our two loves be one, or thou and I   20
Love so alike that none can slacken, none can die.

John Donne (1572–1631)

THE GOOD-MORROW.   4. *seven sleepers' den:* a cave where, according to Christian legend, seven youths escaped persecution and slept for two centuries.

THE SUN RISING

Busy old fool, unruly Sun,
    Why dost thou thus
Through windows and through curtains call on us?
Must to thy motions lovers' seasons run?
    Saucy pedantic wretch, go chide   5
    Late schoolboys and sour prentices,
  Go tell court-huntsmen that the king will ride,
  Call country ants to harvest offices;
Love, all alike, no season knows, nor clime,
Nor hours, days, months, which are the rags of time.   10

    Thy beams so reverend and strong
    Why shouldst thou think?
I could eclipse and cloud them with a wink,
But that I would not lose her sight so long;
    If her eyes have not blinded thine,   15
    Look, and tomorrow late tell me,
  Whether both th' Indias of spice and mine
  Be where thou left'st them, or lie here with me.
Ask for those kings whom thou saw'st yesterday,
And thou shalt hear, "All here in one bed lay."   20

    She's all states, and all princes I;
    Nothing else is.
Princes do but play us; compared to this,
All honor's mimic, all wealth alchemy.
    Thou, Sun, art half as happy as we,   25
    In that the world's contracted thus;
  Thine age asks ease, and since thy duties be
  To warm the world, that's done in warming us.
Shine here to us, and thou art everywhere;
This bed thy center is, these walls thy sphere.   30

John Donne (1572–1631)

VERGISSMEINICHT

Three weeks gone and the combatants gone,
returning over the nightmare ground
we found the place again, and found
the soldier sprawling in the sun.

The frowning barrel of his gun   5
overshadowing. As we came on
that day, he hit my tank with one
like the entry of a demon.

Look. Here in the gunpit spoil
the dishonored picture of his girl   10
who has put: *Steffi.° Vergissmeinicht*   a girl's name
in a copybook gothic script.

We see him almost with content
abased, and seeming to have paid
and mocked at by his own equipment   15
that's hard and good when he's decayed.

But she would weep to see to-day
how on his skin the swart flies move;
the dust upon the paper eye
and the burst stomach like a cave.   20

For here the lover and killer are mingled
who had one body and one heart.
And death who had the soldier singled
has done the lover mortal hurt.

Keith Douglas (1920–1944)

ON HEARING THE AIRLINES WILL USE A PSYCHOLOGICAL PROFILE TO CATCH POTENTIAL SKYJACKERS

They will catch me
as sure as the checkout girls
in every Woolworth's have caught me, the badge
of my imagined theft shining in their eyes.

I will be approaching the ticket counter   5
and knowing myself, myselves,
will effect the nonchalance of a baron.
That is what they'll be looking for.

I'll say "Certainly is nice that the
airlines are taking these precautions,"   10

VERGISSMEINICHT. The German title means "Forget me not." The author, an English
poet, fought with a tank battalion in World War II and was killed in the invasion of
Normandy.

and the man behind the counter
will press a secret button,

there'll be a hand on my shoulder
(this will have happened before in a dream),
and in a back room they'll ask me   15
"Why were you going to do it?"

I'll say "You wouldn't believe
I just wanted to get to Cleveland?"
"No," they'll say.
So I'll tell them everything,   20

the plot to get the Pulitzer Prize
in exchange for the airplane,
the bomb in my pencil,
heroin in the heel of my boot.

Inevitably, it'll be downtown for booking,   25
newsmen pumping me for deprivation
during childhood,
the essential cause.

"There is no one cause for any human act,"
I'll tell them, thinking *finally,*   30
a chance to let the public in
on the themes of great literature.

And on and on, celebrating myself, offering
no resistance, assuming what they assume,
knowing, in a sense, there is no such thing   35
as the wrong man.

Stephen Dunn (b. 1939)

BROADMINDED

Some of my best friends are white boys.
When I meet 'em,
I treat 'em
just the same as if they was people.

Ray Durem (1915–1963)

CONSTANTLY RISKING ABSURDITY

Constantly risking absurdity
                and death
        whenever he performs
                above the heads
                      of his audience   5
the poet like an acrobat
          climbs on rime
              to a high wire of his own making
and balancing on eyebeams
            above a sea of faces   10
      paces his way
           to the other side of day
performing entrechats
          and slight-of-foot tricks
and other high theatrics   15
          and all without mistaking
     any thing
          for what it may not be
For he's the super realist
          who must perforce perceive   20
     taut truth
         before the taking of each stance or step
in his supposed advance
         toward that still higher perch
where Beauty stands and waits   25
        with gravity
          to start her death-defying leap
     And he
    a little charleychaplin man
          who may or may not catch   30
her fair eternal form
         spreadeagled in the empty air
    of existence

                    Lawrence Ferlinghetti (b. 1919)

ACQUAINTED WITH THE NIGHT

I have been one acquainted with the night.
I have walked out in rain – and back in rain.
I have outwalked the furthest city light.

I have looked down the saddest city lane.
I have passed by the watchman on his beat   5
And dropped my eyes, unwilling to explain.

I have stood still and stopped the sound of feet
When far away an interrupted cry
Came over houses from another street,

But not to call me back or say good-by;   10
And further still at an unearthly height
One luminary clock against the sky

Proclaimed the time was neither wrong nor right.
I have been one acquainted with the night.

Robert Frost (1874–1963)

MENDING WALL

Something there is that doesn't love a wall,
That sends the frozen-ground-swell under it
And spills the upper boulders in the sun,
And makes gaps even two can pass abreast.
The work of hunters is another thing: 5
I have come after them and made repair
Where they have left not one stone on a stone,
But they would have the rabbit out of hiding,
To please the yelping dogs. The gaps I mean,
No one has seen them made or heard them made,   10
But at spring mending-time we find them there.
I let my neighbor know beyond the hill;
And on a day we meet to walk the line
And set the wall between us once again.
We keep the wall between us as we go.   15
To each the boulders that have fallen to each.
And some are loaves and some so nearly balls
We have to use a spell to make them balance:
"Stay where you are until our backs are turned!"
We wear our fingers rough with handling them.   20
Oh, just another kind of outdoor game,
One on a side. It comes to little more:
There where it is we do not need the wall:
He is all pine and I am apple orchard.

My apple trees will never get across   25
And eat the cones under his pines, I tell him.
He only says, "Good fences make good neighbors."
Spring is the mischief in me, and I wonder
If I could put a notion in his head:
"*Why* do they make good neighbors? Isn't it   30
Where there are cows? But here there are no cows.
Before I built a wall I'd ask to know
What I was walling in or walling out,
And to whom I was like to give offense.
Something there is that doesn't love a wall,   35
That wants it down." I could say "Elves" to him,
But it's not elves exactly, and I'd rather
He said it for himself. I see him there,
Bringing a stone grasped firmly by the top
In each hand, like an old-stone savage armed.   40
He moves in darkness as it seems to me,
Not of woods only and the shade of trees.
He will not go behind his father's saying,
And he likes having thought of it so well
He says again, "Good fences make good neighbors."   45

Robert Frost (1874–1963)

CONSIDERING THE SNAIL

The snail pushes through a green
night, for the grass is heavy
with water and meets over
the bright path he makes, where rain
has darkened the earth's dark. He   5
moves in a wood of desire,

pale antlers barely stirring
as he hunts. I cannot tell
what power is at work, drenched there
with purpose, knowing nothing.   10
What is a snail's fury? All
I think is that if later

I parted the blades above
the tunnel and saw the thin

trail of broken white across   15
litter, I would never have
imagined the slow passion
to that deliberate progress.

Thom Gunn (b. 1929)

DEAR GOD, THE DAY IS GREY

Dear God, the day is grey. My house
is not in order. Lord, the dust
sifts through my rooms and with my fear,
I sweep mortality, outwear
my brooms, but not this leaning floor   5
which lasts and groans. I, walking here,
still loathe the labors I would love
and hate the self I cannot move.

And God, I know the unshined boards,
the flaking ceiling, various stains   10
that mottle these distempered goods,
the greasy cloths, the jagged tins,
the dog that paws the garbage cans.
I know what laborings, love, and pains,
my blood would will, yet will not give: 15
the knot of hair that clogs the drains
clots in my throat. My dyings thrive.

The refuse, Lord, that I put out
burns in vast pits incessantly.
All piecemeal deaths, trash, undevout   20
and sullen sacrifice, to thee.

Anne Halley (b. 1928)

THE DARKLING THRUSH

I leant upon a coppice gate
    When Frost was specter-gray,
And Winter's dregs made desolate
    The weakening eye of day.
The tangled bine-stems scored the sky   5
    Like strings of broken lyres,
And all mankind that haunted nigh
    Had sought their household fires.

The land's sharp features seemed to be
    the Century's corpse outleant,   10
His crypt the cloudy canopy,
    The wind his death-lament.
The ancient pulse of germ and birth
    Was shrunken hard and dry,
And every spirit upon earth   15
    Seemed fervorless as I.

At once a voice arose among
    The bleak twigs overhead
In a full-hearted evensong
    Of joy illimited;   20
An aged thrush, frail, gaunt, and small,
    In blast-beruffled plume,
Had chosen thus to fling his soul
    Upon the growing gloom.

So little cause for carolings   25
    Of such ecstatic sound
Was written on terrestrial things
    Afar or nigh around,
That I could think there trembled through
    His happy good-night air   30
Some blessed Hope, whereof he knew
    And I was unaware.

December 1900.

Thomas Hardy (1840–1928)

CHANNEL FIRING

That night your great guns, unawares,
Shook all our coffins as we lay,
And broke the chancel window-squares,
We thought it was the Judgment-day

CHANNEL FIRING. 35–36. *Stourton Tower:* memorial at the spot where Alfred the Great resisted the invading Danes in 879; *Camelot:* legendary capital of Arthur's kingdom; *Stonehenge:* mysterious circle of huge stones erected in Wiltshire by very early inhabitants of Britain. The three references move backward in time through the historic, the legendary, and the prehistoric.

And sat upright. While drearisome   5
Arose the howl of wakened hounds:
The mouse let fall the altar-crumb,
The worms drew back into the mounds,

The glebe cow drooled. Till God called, "No;
It's gunnery practice out at sea   10
Just as before you went below;
The world is as it used to be:

"All nations striving strong to make
Red war yet redder. Mad as hatters
They do no more for Christès sake   15
Than you who are helpless in such matters.

"That this is not the judgment-hour
For some of them's a blessed thing,
For if it were they'd have to scour
Hell's floor for so much threatening. . . .   20

"Ha, ha. It will be warmer when
I blow the trumpet (if indeed
I ever do; for you are men,
and rest eternal sorely need)."

So down we lay again. "I wonder,   25
Will the world ever saner be,"
Said one, "than when He sent us under
In our indifferent century!"

And many a skeleton shook his head.
"Instead of preaching forty year,   30
My neighbor Parson Thirdly said,
"I wish I had stuck to pipes and beer."

Again the guns disturbed the hour,
Roaring their readiness to avenge,
As far inland as Stourton Tower,   35
And Camelot, and starlit Stonehenge.

Thomas Hardy (1840–1928)

THE WIFE'S TALE

When I had spread it all on linen cloth
Under the hedge, I called them over.
The hum and gulp of the thresher ran down
And the big belt slewed to a standstill, straw
Hanging undelivered in the jaws.   5
There was such quiet that I heard their boots
Crunching the stubble twenty yards away.

He lay down and said "Give these fellows theirs.
I'm in no hurry," plucking grass in handfuls
And tossing it in the air. "That looks well."   10
(He nodded at my white cloth on the grass.)
"I declare a woman could lay out a field
Though boys like us have little call for cloths."
He winked, then watched me as I poured a cup
And buttered the thick slices that he likes.   15
"It's threshing better than I thought, and mind
It's good clean seed. Away over there and look."
Always this inspection has to be made
Even when I don't know what to look for.

But I ran my hand in the half-filled bags   20
Hooked to the slots. It was hard as shot,
Innumerable and cool. The bags gaped
Where the chutes ran back to the stilled drum
And forks were stuck at angles in the ground
As javelins might mark lost battlefields.   25
I moved between them back across the stubble.

They lay in the ring of their own crusts and dregs
Smoking and saying nothing. "There's a good yield,
Isn't there?" – as proud as if he were the land itself –
"Enough for crushing and for sowing both."   30
And that was it. I'd come and he had shown me
So I belonged no further to the work.
I gathered cups and folded up the cloth
And went. But they still kept their ease
Spread out, unbuttoned, grateful, under the trees.   35

Seamus Heaney (b. 1939)

"MORE LIGHT! MORE LIGHT!"

Composed in the Tower before his execution
These moving verses, and being brought at that time
Painfully to the stake, submitted, declaring thus:
"I implore my God to witness that I have made no crime."

Nor was he forsaken of courage, but the death was horrible,   5
The sack of gunpowder failing to ignite.
His legs were blistered sticks on which the black sap
Bubbled and burst as he howled for the Kindly Light.

And that was but one, and by no means one of the worst;
Permitted at least his pitiful dignity;   10
And such as were by made prayers in the name of Christ,
That shall judge all men, for his soul's tranquility.

We move now to outside a German wood.
Three men are there commanded to dig a hole
In which the two Jews are ordered to lie down   15
And be buried alive by the third, who is a Pole.

Not light from the shrine at Weimar beyond the hill
Nor light from heaven appeared. But he did refuse.
A Lüger settled back deeply in its glove.
He was ordered to change places with the Jews.   20

Much casual death had drained away their souls.
The thick dirt mounted toward the quivering chin.
When only the head was exposed the order came
To dig him out again and to get back in.

"MORE LIGHT! MORE LIGHT!"   Title: These words are sometimes said to have been the last uttered by Goethe (1749–1832), the great German poet and scientist, before his death. 1. *Tower:* the Tower of London, for centuries a place of imprisonment for high-ranking offenders against the English Crown. The account in stanzas 1–3 is composite, but based largely on the death of Bishop Nicholas Ridley, burned at Oxford in 1553.   6. *gunpowder:* used to ignite the faggots and thus make the death occur more quickly.   8. *Kindly Light:* "Lead, Kindly Light" are the opening words of a famous hymn ("The Pillar of Cloud") by Cardinal Newman (1801–1890).   13. *German wood:* Stanzas 4–8 give an accurate account of an incident that occurred at Buchenwald in 1944.   17. *Weimar:* the intellectual center of Germany during the late eighteenth and early nineteenth centuries; Goethe died there. It is near Buchenwald.

No light, no light in the blue Polish eye.   25
When he finished a riding boot packed down the earth.
The Lüger hovered lightly in its glove.
He was shot in the belly and in three hours bled to death.

No prayers or incense rose up in those hours
Which grew to be years, and every day came mute   30
Ghosts from the ovens, sifting through crisp air,
And settled upon his eyes in a black soot.

Anthony Hecht (b. 1923)

THE CHESTNUT CASTS HIS FLAMBEAUX

The chestnut casts his flambeaux, and the flowers
    Stream from the hawthorn on the wind away,
The doors clap to, the pane is blind with showers.
    Pass me the can, lad; there's an end of May.

There's one spoilt spring to scant our mortal lot,   5
    One season ruined of our little store.
May will be fine next year as like as not:
    Oh ay, but then we shall be twenty-four.

We for a certainty are not the first
    Have sat in taverns while the tempest hurled   10
Their hopeful plans to emptiness, and cursed
    Whatever brute and blackguard made the world.

It is in truth iniquity on high
    To cheat our sentenced souls of aught they crave,
And mar the merriment as you and I   15
    Fare on our long fool's errand to the grave.

Iniquity it is; but pass the can.
    My lad, no pair of kings our mothers bore;
Our only portion is the estate of man:
    We want the moon, but we shall get no more.   20

If here today the cloud of thunder lours
    Tomorrow it will hie on far behests;
The flesh will grieve on other bones than ours
    Soon, and the soul will mourn in other breasts.

The troubles of our proud and angry dust   25
   Are from eternity, and shall not fail.
Bear them we can, and if we can we must.
   Shoulder the sky, my lad, and drink your ale.

A. E. Housman (1859–1936)

TO AN ATHLETE DYING YOUNG

The time you won your town the race
We chaired you through the market-place;
Man and boy stood cheering by,
And home we brought you shoulder-high.

To-day, the road all runners come,   5
Shoulder-high, we bring you home,
And set you at your threshold down,
Townsman of a stiller town.

Smart lad, to slip betimes away
From fields where glory does not stay   10
And early though the laurel grows
It withers quicker than the rose.

Eyes the shady night has shut
Cannot see the record cut,
And silence sounds no worse than cheers   15
After earth has stopped the ears:

Now you will not swell the rout
Of lads that wore their honors out,
Runners whom renown outran
And the name died before the man.   20

So set, before its echoes fade,
The fleet foot on the sill of shade,
And hold to the low lintel up
The still-defended challenge-cup.

And round that early-laurelled head   25
Will flock to gaze the strengthless dead,
And find unwithered on its curls
The garland briefer than a girl's.

A. E. Housman (1859–1936)

PIKE

Pike, three inches long, perfect
Pike in all parts, green tigering the gold.
Killers from the egg: the malevolent aged grin.
They dance on the surface among the flies.

Or move, stunned by their own grandeur   5
Over a bed of emerald, silhoutte
Of submarine delicacy and horror.
A hundred feet long in their world.

In ponds, under the heat-struck lily pads –
Gloom of their stillness: 10
Logged on last year's black leaves, watching upwards.
Or hung in an amber cavern of weeds

The jaws' hooked clamp and fangs
Not to be changed at this date;
A life subdued to its instrument;   15
The gills kneading quietly, and the pectorals.

Three we kept behind glass,
Jungled in weed: three inches, four,
And four and a half: fed fry to them –
Suddenly there were two. Finally one.   20

With a sag belly and the grin it was born with.
And indeed they spare nobody.
Two, six pounds each, over two feet long,
High and dry and dead in the willow-herb –

One jammed past its gills down the other's gullet: 25
The outside eye stared: as a vice locks –
The same iron in this eye
Though its film shrank in death.

A pond I fished, fifty yards across,
Whose lilies and muscular tench   30
Had outlasted every visible stone
Of the monastery that planted them –

Stilled legendary depth:
It was as deep as England. It held

Pike too immense to stir, so immense and old   35
That past nightfall I dared not cast

But silently cast and fished
With the hair frozen on my head
For what might move, for what eye might move.
The still splashes on the dark pond,   40

Owls hushing the floating woods
Frail on my ear against the dream
Darkness beneath night's darkness had freed,
That rose slowly towards me, watching.

Ted Hughes (b. 1930)

WIND

This house has been far out at sea all night,
The woods crashing through darkness, the booming hills,
Winds stampeding the fields under the window
Floundering black astride and blinding wet

Till day rose; then under an orange sky   5
The hills had new places, and wind wielded
Blade-like, luminous black and emerald,
Flexing like the lens of a mad eye.

At noon I scaled along the house-side as far as
The coal-house door. Once I looked up –   10
Through the brunt wind that dented the balls of my eyes
The tent of the hills drummed and strained its guyrope,

The fields quivering, the skyline a grimace,
At any second to bang and vanish with a flap:
The wind flung a magpie away and a black-   15
Back gull bent like an iron bar slowly. The house

Rang like some fine green goblet in the note
That any second would shatter it. Now deep
In chairs, in front of the great fire, we grip
Our hearts and cannot entertain book, thought,   20

Or each other. We watch the fire blazing,
And feel the roots of the house move, but sit on,

Seeing the window tremble to come in,
Hearing the stones cry out under the horizons.

Ted Hughes (b.1930)

APPROACHING THE CASTLE

The riches we find inside will be in rich light
pulsing off walls of gold. For every man,
at least two girls, banquets featuring
Yugoslavian tuna in spiced tomato oil
and roasted Kashmir pig. A Sicilian liqueur   5
will leave us clear the morning after.
In the moat, five pound cutthroat trout,
no limit, no license required, a bait
that always works. In our excitement
we feel wind spurring our horses. The towers   10
ride high above us like orchestrated stars.

The drawbridge is down, the gate unguarded,
the coat of arms on the wall faded from rain.
Why is entry so easy? Why no sound?
We were told the court band plays heart thumping jazz   15
and clowns imported from France make laughter
a legend. Best we circle the castle
and think. Word was, the king would greet us
at the gate and roses shower from minarets.
We would ride in to trumpets and applause.   20

This winter, many have fallen. Supplies
are low. Those who came down with fever
headed back home. The governor sent word.
He advised us to go in, take notes and send back
a full report. We held several meetings   25
in the swamp and talked about entering.
Once, we decided to try it but stopped short,
intimidated somehow by the banner
saying "Welcome", one side
loose in the wind and slapping stone.   30

Richard Hugo (b. 1923)

THE DEATH OF THE BALL TURRET GUNNER

From my mother's sleep I fell into the State,
And I hunched in its belly till my wet fur froze.
Six miles from earth, loosed from its dream of life,
I woke to black flak and the nightmare fighters.
When I died they washed me out of the turret with a hose.

Randall Jarrell (1914–1965)

LA BELLE DAME SANS MERCI

O, what can ail thee, knight-at-arms,
    Alone and palely loitering?
The sedge has withered from the lake,
    And no birds sing.

O, what can ail thee, knight-at-arms,   5
    So haggard and so woe-begone?
The squirrel's granary is full,
    And the harvest's done.

I see a lily on thy brow,
    With anguish moist and fever dew;   10
And on thy cheeks a fading rose
    Fast withereth too.

I met a lady in the meads,
    Full beautiful – a faery's child,
Her hair was long, her foot was light,   15
    And her eyes were wild.

I made a garland for her head,
    And bracelets too, and fragrant zone;
She looked at me as she did love,
    And made sweet moan.   20

I set her on my pacing steed,
    And nothing else saw all day long;
For sidelong would she bend, and sing
    A faery's song.

LA BELLE DAME SANS MERCI.   The title means "The beautiful woman without mercy."

She found me roots of relish sweet,   25
    And honey wild, and manna dew,
And sure in language strange she said –
    "I love thee true."

She took me to her elfin grot,
    And there she wept and sighed full sore,   30
And there I shut her wild wild eyes
    With kisses four.

And there she lullèd me asleep
    And there I dreamed – Ah! woe betide!
The latest dream I ever dreamed   35
    On the cold hill side.

I saw pale kings and princes too,
    Pale warriors, death-pale were they all;
They cried – "La Belle Dame sans Merci
    Hath thee in thrall!"   40

I saw their starved lips in the gloam
    With horrid warning gapèd wide,
And I awoke and found me here
    On the cold hill's side.

And this is why I sojourn here   45
    Alone and palely loitering,
Though the sedge has withered from the lake,
    And no birds sing.

John Keats (1795–1821)

ODE ON A GRECIAN URN

Thou still unravished bride of quietness,
    Thou foster-child of silence and slow time,
Sylvan historian, who canst thus express
    A flowery tale more sweetly than our rhyme:
What leaf-fringed legend haunts about thy shape   5

ODE ON A GRECIAN URN. 49–50. In the 1820 edition of Keats's poems the words "Beauty is truth, truth beauty" were enclosed in quotation marks, and the poem is often reprinted that way. It is now generally agreed, however, on the basis of examination of contemporary transcripts of Keats's poem, that Keats intended for the entire last two lines of the poem to be spoken by the Urn.

Of deities or mortals, or of both,
   In Tempe or the dales of Arcady?
What men or gods are these? What maidens loth?
What mad pursuit? What struggle to escape?
   What pipes and timbrels? What wild ecstasy?   10

Heard melodies are sweet, but those unheard
   Are sweeter; therefore, ye soft pipes, play on;
Not to the sensual ear, but, more endeared,
   Pipe to the spirit ditties of no tone:
Fair youth, beneath the trees, thou canst not leave   15
   Thy song, nor ever can those trees be bare;
      Bold Lover, never, never canst thou kiss,
Though winning near the goal – yet, do not grieve;
      She cannot fade, though thou hast not thy bliss,
   For ever wilt thou love, and she be fair!   20

Ah, happy, happy boughs! that cannot shed
   Your leaves, nor ever bid the Spring adieu;
And, happy melodist, unwearied,
   For ever piping songs for ever new;
More happy love! more happy, happy love!   25
   For ever warm and still to be enjoyed,
      For ever panting and for ever young;
All breathing human passion far above,
   That leaves a heart high-sorrowful and cloyed,
      A burning forehead, and a parching tongue.   30

Who are these coming to the sacrifice?
   To what green altar, O mysterious priest,
Lead'st thou that heifer lowing at the skies,
   And all her silken flanks with garlands drest?
What little town by river or sea shore,   35
   Or mountain-built with peaceful citadel,
      Is emptied of its folks, this pious morn?
And, little town, thy streets for evermore
   Will silent be; and not a soul to tell
      Why thou art desolate, can e'er return.   40

O Attic shape! Fair attitude! with brede
   Of marble men and maidens overwrought,
With forest branches and the trodden weed;

Thou, silent form, dost tease us out of thought
    As doth eternity: Cold Pastoral!   45
        When old age shall this generation waste,
            Thou shalt remain, in midst of other woe
        Than ours, a friend to man, to whom thou say'st,
    Beauty is truth, truth beauty, – that is all
        Ye know on earth, and all ye need to know.   50

John Keats (1795–1821)

ODE TO A NIGHTINGALE

I

My heart aches, and a drowsy numbness pains
    My sense, as though of hemlock° I had drunk,   a poisonous drink
Or emptied some dull opiate to the drains
    One minute past, and Lethe-wards had sunk:
'Tis not through envy of thy happy lot,   5
    But being too happy in thine happiness, –
        That thou, light-wingèd Dryad° of the trees,   a wood nymph
            In some melodious plot
    Of beechen green, and shadows numberless,
        Singest of summer in full-throated ease.   10

II

O, for a drought of vintage! that hath been
    Cooled a long age in the deep-delvèd earth,
Tasting of Flora° and the country green,   goddess of flowers
    Dance, and Provençal song, and sunburnt mirth!
O for a beaker full of the warm South,   15
    Full of the true, the blushful Hippocrene,
        With beaded bubbles winking at the brim,
            And purple-stainèd mouth;
    That I might drink, and leave the world unseen,
        And with thee fade away into the forest dim: 20

ODE TO A NIGHTINGALE.   4. *Lethe:* river of forgetfulness in the Greek underworld.
14. *Provençal:* Provence, a wine-growing region in southern France famous, in the Middle
Ages, for troubadours.   16. *Hippocrene:* fountain of the Muses on Mt. Helicon in Greece.
32. *Bacchus . . . pards:* Bacchus, god of wine, had a chariot drawn by leopards.
66. *Ruth:* see Bible, Ruth 2.

III

Fade far away, dissolve, and quite forget
　　What thou among the leaves hast never known,
The weariness, the fever, and the fret
　　Here, where men sit and hear each other groan;
Where palsy shakes a few, sad, last gray hairs,　　　　　　　　　25
　　　Where youth grows pale, and specter-thin, and dies;
　　　　　Where but to think is to be full of sorrow
　　　　　　And leaden-eyed despairs,
　　　Where Beauty cannot keep her lustrous eyes,
　　　　Or new Love pine at them beyond to-morrow.　　　　　30

IV

Away! away! for I will fly to thee,
　　Not charioted by Bacchus and his pards,
But on the viewless° wings of Poesy,　　　　　　　　　invisible
　　Though the dull brain perplexes and retards:
Already with thee! tender is the night,　　　　　　　　　35
　　And haply the Queen-Moon is on her throne,
　　　Clustered around by all her starry Fays;
　　　　　But here there is no light,
　　Save what from heaven is with the breezes blown
　　　Through verdurous glooms and winding mossy ways.　　40

V

I cannot see what flowers are at my feet,
　　Nor what soft incense hangs upon the boughs,
But, in embalmèd° darkness, guess each sweet　　　　　perfumed
　　Wherewith the seasonable month endows
The grass, the thicket, and the fruit-tree wild;　　　　　45
　　White hawthorn, and the pastoral eglantine;
　　　Fast fading violets covered up in leaves;
　　　　　And mid-May's eldest child,
　　The coming musk-rose, full of dewy wine,
　　　The murmurous haunt of flies on summer eves.　　　　50

VI

Darkling° I listen; and, for many a time   *in darkness*
    I have been half in love with easeful Death,
Called him soft names in many a musèd rhyme,
    To take into the air my quiet breath;
Now more than ever seems it rich to die,   55
    To cease upon the midnight with no pain,
        While thou art pouring forth thy soul abroad
            In such an ecstasy!
    Still wouldst thou sing, and I have ears in vain –
    To thy high requiem become a sod.   60

VII

Thou wast not born for death, immortal Bird!
    No hungry generations tread thee down;
The voice I hear this passing night was heard
    In ancient days by emperor and clown:
Perhaps the self-same song that found a path   65
    Through the sad heart of Ruth, when, sick for home,
        She stood in tears amid the alien corn;
            The same that oft-times hath
    Charmed magic casements, opening on the foam
    Of perilous seas, in faery lands forlorn.   70

VIII

Forlorn! the very word is like a bell
    To toll me back from thee to my sole self!
Adieu! the fancy cannot cheat so well
    As she is famed to do, deceiving elf.
Adieu! adieu! thy plaintive anthem fades   75
    Past the near meadows, over the still stream,
        Up the hill-side; and now 'tis buried deep
            In the next valley-glades:
    Was it a vision, or a waking dream?
    Fled is that music: – Do I wake or sleep?   80

John Keats (1795–1821)

SHEEPDOG TRIALS IN HYDE PARK

A shepherd stands at one end of the arena.
Five sheep are unpenned at the other. His dog runs out
In a curve to behind them, fetches them straight to the shepherd,
Then drives the flock round a triangular course
Through a couple of gates and back to his master; two   5
Must be sorted there from the flock, then all five penned.
Gathering, driving away, shedding and penning
Are the plain words for a miraculous game.

An abstract game. What can the sheepdog make of such
Simplified terrain? – no hills, dales, bogs, walls, tracks,   10
Only a quarter-mile plain of grass, dumb crowds
Like crowds on hoardings around it, and behind them
Traffic or mounds of lovers and children playing.
Well, the dog is no landscape-fancier; his whole concern
Is with his master's whistle, and of course   15
With the flock – sheep are sheep anywhere for him.

The sheep are the chanciest element. Why, for instance,
Go through this gate when there's on either side of it
No wall or hedge but huge and viable space?
Why not eat the grass instead of being pushed around it?   20
Like blobs of quicksilver on a tilting board
The flock erratically runs, dithers, breaks up,
Is reassembled: their ruling idea is the dog;
And behind the dog, though they know it not yet, is a shepherd.

The shepherd knows that time is of the essence   25
But haste calamitous. Between dog and sheep
There is always an ideal distance, a perfect angle;
But these are constantly varying, so the man
Should anticipate each move through the dog, his medium.
The shepherd is the brain behind the dog's brain,   30
But his control of dog, like dog's of sheep,
Is never absolute – that's the beauty of it

For beautiful it is. The guided missiles,
The black-and-white angels follow each quirk and jink of
The evasive sheep, play grandmother's steps behind them,   35
Freeze to the ground, or leap to head off a straggler
Almost before it knows that it wants to stray,

As if radar-controlled. But they are not machines –
You can feel them feeling mastery, doubt, chagrin:
Machines don't frolic when their job is done.   40

What's needfully done in the solitude of sheep-runs –
Those tough, real tasks – becomes this stylized game,
A demonstration of intuitive wit
Kept natural by the saving grace of error.
To lift, to fetch, to drive, to shed, to pen   45
Are acts I recognize, with all they mean
Of shepherding the unruly, for a kind of
Controlled woolgathering is my work too.

C. Day Lewis (1904–1972)

MR. EDWARDS AND THE SPIDER

I saw the spiders marching through the air,
Swimming from tree to tree that mildewed day
    In latter August when the hay
    Came creaking to the barn. But where
        The wind is westerly.   5
Where gnarled November makes the spiders fly
Into the apparitions of the sky,
    They purpose nothing but their ease and die
Urgently beating east to sunrise and the sea;

    What are we in the hands of the great God?   10
It was in vain you set up thorn and briar
    In battle array against the fire
    And treason crackling in your blood;
        For the wild thorns grow tame
And will do nothing to oppose the flame;   15
    Your lacerations tell the losing game
    You play against a sickness past your cure.
How will the hands be strong? How will the heart endure?

MR. EDWARDS AND THE SPIDER.   Title: Jonathan Edwards, Puritan preacher and theologian (1703–1758), as a boy of eleven wrote an essay describing how spiders are borne on the wind, at the end of a strand of web, toward the sea, where they die. The images in the poem are taken from this essay and from his famous sermons "Sinners in the Hands of an Angry God" and "The Future Punishment of the Wicked." 38. *Joseph (or Josiah) Hawley:* leader of the faction that got Edwards dismissed from his pastorate in Northhampton, Mass.

A very little thing, a little worm,
Or hourglass-blazoned spider, it is said,   20
      Can kill a tiger. Will the dead
      Hold up his mirror and affirm
            To the four winds the smell
And flash of his authority? It's well
If God who holds you to the pit of hell,   25
Much as one holds a spider, will destroy,
Baffle and dissipate your soil. As a small boy

On Windsor Marsh, I saw the spider die
When thrown into the bowels of fierce fire:
      There's no long struggle, no desire   30
      To get up on its feet and fly —
            It stretches out its feet
And dies. This is the sinner's last retreat;
Yes, and no strength exerted on the heat
Then sinews the abolished will, when sick   35
And full of burning, it will whistle on a brick.

But who can plumb the sinking of that soul?
Josiah Hawley, picture yourself cast
      Into a brick-kiln where the blast
      Fans your quick vitals to a coal —   40
            If measured by a glass
How long would it seem burning! Let there pass
A minute, ten, ten trillion; but the blaze
Is infinite, eternal: this is death,
To die and know it. This is the Black Widow, death.   45

Robert Lowell (b. 1917)

PORTRAIT OF A GIRL WITH COMIC BOOK

Thirteen's no age at all. Thirteen is nothing.
It is not wit, or powder on the face,
Or Wednesday matinées, or misses' clothing,
Or intellect, or grace.
Twelve has its tribal customs. But thirteen   5
Is neither boys in battered cars nor dolls,
Not *Sara Crewe,* or movie magazine,
Or pennants on the walls.

Thirteen keeps diaries and tropical fish
(A month, at most); scorns jumpropes in the spring;   10
Could not, would fortune grant it, name its wish;
Wants nothing, everything;
Has secrets from itself, friends it despises;
Admits none to the terrors that it feels;
Owns half a hundred masks but no disguises;   15
And walks upon its heels.

Thirteen's anomalous—not that, not this:
Not folded bud, or wave that laps a shore,
Or moth proverbial from the chrysalis.
Is the one age defeats the metaphor.   20
Is not a town, like childhood, strongly walled
But easily surrounded; is no city.
Nor, quitted once, can it be quite recalled—
Not even with pity.

Phyllis McGinley (b. 1905)

OH, OH, YOU WILL BE SORRY FOR THAT WORD

Oh, Oh, you will be sorry for that word!
Give back my book and take my kiss instead.
Was it my enemy or my friend I heard,
"What a big book for such a little head!"
Come, I will show you now my newest hat,   5
And you may watch me purse my mouth and prink!
Oh, I shall love you still, and all of that.
I never again shall tell you what I think.
I shall be sweet and crafty, soft and sly;
You will not catch me reading any more: 10
I shall be called a wife to pattern by;
And some day when you knock and push the door,
Some sane day, not too bright and not too stormy,
I shall be gone, and you may whistle for me.

Edna St. Vincent Millay (1892–1950)

THE HORSES

Barely a twelvemonth after
The seven days war that put the world to sleep,
Late in the evening the strange horses came.

By then we had made our covenant with silence,
But in the first few days it was so still   5
We listened to our breathing and were afraid.
On the second day
The radios failed; we turned the knobs; no answer.
On the third day a warship passed us, heading north,
Dead bodies piled on the deck. On the sixth day   10
A plane plunged over us into the sea. Thereafter
Nothing. The radios dumb;
And still they stand in corners of our kitchens,
And stand, perhaps, turned on, in a million rooms
All over the world. But now if they should speak,   15
If on a sudden they should speak again,
If on the stroke of noon a voice should speak,
We would not listen, we would not let it bring
That old bad world that swallowed its children quick
At one great gulp. We would not have it again.   20
Sometimes we think of the nations lying asleep,
Curled blindly in impenetrable sorrow,
And then the thought confounds us with its strangeness.

The tractors lie about our fields; at evening
They look like dank sea-monsters couched and waiting.   25
We leave them where they are and let them rust.
"They'll moulder away and be like other loam."
We make our oxen drag our rusty ploughs,
Long laid aside. We have gone back
Far past our fathers' land.

                  And then, that evening   30
Late in the summer the strange horses came.
We heard a distant tapping on the road,
A deepening drumming; it stopped, went on again
And at the corner changed to hollow thunder.
We saw the heads   35
Like a wild wave charging and were afraid.
We had sold our horses in our fathers' time
To buy new tractors. Now they were strange to us
As fabulous steeds set on an ancient shield
Or illustrations in a book of knights.   40

We did not dare go near them. Yet they waited,
Stubborn and shy, as if they had been sent
By an old command to find our whereabouts
And that long-lost archaic companionship.
In the first moment we had never a thought   45
That they were creatures to be owned and used.
Among them were some half-a-dozen colts
Dropped in some wilderness of the broken world,
Yet new as if they had come from their own Eden.
Since then they have pulled our ploughs and borne our loads,   50
But that free servitude still can pierce our hearts.
Our life is changed; their coming our beginning.

Edwin Muir (1887–1959)

LOVE POEM

My clumsiest dear, whose hands shipwreck vases,
At whose quick touch all glasses chip and ring,
Whose palms are bulls in china, burs in linen,
And have no cunning with any soft thing

Except all ill-at-ease fidgeting people: 5
The refugee uncertain at the door
You make at home; deftly you steady
The drunk clambering on his undulant floor.

Unpredictable dear, the taxi drivers' terror,
Shrinking from far headlights pale as a dime   10
Yet leaping before red apoplectic streetcars –
Misfit in any space. And never on time.

A wrench in clocks and the solar system. Only
With words and people and love you move at ease.
In traffic of wit expertly manoeuvre   15
And keep us, all devotion, at your knees.

Forgetting your coffee spreading on our flannel,
Your lipstick grinning on our coat,
So gayly in love's unbreakable heaven
Our souls on glory of spilt bourbon float.   20

Be with me, darling, early and late. Smash glasses –
I will study wry music for your sake.
For should your hands drop white and empty
All the toys of the world would break.

John Frederick Nims (b. 1914)

THE MILL

The miller's wife had waited long,
　　The tea was cold, the fire was dead;
And there might yet be nothing wrong
　　In how he went and what he said:
"There are no millers any more,"　　　　　　　　5
　　Was all that she had heard him say;
And he had lingered at the door
　　So long that it seemed yesterday.

Sick with a fear that had no form
　　She knew that she was there at last;　　　　　10
And in the mill there was a warm
　　And mealy fragrance of the past.
What else there was would only seem
　　To say again what he had meant;
And what was hanging from a beam　　　　　　　15
　　Would not have heeded where she went.

And if she thought it followed her,
　　She may have reasoned in the dark
That one way of the few there were
　　Would hide her and would leave no mark:　　20
Black water, smooth above the weir
　　Like starry velvet in the night,
Though ruffled once, would soon appear
　　The same as ever to the sight.

Edwin Arlington Robinson (1869–1935)

MR. FLOOD'S PARTY

Old Eben Flood, climbing alone one night
Over the hill between the town below
And the forsaken upland hermitage
That held as much as he should ever know
On earth again of home, paused warily.   5
The road was his with not a native near;
And Eben, having leisure, said aloud,
For no man else in Tilbury Town to hear:

"Well, Mr. Flood, we have the harvest moon
Again, and we may not have many more;   10
The bird is on the wing, the poet says,
And you and I have said it here before.
Drink to the bird." He raised up to the light
The jug that he had gone so far to fill,
And answered huskily: "Well, Mr. Flood,   15
Since you propose it, I believe I will."

Alone, as if enduring to the end
A valiant armor of scarred hopes outworn,
He stood there in the middle of the road
Like Roland's ghost winding a silent horn.   20
Below him, in the town among the trees,
Where friends of other days had honored him,
A phantom salutation of the dead
Rang thinly till old Eben's eyes were dim.

Then, as a mother lays her sleeping child   25
Down tenderly, fearing it may awake,
He set the jug down slowly at his feet
With trembling care, knowing that most things break;
And only when assured that on firm earth
It stood, as the uncertain lives of men   30

MR. FLOOD'S PARTY.   11. *bird:* Mr. Flood is quoting from *The Rubáiyát of Omar Khayyám,*
"The bird of Time . . . is on the wing."   20. *Roland:* hero of the French ˜epic poem
The Song of Roland. He died fighting a rearguard action for Charlemagne against the
Moors in Spain; before his death he sounded a call for help on his famous horn, but the
king's army arrived too late.

Assuredly did not, he paced away,
And with his hand extended paused again:

"Well, Mr. Flood, we have not met like this
In a long time; and many a change has come
To both of us, I fear, since last it was   35
We had a drop together. Welcome home!"
Convivially returning with himself,
Again he raised the jug up to the light;
And with an acquiescent quaver said:
"Well, Mr. Flood, if you insist, I might.   40

"Only a very little, Mr. Flood –
For auld lang syne. No more, sir; that will do."
So, for the time, apparently it did,
And Eben evidently thought so too;
For soon amid the silver loneliness   45
Of night he lifted up his voice and sang,
Secure, with only two moons listening,
Until the whole harmonious landscape rang –

"For auld lang syne." The weary throat gave out,
The last word wavered, and the song was done.   50
He raised again the jug regretfully
And shook his head, and was again alone.
There was not much that was ahead of him,
And there was nothing in the town below –
Where strangers would have shut the many doors   55
That many friends had opened long ago.

Edwin Arlington Robinson (1869–1935)

I KNEW A WOMAN

I knew a woman, lovely in her bones,
When small birds sighed, she would sigh back at them;
Ah, when she moved, she moved more ways than one:
The shapes a bright container can contain!
Of her choice virtues only gods should speak,   5
Or English poets who grew up on Greek
(I'd have them sing in chorus, cheek to cheek).

How well her wishes went! She stroked my chin,
She taught me Turn, and Counter-turn, and Stand;
She taught me Touch, that undulant white skin; 10
I nibbled meekly from her proffered hand;
She was the sickle; I, poor I, the rake,
Coming behind her for her pretty sake
(But what prodigious mowing we did make).

Love likes a gander, and adores a goose: 15
Her full lips pursed, the errant note to seize;
She played it quick, she played it light and loose;
My eyes, they dazzled at her flowing knees;
Her several parts could keep a pure repose,
Or one hip quiver with a mobile nose 20
(She moved in circles, and those circles moved).

Let seed be grass, and grass turn into hay:
I'm martyr to a motion not my own;
What's freedom for? To know eternity.
I swear she cast a shadow white as stone. 25
But who would count eternity in days?
These old bones live to learn her wanton ways:
(I measure time by how a body sways).

Theodore Roethke (1908–1963)

THE WAKING

I wake to sleep, and take my waking slow.
I feel my fate in what I cannot fear.
I learn by going where I have to go.

We think by feeling. What is there to know?
I hear my being dance from ear to ear. 5
I wake to sleep, and take my waking slow.

Of those so close beside me, which are you?
God bless the Ground! I shall walk softly there,
And learn by going where I have to go.

Light takes the Tree; but who can tell us how? 10
The lowly worm climbs up a winding stair;
I wake to sleep, and take my waking slow.

Great Nature has another thing to do
To you and me; so take the lively air,
And, lovely, learn by going where to go.   15

This shaking keeps me steady. I should know.
What falls away is always. And is near.
I wake to sleep, and take my waking slow.
I learn by going where I have to go.

Theodore Roethke (1908–1963)

SILENT NOON

Your hands lie open in the long fresh grass, –
The finger-points look through like rosy blooms:
Your eyes smile peace. The pasture gleams and glooms
'Neath billowing skies that scatter and amass.
All round our nest, far as the eye can pass,   5
Are golden kingcup-fields with silver edge
Where the cow-parsley skirts the hawthorne-hedge.
'Tis visible silence, still as the hour-glass.

Deep in the sun-searched growths the dragon-fly
Hangs like a blue thread loosened from the sky: –   10
So this winged hour is dropped to us from above.
Oh! clasp we to our hearts, for deathless dower,
This close-companioned inarticulate hour
When twofold silence was the song of love.

Dante Gabriel Rossetti (1828–1882)

FEAR NO MORE

Fear no more the heat o' the sun,
    Nor the furious winter's rages;
Thou thy worldly task hast done,
    Home art gone, and ta'en thy wages.
Golden lads and girls all must,   5
As chimney-sweepers, come to dust.

Fear no more the frown o' the great;
    Thou art past the tyrant's stroke;
Care no more to clothe and eat;

To thee the reed is as the oak.   10
The scepter, learning, physic,° must   art of healing
All follow this, and come to dust.

Fear no more the lightning-flash,
    Nor the all-dreaded thunder-stone;°   thunderbolt
Fear not slander, censure rash;   15
    Thou has finished joy and moan.
All lovers young, all lovers must
Consign to thee,° and come to dust.   yield to your condition

William Shakespeare (1564–1616)

LET ME NOT TO THE MARRIAGE OF TRUE MINDS

Let me not to the marriage of true minds
Admit impediments. Love is not love
Which alters when it alteration finds,
Or bends with the remover to remove,
O no! it is an ever-fixèd mark   5
That looks on tempests and is never shaken;
It is the star to every wandering bark,
Whose worth's unknown, although his height be taken.
Love's not Time's fool, though rosy lips and cheeks
Within his bending sickle's compass come;   10
Love alters not with his brief hours and weeks,
But bears it out even to the edge of doom.
    If this be error and upon me proved,
    I never writ, nor no man ever loved.

William Shakespeare (1564–1616)

MY MISTRESS' EYES ARE NOTHING LIKE THE SUN

My mistress' eyes are nothing like the sun;
Coral is far more red than her lips' red:
If snow be white, why then her breasts are dun;
If hairs be wires, black wires grow on her head.   4
I have seen roses damasked,° red and white,   of different colors
But no such roses see I in her cheeks;
And in some perfumes is there more delight
Than in the breath that from my mistress reeks.

I love to hear her speak, yet well I know
That music hath a far more pleasing sound: 10
I grant I never saw a goddess go, –
My mistress, when she walks, treads on the ground.
    And yet, by heaven, I think my love as rare
    As any she belied with false compare.

William Shakespeare (1564–1616)

TELEPHONE CONVERSATION

The price seemed reasonable, location
Indifferent. The landlady swore she lived
Off premises. Nothing remained
But self-confession. "Madam," I warned,
"I hate a wasted journey – I am African."   5
Silence. Silenced transmission of
Pressurized good-breeding. Voice, when it came,
Lipstick-coated, long gold-rolled
Cigarette-holder tipped. Caught I was, foully.
"HOW DARK?" . . . I had not misheard . . . "ARE YOU LIGHT   10
OR VERY DARK?" Button B. Button A. Stench
Of rancid breath of public hide-and-speak.
Red booth. Red pillar box. Red double-tiered
Omnibus squelching tar. It *was* real! Shamed
By ill-mannered silence, surrender   15
Pushed dumbfounded to beg simplification.
Considerate she was, varying the emphasis –
"ARE YOU DARK? OR VERY LIGHT?" Revelation came.
"You mean – like plain or milk chocolate?"
Her assent was clinical, crushing in its light   20
Impersonality. Rapidly, wave-length adjusted,
I chose. "West African sepia" – and as afterthought,
"Down in my passport." Silence for spectroscopic
Flight of fancy, till truthfulness clanged her accent
Hard on the mouthpiece. "WHAT'S THAT?" conceding   25
"DON'T KNOW WHAT THAT IS." "Like brunette."
"THAT'S DARK, ISN'T IT?" "Not altogether.
Facially, I am brunette, but madam, you should see
The rest of me. Palm of my hand, soles of my feet

Are a peroxide blonde. Friction, caused –   30
Foolishly madam – by sitting down, has turned
My bottom raven black – One moment, madam! – sensing
Her receiver rearing on the thunderclap
About my ears – "Madam," I pleaded, "wouldn't you rather
See for yourself?"   35

Wole Soyinka (b. 1935)

AT THE UN-NATIONAL MONUMENT
ALONG THE CANADIAN BORDER

This is the field where the battle did not happen,
where the unknown soldier did not die.
This is the field where grass joined hands,
where no monument stands,
and the only heroic thing is the sky.   5

Birds fly here without any sound,
unfolding their wings across the open.
No people killed – or were killed – on this ground
hallowed by neglect and an air so tame
that people celebrate it by forgetting its name.   10

William Stafford (b. 1914)

PETER QUINCE AT THE CLAVIER

I

Just as my fingers on these keys
Make music, so the self-same sounds
On my spirit make a music, too.

Music is feeling, then, not sound;
And thus it is that what I feel,   5
Here in this room, desiring you,

Thinking of your blue-shadowed silk,
Is music. It is like the strain
Waked in the elders by Susanna:

PETER QUINCE AT THE CLAVIER.   The story of Susanna and the Elders is to be found in
the *Apocrypha* and in the *Douay Bible* (Daniel, 13). The name Peter Quince comes from
Shakespeare's *Midsummer Night's Dream.*

Of a green evening, clear and warm,   10
She bathed in her still garden, while
The red-eyed elders, watching, felt
The bases of their beings throb
In witching chords, and their thin blood
Pulse pizzicati of Hosanna.   15

II

In the green water, clear and warm,
Susanna lay.
She searched
The touch of springs,
And found   20
Concealed imaginings.
She sighed,
For so much melody.

Upon the bank, she stood
In the cool   25
Of spent emotions,
She felt, among the leaves,
The dew
Of old devotions.

She walked upon the grass,   30
Still quavering.
The winds were like her maids
On timid feet,
Fetching her woven scarves,
Yet wavering.   35

A breath upon her hand
Muted the night.
She turned –
A cymbal crashed,
And roaring horns.   40

III

Soon, with a noise like tambourines,
Came her attendant Byzantines.

They wondered why Susanna cried
Against the elders by her side;

And as they whispered, the refrain   45
Was like a willow swept by rain.

Anon, their lamps' uplifted flame
Revealed Susanna and her shame.

And then, the simpering Byzantines
Fled with a noise like tambourines.   50

IV

Beauty is momentary in the mind—
The fitful tracing of a portal;
But in the flesh it is immortal.

The body dies; the body's beauty lives.
So evenings die, in their green going,   55
A wave, interminably flowing.
So gardens die, their meek breath scenting
The cowl of Winter, done repenting.
So maidens die, to the auroral
Celebration of a maiden's choral.   60

Susanna's music touched the bawdy strings
Of those white elders; but, escaping,
Left only Death's ironic scraping.
Now, in its immortality, it plays
On the clear viol of her memory,   65
And makes a constant sacrament of praise.

Wallace Stevens (1879–1955)

THE WATCH

When I
took my
watch to the watchfixer I
felt privileged but also pained to watch the operation. He
had long fingernails and a voluntary squint. He   5
fixed a magnifying cup over his
squint eye. He

undressed my
watch. I
watched him   10
split her
in three layers and lay her
middle – a quivering viscera – in a circle on a little plinth. He
shoved shirtsleeves up and leaned like an ogre over my
naked watch. With critical pincers he   15
poked and stirred. He
lifted out little private things with a magnet too tiny for me
to watch almost. "Watch out!" I
almost said. His
eye watched, enlarged, the secrets of my   20
watch, and I
watched anxiously. Because what if he
touched her
ticker too rough, and she
gave up the ghost out of pure fright? Or put her   25
things back backwards so she'd
run backwards after this? Or he
might lose a minuscule part, connected to her
exquisite heart, and mix her
up, instead of fix her.   30

And all the time,
all the time-
pieces on the walls, on the shelves, told the time,
told the time
in swishes and ticks,   35
swishes and ticks,
and seemed to be gloating, as they watched and told. I
felt faint, I
was about to lose my
breath – my   40
ticker going lickety-split – when watchfixer clipped her
three slices together with a gleam and two flicks of his
tools like chopsticks. He
spat out his
eye, lifted her   45
high, gave her

a twist, set her
hands right, and laid her
little face, quite as usual, in its place on my
wrist.   50

May Swenson (b. 1919)

A DESCRIPTION OF THE MORNING

Now hardly here and there a hackney-coach
Appearing, showed the ruddy morn's approach.
Now Betty from her master's bed had flown,
And softly stole to discompose her own.
The slip-shod 'prentice from his master's door   5
Had pared the dirt, and sprinkled round the floor.
Now Moll had whirled her mop with dextrous airs,
Prepared to scrub the entry and the stairs.
The youth with broomy stumps began to trace
The kennel's edge, where wheels had worn the place.   10
The small-coal man was heard with cadence deep,
Till downed in shriller notes of chimney-sweep.
Duns at his lordship's gate began to meet;
And Brickdust Moll had screamed through half the street.
The turnkey now his flock returning sees,   15
Duly let out a-nights to steal for fees.
The watchful bailiffs take their silent stands;
And schoolboys lag with satchels in their hands.

Jonathan Swift (1667–1745)

DO NOT GO GENTLE INTO THAT GOOD NIGHT

Do not go gentle into that good night,
Old age should burn and rave at close of day;
Rage, rage against the dying of the light.

Though wise men at their end know dark is right,
Because their words had forked no lightning they   5
Do not go gentle into that good night.

A DESCRIPTION OF THE MORNING.   9. *youth:* he is apparently searching for salvage.
10. *kennel:* gutter.   14. *Brickdust:* red-complexioned.

Good men, the last wave by, crying how bright
Their frail deeds might have danced in a green bay,
Rage, rage against the dying of the light.

Wild men who caught and sang the sun in flight,   10
And learn, too late, they grieved it on its way
Do not go gentle into that good night.

Grave men, near death, who see with blinding sight
Blind eyes could blaze like meteors and be gay,
Rage, rage against the dying of the light.   15

And you, my father, there on the sad height,
Curse, bless, me now with your fierce tears, I pray.
Do not go gentle into that good night.
Rage, rage against the dying of the light.

Dylan Thomas (1914–1953)

FERN HILL

Now as I was young and easy under the apple boughs
About the lilting house and happy as the grass was green,
    The night above the dingle starry,
        Time let me hail and climb
    Golden in the heydays of his eyes,   5
And honored among wagons I was prince of the apple towns
And once below a time I lordly had the trees and leaves
        Trail with daisies and barley
    Down the rivers of the windfall light.

And as I was green and carefree, famous among the barns   10
About the happy yard and singing as the farm was home,
    In the sun that is young once only,
        Time let me play and be
    Golden in the mercy of his means,
And green and golden I was huntsman and herdsman, the calves 15
Sang to my horn, the foxes on the hills barked clear and cold,
        And the sabbath rang slowly
    In the pebbles of the holy streams.

All the sun long it was running, it was lovely, the hay
Fields high as the house, the tunes from the chimneys, it was air   20
   And playing, lovely and watery
      And fire green as grass.
   And nightly under the simple stars
As I rode to sleep the owls were bearing the farm away,
All the moon long I heard, blessed among stables, the nightjars   25
   Flying with the ricks, and the horses
      Flashing into the dark.

And then to awake, and the farm, like a wanderer white
With the dew, come back, the cock on his shoulder: it was all
   Shining, it was Adam and maiden,   30
      The sky gathered again
   And the sun grew round that very day.
So it must have been after the birth of the simple light
In the first, spinning place, the spellbound horses walking warm
   Out of the whinnying green stable   35
      On to the fields of praise.

And honored among foxes and pheasants by the gay house
Under the new made clouds and happy as the heart was long,
   In the sun born over and over,
      I ran my heedless ways,   40
   My wishes raced through the house high hay
And nothing I cared, at my sky blue trades, that time allows
In all his tuneful turning so few and such morning songs
   Before the children green and golden
      Follow him out of grace,   45

Nothing I cared, in the lamb white days, that time would take me
Up to the swallow thronged loft by the shadow of my hand,
   In the moon that is always rising,
      Nor that riding to sleep
   I should hear him fly with the high fields   50
And wake to the farm forever fled from the childless land.
Oh as I was young and easy in the mercy of his means,
      Time held me green and dying
   Though I sang in my chains like the sea.

Dylan Thomas (1914–1953)

THE GALLOWS

There was a weasel lived in the sun
With all his family,
Till a keeper shot him with his gun
And hung him up on a tree,
Where he swings in the wind and the rain   5
In the sun and in the snow,
Without pleasure, without pain,
On the dead oak tree bough.

There was a crow who was no sleeper,
But a thief and a murderer   10
Till a very late hour; and this keeper
Made him one of the things that were,
To hang and flap in the rain and wind,
In the sun and in the snow.
There are no more sins to be sinned   15
On the dead oak tree bough.

There was a magpie, too,
Had a long tongue and a long tail;
He could both talk and do –
But what did that avail?   20
He, too, flaps in the wind and rain
Alongside weasel and crow.
Without pleasure, without pain,
On the dead oak tree bough.

And many other beasts,   25
And birds, skin, bone and feather,
Have been taken from their feasts
And hung up there together,
To swing and have endless leisure
In the sun and in the snow,   30
Without pain, without pleasure,
On the dead oak tree bough.

Edward Thomas (1878–1917)

SEA GRAPES

That sail in cloudless light
which tires of islands,
a schooner beating up the Caribbean

for home, could be Odysseus
home-bound through the Acgean,   5
just as that husband's

sorrow under the sea-grapes, repeats
the adulterer's hearing Nausicaa's name
in every gull's outcry.

But whom does this bring peace? The classic war   10
between a passion and responsibility
is never finished, and has been the same

to the sea-wanderer and the one on shore,
now wriggling on his sandals to walk home,
since Troy sighed its last flame,   15

and the blind giant's boulder heaved the trough
from which The Odyssey's hexameters come
to finish up as Caribbean surf.

The classics can console. But not enough.

Derek Walcott (b. 1930)

A NOISELESS PATIENT SPIDER

A noiseless patient spider,
I marked where on a little promontory it stood isolated,
Marked how to explore the vacant vast surrounding,
It launched forth filament, filament, filament, out of itself,
Ever unreeling them, ever tirelessly speeding them.   5

And you O my soul where you stand,
Surrounded, detached, in measureless oceans of space,
Ceaselessly musing, venturing, throwing, seeking the spheres to connect them,
Till the bridge you will need be formed, till the ductile anchor hold,
Till the gossamer thread you fling catch somewhere, O my soul.   10

Walt Whitman (1819–1892)

WHEN I HEARD THE LEARN'D ASTRONOMER

When I heard the learn'd astronomer,
When the proofs, the figures, were ranged in columns before me,
When I was shown the charts and diagrams, to add, divide, and measure them,

When I sitting heard the astronomer where he lectured with much applause in
    the lecture-room,
How soon unaccountable I became tired and sick,
Till rising and gliding out I wandered off by myself,
In the mystical moist night-air, and from time to time,
Looked up in perfect silence at the stars.

Walt Whitman (1819–1892)

THE MILL

        The spoiling daylight inched along the bar-top,
        Orange and cloudy, slowly igniting lint,
        And then that glow was gone, and still your voice,
        Serene with failure and with the ease of dying,
        Rose from the shades that more and more became you.   5
        Turning among its images, your mind
        Produced the names of streets, the exact look
        Of lilacs, 1903, in Cincinnati,
        – Random, as if your testament were made,
        The round sums all bestowed, and now you spent   10
        Your pocket change, so as to be rid of it.
        Or was it that you half-hoped to surprise
        Your dead life's sound and sovereign anecdote?
        What I remember best is the wrecked mill
        You stumbled on in Tennessee; or was it   15
        Somewhere down in Brazil? It slips my mind
        Already. But there it was in a still valley
        Far from the towns. No road or path came near it.
        If there had been a clearing now it was gone,
        And all you found amidst the choke of green   20
        Was three walls standing, hurdled by great vines
        And thatched by height on height of hushing leaves.
        But still the mill-wheel turned! its crazy buckets
        Creaking and lumbering out of the clogged race
        And sounding, as you said, as if you'd found   25
        Time all alone and talking to himself
        In his eternal rattle.
                      How should I guess
        Where they are gone to, now that you are gone,
        Those fading streets and those most fragile lilacs,

Those fragmentary views, those times of day?　　　　30
All that I can be sure of is the mill-wheel.
It turns and turns in my mind, over and over.

Richard Wilbur (b. 1921)

THE RED WHEELBARROW

so much depends
upon

a red wheel
barrow

glazed with rain
water

beside the white
chickens.

William Carlos Williams (1883–1963)

THE SOLITARY REAPER

Behold her, single in the field,
Yon solitary Highland lass!
Reaping and singing by herself;
Stop here, or gently pass!
Alone she cuts and binds the grain,　　　　5
And sings a melancholy strain;
O listen! for the vale profound
Is overflowing with the sound.

No nightingale did ever chaunt
More welcome notes to weary bands　　　　10
Of travellers in some shady haunt
Among Arabian sands.
A voice so thrilling ne'er was heard
In springtime from the cuckoo-bird,
Breaking the silence of the seas　　　　15
Among the farthest Hebrides.

THE SOLITARY REAPER.　2. *Highland:* Scottish upland. The girl is singing in the Highland language, a form of Gaelic, quite different from English.　16. *Hebrides:* islands off the northwest tip of Scotland.

Will no one tell me what she sings? –
Perhaps the plaintive numbers° flow   measures
For old, unhappy, far-off things,
And battles long ago.   20
Or is it some more humble lay,°   song
Familiar matter of today?
Some natural sorrow, loss, or pain,
That has been, and may be again?

Whate'er the theme, the maiden sang   25
As if her song could have no ending;
I saw her singing at her work,
And o'er the sickle bending –
I listened, motionless and still;
And, as I mounted up the hill,   30
The music in my heart I bore
Long after it was heard no more.

William Wordsworth (1770–1850)

THERE WAS A BOY

There was a Boy; ye knew him well, ye cliffs
And islands of Winander! – many a time,
At evening, when the earliest stars began
To move along the edges of the hills,
Rising or setting, would he stand alone,   5
Beneath the trees, or by the glimmering lake;
And there, with fingers interwoven, both hands
Pressed closely palm to palm and to his mouth
Uplifted, he, as through an instrument,
Blew mimic hootings to the silent owls,   10
That they might answer him. – And they would shout
Across the watery vale, and shout again,
Responsive to his call, – with quivering peals,
And long halloos, and screams, and echoes loud
Redoubled and redoubled; concourse wild   15
Of jocund din! And, when there came a pause
Of silence such as baffled his best skill:

Then, sometimes, in that silence, while he hung
Listening, a gentle shock of mild surprise
Has carried far into his heart the voice   20
Of mountain-torrents; or the visible scene
Would enter unawares into his mind
With all its solemn imagery, its rocks,
Its woods, and that uncertain heaven received
Into the bosom of the steady lake.   25

   This boy was taken from his mates, and died
In childhood, ere he was full twelve years old.
Pre-eminent in beauty is the vale
Where he was born and bred: the churchyard hangs
Upon a slope above the village-school;   30
And, through that churchyard when my way has led
On summer-evenings, I believe that there
A long half-hour together I have stood
Mute – looking at the grave in which he lies!

                          William Wordsworth (1770–1850)

THE WORLD IS TOO MUCH WITH US

The world is too much with us; late and soon,
Getting and spending, we lay waste our powers:
Little we see in Nature that is ours;
We have given our hearts away, a sordid boon!
The Sea that bares her bosom to the moon;   5
The winds that will be howling at all hours,
And are up-gathered now like sleeping flowers;
For this, for everything, we are out of tune;
It moves us not. – Great God! I'd rather be
A Pagan suckled in a creed outworn;   10
So might I, standing on this pleasant lea,
Have glimpses that would make me less forlorn;
Have sight of Proteus rising from the sea;
Or hear old Triton blow his wreathèd horn.

                          William Wordsworth (1770–1850)

PURITAN SONNET

Down to the Puritan marrow of my bones
There's something in this richness that I hate.
I love the look, austere, immaculate,
Of landscapes drawn in pearly monotones.
There's something in my very blood that owns   5
Bare hills, cold silver on a sky of slate,
A thread of water, churned to milky spate
Streaming through slanted pastures fenced with stones.

I love those skies, thin blue or snowy gray,
Those fields sparse-planted, rendering meager sheaves;   10
That spring, briefer than apple-blossom's breath,
Summer, so much too beautiful to stay,
Swift autumn, like a bonfire of leaves,
And sleepy winter, like the sleep of death.

Elinor Wylie (1885–1928)

ADAM'S CURSE

We sat together at one summer's end,
That beautiful mild woman, your close friend,
And you and I, and talked of poetry.
I said, "A line will take us hours maybe;
Yet if it does not seem a moment's thought,   5
Our stitching and unstitching has been naught.

Better go down upon your marrow-bones
And scrub a kitchen pavement, or break stones
Like an old pauper, in all kinds of weather;
For to articulate sweet sounds together   10
Is to work harder than all these, and yet
Be thought an idler by the noisy set
Of bankers, schoolmasters, and clergymen
The martyrs call the world."
                And thereupon
That beautiful mild woman for whose sake   15
There's many a one shall find out all heartache
On finding that her voice is sweet and low
Replied, "To be born woman is to know—

Although they do no talk of it at school –
That we must labor to be beautiful."   20

I said, "It's certain there is no fine thing
Since Adam's fall but needs much laboring.
There have been lovers who thought love should be
So much compounded of high courtesy
That they would sigh and quote with learned looks   25
Precedents out of beautiful old books;
Yet now it seems an idle trade enough."

We sat grown quiet at the name of love;
We saw the last embers of daylight die,
And in the trembling blue-green of the sky   30
A moon, worn as if it had been a shell
Washed by time's waters as they rose and fell
About the stars and broke in days and years.

I had a thought for no one's but your ears:
That you were beautiful, and that I strove   35
To love you in the old high way of love;
That it had all seemed happy, and yet we'd grown
As weary-hearted as that hollow moon.

William Butler Yeats (1865–1939)

SAILING TO BYZANTIUM

I

That is no country for old men. The young
In one another's arms, birds in the trees
– Those dying generations – at their song,
The salmon-falls, the mackerel-crowded seas,
Fish, flesh, or fowl, commend all summer long   5
Whatever is begotten, born, and dies.
Caught in that sensual music all neglect
Monuments of unageing intellect.

SAILING TO BYZANTIUM. *Byzantium:* Ancient eastern capital of the Holy Roman Empire; here symbolically a holy city of the imagination.   1. *That:* Ireland, or the ordinary sensual world.   27–31. *such . . . Byzantium:* The Byzantine Emperor Theophilus had made for himself mechanical golden birds which sang upon the branches of a golden tree.

II

An aged man is but a paltry thing,
A tattered coat upon a stick, unless   10
Soul clap its hands and sing, and louder sing
For every tatter in its mortal dress,
Nor is there singing school but studying
Monuments of its own magnificence;
And therefore I have sailed the seas and come   15
To the holy city of Byzantium.

III

O sages standing in God's holy fire
As in the gold mosaic of a wall,
Come from the holy fire, perne in a gyre,°   spin in spiraling or
And be the singing-masters of my soul.   cone-shaped flight
Consume my heart away; sick with desire   21
And fastened to a dying animal
It knows not what it is; and gather me
Into the artifice of eternity.

IV

Once out of nature I shall never take   25
My bodily form from any natural thing,
But such a form as Grecian goldsmiths make
Of hammered gold and gold enamelling
To keep a drowsy Emperor awake;
Or set upon a golden bough to sing   30
To lords and ladies of Byzantium
Of what is past, or passing, or to come.

William Butler Yeats (1865–1939)

GLOSSARY
OF POETIC TERMS

The definitions in this glossary sometimes repeat and sometimes differ in language from those in the text. Where they differ, the intention is to give a fuller sense of the term's meaning by allowing the reader a double perspective on it. Page numbers refer to discussion in the text, which in most but not all cases is fuller than that in the glossary.

Accent.   In this book, the same as *stress.* A syllable given more prominence in pronunciation than its neighbors is said to be accented.   180–87

Allegory.   A narrative or description having a second meaning beneath the surface one.   88–89

Alliteration.   The repetition at close intervals of the initial consonant sounds of accented syllables or important words (for example, *m*ap–*m*oon, *k*ill–*c*ode, *p*reach–ap*p*rove). Important words and accented syllables beginning with vowels may also be said to alliterate with each other inasmuch as they all have the same lack of an initial consonant sound (for example, "*I*nebri*a*te of *a*ir am *I*").   167–68, 169–70, 172–73

Allusion.   A reference, explicit or implicit, to something in previous literature or history. (The term is reserved by some writers for implicit references only, such as those in "On His Blindness," 127, and "In the Garden," 135; but the distinction between the two kinds of reference is not always clear-cut.)   122–26

Anapest.   A metrical foot consisting of two unaccented syllables followed by one accented syllable (for example, ŭn-dĕr-stānd).   182

Anapestic meter.   A meter in which a majority of the feet are anapests. (But see *Triple meter.*)   182, 220

Apostrophe.   A figure of speech in which someone absent or dead or something nonhuman is addressed as if it were alive and present and could reply.   65

Approximate rime (known also as *imperfect rime, near rime, slant rime,* or *oblique rime*).   A term used for words in a riming pattern that have some kind of sound correspondence but are not perfect rimes. See *Rime.* Approximate rimes occur occasionally in patterns where most of the rimes are perfect (for example, arrayed–said in "Richard Cory," 42), and sometimes are used systematically in place of perfect rime (for example, "Mr. Z," 117).   168, 169–70

Assonance.   The repetition at close intervals of the vowel sounds of accented syllables or important words (for example, h*a*t–r*a*n–*a*mber, v*ei*n–m*a*de).   167–68, 169–70

Ballad.   A fairly short narrative poem written in a songlike stanzaic form.   13
Ballad stanza.   See pages 13–14 (Question 4), and 223 (Exercise 1).
Blank verse.   Unrimed iambic pentameter.   187

Cacophony.   A harsh, discordant, unpleasant-sounding choice and arrangement of sounds.   202–03

Caesura.   See *Grammatical pause* and *Rhetorical pause.*

Connotation.   What a word suggests beyond its basic definition, a word's overtones of meaning.   35–42

Consonance.   The repetition at close intervals of the final consonant sounds of accented syllables or important words (for example, boo*k*–pla*qu*e–thic*k*er).   167–68, 169–70

Continuous form.   That form of a poem in which the lines follow each other without formal grouping, the only breaks being dictated by units of meaning.   217–18

Couplet.   Two successive lines, usually in the same meter, linked by rime. 189 (Question 2), 222

Dactyl.   A metrical foot consisting of one accented syllable followed by two unaccented syllables (for example, mēr-rǐ-lў).   182

Dactylic meter.   A meter in which a majority of the feet are dactyls. (But see *Triple meter.*)   182

Denotation.   The basic definition or dictionary meaning of a word.   35–42

Didactic poetry.   Poetry having as a primary purpose to teach or preach.   241

Dimeter.   A metrical line containing two feet.   182

Dipodic foot.   The basic foot of *dipodic verse,* consisting (when complete) of an unaccented syllable, a lightly accented syllable, an unaccented syllable, and a heavily accented syllable, in that succession. However, dipodic verse accommodates a tremendous amount of variety, as shown by the examples in the text.   194, 196

Dipodic verse.   A meter in which there is a perceptible alternation between light and heavy stresses. See *Dipodic foot.*   194, 196

Double rime.   A rime in which the repeated vowel sound is in the second last syllable of the words involved (for example, politely–rightly–spritely); one form of *feminine rime.*   176

Dramatic framework.   The situation, whether actual or fictional, realistic or fanciful, in which an author places his or her characters in order to express the theme.   22–25

Dramatic irony.   See *Irony.*

Duple meter.   A meter in which a majority of the feet contain two syllables. Iambic and trochaic are both duple meters.   182

End rime.   Rimes that occur at the ends of lines.   168

End-stopped line.   A line that ends with a natural speech pause, usually marked by punctuation.   188

English (or Shakespearean) sonnet.   A sonnet riming *ababcdcdefefgg.* Its content or structure ideally parallels the rime scheme, falling into three coordinate quatrains and a concluding couplet; but it is often structured, like the Italian sonnet, into octave and sestet, the principal break in thought coming at the end of the eighth line.   222–23, 224 (Exercise 4)

Euphony.   A smooth, pleasant-sounding choice and arrangement of sounds.   202–03

Expected rhythm.   The metrical expectation set up by the basic meter of a poem.   185–86

Extended figure.   A figure of speech (usually metaphor, simile, personification, or apostrophe) sustained or developed through a considerable number of lines or through a whole poem. Also called a *sustained figure.*   72

Feminine rime.   A rime in which the repeated accented vowel is in either the second or third last syllable of the words involved (for example, ceiling–appealing; hurrying–scurrying).   168, 176 (Question 5)

Figurative language.   Language employing figures of speech; language that cannot be taken literally or only literally.   60–70, 80–91, 101–10

Figure of speech.   Broadly, any way of saying something other than the ordinary way; more narrowly (and for the purposes of this book) a way of saying one thing and meaning another.   60–71, 80–91, 101–10

Fixed form.   Any form of poem in which the length and pattern are prescribed by previous usage or tradition, such as *sonnet, limerick, villanelle, haiku,* and so on.   220–24

Folk ballad.   A narrative poem designed to be sung, composed by an anonymous author, and transmitted orally for years or generations before being written down. It has usually undergone modification through the process of oral transmission.   12

Foot. The basic unit used in the scansion or measurement of verse. A foot usually contains one accented syllable and one or two unaccented syllables, but the *monosyllabic foot,* the *spondaic foot (spondee),* and the *dipodic foot* are all modifications of this principle. 183–84, 194, 196

Form. The external pattern or shape of a poem, describable without reference to its content, as *continuous form, stanzaic form, fixed form* (and their varieties), *free verse,* and *syllabic verse.* 187, 217–24, 227, 228. See *Structure.*

Free verse. Non-metrical verse. Poetry written in free verse is arranged in lines, may be more or less rhythmical, but has no fixed metrical pattern or expectation. 187

Grammatical pause (also called *caesura*). A pause introduced into the reading of a line by a mark of punctuation. Grammatical pauses do not affect scansion. 186

Haiku. A three-line poem, Japanese in origin, narrowly conceived of as a fixed form in which the lines contain respectively 5, 7, and 5 syllables (in American practice this requirement is frequently dispensed with). Haiku are generally concerned with some aspect of nature and present a single image or two juxtaposed images without comment, relying on suggestion rather than on explicit statement to communicate their meaning. 228

Heard rhythm. The actual rhythm of a metrical poem as we hear it when it is read naturally. The heard rhythm mostly conforms to but sometimes departs from or modifies the *expected rhythm.* 185–86

Heptameter. A metrical line containing seven feet. 182

Hexameter. A metrical line containing six feet. 182

Hyperbole. See *Overstatement.*

Iamb. A metrical foot consisting of one unaccented syllable followed by one accented syllable (for example, rĕ-hēarse). 182

Iambic meter. A meter in which the majority of feet are iambs. The most common English meter. 182

Imagery. The representation through language of sense experience. 50–53

Internal rime. A rime in which one or both of the rime-words occur *within* the line. 168

Irony. A situation, or a use of language, involving some kind of incongruity or discrepancy. 106. Three kinds of irony are distinguished in this book:

Verbal irony. A figure of speech in which what is meant is the opposite of what is said. 104–106

Dramatic irony. A device by which the author implies a different meaning from that intended by the speaker (or by *a* speaker) in a literary work. 107–09

Irony of situation (or *Situational irony*). A situation in which there is an incongruity between actual circumstances and those that would seem appropriate or between what is anticipated and what actually comes to pass. 106, 108–09

Italian (or Petrarchan) sonnet. A sonnet consisting of an octave riming *abbaabba* and of a sestet using any arrangement of two or three additional rimes, such as *cdcdcd* or *cdecde.* 221–22, 224 (Exercise 4).

Limerick. A fixed form consisting of five lines of anapestic meter, the first two trimeter, the next two dimeter, the last line trimeter, riming *aabba;* used exclusively for humorous or nonsense verse. 220–21, 224–25

Masculine rime (also known as *Single rime*). A rime in which the repeated accented vowel sound is in the final syllable of the words involved (for example, dance–pants, scald–recalled). 168, 176 (Question 5).

Metaphor. A figure of speech in which an implicit comparison is made between two things essentially unlike. It may take one of four forms: (1) that in which the literal term and the figurative term are both *named;* (2) that in which the literal term is *named* and the figurative term *implied;* (3) that in which the literal term is *implied* and the figurative term *named;* (4) that in which both the literal and the figurative terms are *implied.* 61–64, 68–70

Meter. Regularized rhythm; an arrangement of language in which the accents occur at apparently equal intervals in time. 180–88

Metonymy. A figure of speech in which some significant aspect or detail of an experience is used to represent the whole experience. In this book the single term *metonymy* is used for what are sometimes distinguished as two separate figures: *synechdoche* (the use of the part for the whole) and *metonymy* (the use of something closely related for the thing actually meant). 67–68

Metrical pause. A pause that supplies the place of an expected accented syllable. Unlike *grammatical* and *rhetorical pauses,* metrical pauses affect scansion. 197

Monometer. A metrical line containing one foot. 182

Monosyllabic foot. A foot consisting of a single accented syllable (for example, shīne). 182

Octameter. A metrical line containing eight feet. 182

Octave. (1) An eight-line stanza. (2) The first eight lines of a sonnet, especially one structured in the manner of an Italian sonnet. 221

Onomatopoeia. The use of words that supposedly mimic their meaning in their sound (for example, boom, click, plop). 200–01

Onomatopoetic language. Language employing *onomatopoeia.*

Overstatement (or *hyperbole*). A figure of speech in which exaggeration is used in the service of truth. 102–04

Oxymoron. A compact paradox, one in which two successive words apparently contradict each other. 191

Paradox. A statement or situation containing apparently contradictory or incompatible elements. 101–02

Paradoxical situation. A situation containing apparently but not actually incompatible elements. The celebration of a fifth birthday anniversary by a twenty-year-old man is paradoxical but explainable if the man was born on February 29. The Christian doctrines that Christ was born of a virgin and is both God and man are, for a Christian believer, paradoxes (that is, apparently impossible but true). 101

Paradoxical statement (or *verbal paradox*). A figure of speech in which an apparently self-contradictory statement is nevertheless found to be true. 101–02

Paraphrase. A restatement of the content of a poem designed to make its *prose meaning* as clear as possible. 27–28

Pentameter. A metrical line containing five feet. 181

Personification. A figure of speech in which human attributes are given to an animal, object, or concept. 64–65

Petrarchan sonnet. See *Italian sonnet.*

Phonetic intensive. A word whose sound, by an obscure process, to some degree suggests its meaning. As differentiated from *onomatopoetic* words, the meanings of phonetic intensives do not refer to sounds. 200–01

Prose. Non-metrical language; the opposite of *verse.* 180–81

Prose meaning. That part of a poem's *total meaning* that can be separated and expressed through paraphrase. 136–40

Quatrain. (1) A four-line stanza. (2) A four-line division of a sonnet marked off by its rime scheme. 222

Refrain. A repeated word, phrase, line, or group of lines, normally at some fixed position in a poem written in stanzaic form. 169, 173 (Exercise), 220

Rhetorical pause (also known as *caesura*). A natural pause, unmarked by punctuation, introduced into the reading of a line by its phrasing or syntax. Rhetorical pauses do not affect scansion. 186

Rhetorical poetry. Poetry using artificially eloquent language, that is, language too high-flown for its occasion and unfaithful to the full complexity of human experience. 240–41

Rhythm. Any wavelike recurrence of motion or sound. 180–81

Rime (or *Rhyme*). The repetition of the accented vowel sound and all succeeding sounds in important or importantly positioned words (for example, old–cold, vane–reign, court–report, order–recorder). The above definition applies to *perfect rime* and assumes that the accented vowel sounds involved are preceded by differing consonant sounds. If the preceding consonant sound is the same (for example, manse–romance, style–stile), or if there is no preceding consonant sound in either word (for example, aisle–isle, alter–altar), or if the same word is repeated in the riming position (for example, hill–hill), the words are called *identical rimes.* Both *perfect rimes* and *identical rimes* are to be distinguished from *approximate rimes.* 168, 170

Rime scheme. Any fixed pattern of rimes characterizing a whole poem or its stanzas. 220

Run-on line. A line which has no natural speech pause at its end, allowing the sense to flow uninterruptedly into the succeeding line. 188

Sarcasm. Bitter or cutting speech; speech intended by its speaker to give pain to the person addressed. 104–05

Satire. A kind of literature that ridicules human folly or vice with the purpose of bringing about reform or of keeping others from falling into similar folly or vice. 104–05

Scansion. The process of measuring verse, that is, of marking accented and unaccented syllables, dividing the lines into feet, identifying the metrical pattern, and noting significant variations from that pattern. 182

Sentimental poetry. Poetry aimed primarily at stimulating the emotions rather than at communicating experience honestly and freshly. 240

Sestet. (1) A six-line stanza. (2) The last six lines of a sonnet structured on the Italian model. 221

Shakespearean sonnet. See *English sonnet.*

Simile. A figure of speech in which an explicit comparison is made between two things essentially unlike. The comparison is made explicit by the use of some such word or phrase as *like, as, than, similar to, resembles,* or *seems.* 61

Single rime. See *Masculine rime.*

Situational irony. See *Irony.*

Sonnet. A fixed form of fourteen lines, normally iambic pentameter, with a rime scheme conforming to or approximating one of two main types—the *Italian* or the *English.* 221–24

Spondee. A metrical foot consisting of two syllables equally or almost equally accented (for example, trūe–blūe). 182

Stanza. A group of lines whose metrical pattern (and usually its rime scheme as well) is repeated throughout a poem. 182, 218–20

Stanzaic form. The form taken by a poem when it is written in a series of units having the same number of lines and usually other characteristics in common, such as metrical pattern or rime scheme. 218–20

Stress. In this book, the same as *Accent.* But see 181 (footnote).

Structure. The internal organization of a poem's content. See *Form.*

Sustained figure. See *Extended figure.*

Syllabic verse. Verse measured by the number of syllables rather than the number of feet per line. 227 (Question 4). Also, see *Haiku.*

Symbol. A figure of speech in which something (object, person, situation, or action) means more than what it is. A symbol, in other words, may be read both literally and metaphorically. 80–88, 91 (Exercise).

Synechdoche. A figure of speech in which a part is used for the whole. In this book it is subsumed under the term *Metonymy.* 67–68

Terza rima. See 224 (Exercise 3).

Tetrameter. A metrical line containing four feet. 182

Theme. The central idea of a literary work. 26

Tone. The writer's or speaker's attitude toward his subject, his audience, or himself; the emotional coloring, or emotional meaning, of a work. 151–55

Total meaning. The total experience communicated by a poem. It includes all those dimensions of experience by which a poem communicates—sensuous, emotional, imaginative, and intellectual—and it can be communicated in no other words than those of the poem itself. 136–40

Trimeter. A metrical line containing three feet. 182

Triple meter. A meter in which a majority of the feet contain three syllables. (Actually, if more than 25% of the feet in a poem are triple, its effect is more triple than duple, and it ought perhaps to be referred to as triple meter.) Anapestic and dactylic are both triple meters. 182

Triple rime. A rime in which the repeated accented vowel sound is in the third last syllable of the words involved (for example, gainfully–disdainfully); one form of *feminine rime.* 176

Trochaic meter. A meter in which the majority of feet are trochees. 182

Trochee. A metrical foot consisting of one accented syllable followed by one unaccented syllable (for example, bār-tĕr). 182

Understatement. A figure of speech that consists of saying less than one means, or of saying what one means with less force than the occasion warrants. 103–04

Verbal irony. See *Irony.*

Verse. Metrical language; the opposite of *prose.* 180–81

Villanelle. See 224 (Exercise 2).

INDEX OF AUTHORS, TITLES, AND FIRST LINES

Authors' names appear in capitals, titles of poems in italics, and first lines of poems in roman type. Numbers in roman type indicate the page of the selection, and italic numbers indicate discussion of the poem.

A   7
B   8
C   9
D   0
E   1
F   2
G   3
H   4
I   5
J   6